Death sits on my Shoulder

by Richard Selley

Acknowledgements

This book would not have been possible without an enormous amount of medical, practical and emotional support. Firstly, I must thank the army of health professionals, including my doctors, nurses, neuropsychologist, speech and language therapist, dietician, and physiotherapists, who have helped me throughout my journey with MND. I also owe a huge debt of thanks to Morag and her team of palliative care nurses, therapists, and volunteers at the Cornhill Macmillan Hospice in Perth — their kindness and friendship has been incredible. Without the daily support of my carers, I would never have coped. Lorraine, Demi, Susan, Kara, Neschka and several others from Rigifa Care Services have looked after me with great understanding, patience, and humour — I thank you all. Over the last two years, writing my blog has become more and more challenging. It is largely thanks to the encouragement of my family and friends, including a large number of my former pupils, that I have kept going — your support has been invaluable. Since we moved to Glenalmond, the school community has shown me a great deal of kindness — my thanks go to them all, and to Judith in particular; she has been a great friend. A special thank you goes to my daughter, Lorna, and my brother, Peter. They took on the proofreading and formatting of my final draft, and without their help, there would be no book. Finally, and most importantly, I thank my wife, Elaine. From chapter one, she has been a tower of strength, and her unconditional love and support have meant more to me than words could ever say.

Preface

Motor Neurone Disease (MND) is a rare condition that affects the nerves (motor neurons) in the brain and spinal cord. When these nerves become damaged they stop sending messages to the muscles that enable us to move our limbs, speak, swallow and breathe. MND is a progressive disease for which there is there is no known cure, and no effective treatment.

My life with MND began some time before I knew it. This diary is based on a blog that I began soon after my diagnosis. It describes my journey to that diagnosis and my attempts to cope with the disease since then. Public awareness of MND has grown recently, particularly since campaigns like the ice bucket challenge. So, why am I writing more about it? Firstly, and perhaps selfishly, I am doing it for myself. I have found that writing about my experiences has helped me to come to terms with having a terminal illness. Secondly, although MND symptoms vary, I hope this diary might help fellow sufferers, their carers, and anyone else who is interested, to better understand the challenges that come with this disease, or any other terminal condition.

All proceeds from the sale of this book will go towards funding research into finding a cure for MND.

Contents

CHAPTER ONE

The Journey to Diagnosis

May 2012

I was having a beer with my brother-in-law, Ed, in The Sheep Heid, my local pub in Duddingston, Scotland. I went to pick up my glass in my right hand and was surprised when it slipped between my forefinger and thumb.

December 2012

My grip in my right hand was not improving and I also noticed that I had some nodules in my palm. I went to see my GP. After describing my problem, he examined my hand and told me I had two things wrong with me: a touch of arthritis and something called a "Dupuytren's contracture". He explained that there was nothing much that could be done for the former, and that the latter did not look serious enough to recommend a surgical procedure.

June 2013

By this time, the grip between my left thumb and forefinger was also weaker. I noticed that I was having difficulty opening a jar of pickled onions with either hand, and I couldn't hold a full pint glass without tucking my little finger underneath the glass to support it. I went back to my GP. He was sympathetic but said I had the same problems with my left hand as I had with my right. He asked if I was still comfortable driving or playing golf, and I told him that I had no problems with either. He said I should monitor the situation and come back if things got worse.

December 2013

Just before Christmas I went to turn off a light and I missed the switch with my finger. I thought this was strange but decided it was probably nothing. My wife, Elaine, said I should get it checked out but I decided to leave it.

March 2014

I reached for a wine glass off a shelf, missed the stem, and knocked the glass to the floor. I couldn't understand quite how I had managed to do this but I put it down to clumsiness.

April 2014

I was determined to play in more golf medals so that I could keep my handicap, so I entered a Wednesday competition. Despite having spent many hours hitting balls on the practice area over the winter, I played very poorly indeed. My playing partners were patient but I was a little upset when one of them asked me if I was a beginner. I told him that three years earlier I had actually won a medal playing off a lower handicap, but I could see that he found this hard to believe. Towards the end of the round I slipped when stepping off a tee area and fell to the ground. I was determined to finish so I carried on, but when the net scores for the competition came out the next day, I was last.

July 2014

Whilst on holiday in Kefalonia, I was taking pictures of the mountains with my phone. Standing on a causeway with my back to the sea, I started fooling around, pretending to lose my balance near the edge. As I moved back, I went to steady myself but I couldn't stop. I fell backwards and hit my head on the concrete. I was quite shaken but decided that I had just been stupid.

August 2014

I noticed that my grip between thumb and forefinger, in both hands, seemed to be weaker. This varied, however, from day to day. I was finding it more difficult to lift a cup of coffee in one hand. When shopping, I struggled to grasp coins from my jacket pocket and then found it hard to pick up my change from the counter. I also broke a plate by dropping it on the floor. I became increasingly frustrated and angry about my clumsiness and decided to go back to my GP.

My GP told me that as my symptoms were not improving, he thought I should see a hand specialist. A referral came through within two weeks and I attended an evening clinic at St. John's Hospital in Livingston. The consultant listened to my story, examined my hand, and said I should have an x-ray straight away. As soon as this was done, I was taken back to see her again. She told me that the x-ray was clear, and then said, "I think you may have something more complicated." She explained that we needed to see if the nerves in my arm might be causing the problem. She said she would make an ultra-sound appointment and arrange for me to have something called a nerve conduction test. She explained that the first appointment should come through very soon, but that there was a long waiting list for the second test.

September 2014

I went for my ultra-sound appointment at Edinburgh Royal Infirmary and the doctor said he couldn't find anything unusual. I asked him if he had any idea how long it would be before I might get my nerve conduction test. I realised this was a fairly silly question, because he probably didn't even know that I was going to have such a test. He told me to ring the appointments number for the Western General if I hadn't heard anything by the end of October. As I tried to pay for my parking fare at the machine, I got very frustrated by my inability to get the right money out of my pocket. Other people were waiting behind me and I spilled coins all over the ground. A very kind lady bent down and helped me pick them up, but in my hurry to get away I failed to thank her properly. On the way home I got more worried about my condition. I decided to do what doctors always advise against; namely, look for information online.

The next day I was alone in the house, except for the ever-present Sam. She's a dachshund, who was supposed to belong to my stepson, Cameron, but at that time spent most of her days on my lap. I nudged her aside and typed "nerve problems" into Google. A variety of things came up, including neuropathy, carpal tunnel, and shingles. Most medical sites seemed to concentrate on nerves and pain, and as I wasn't experiencing any pain, I gradually widened my search to include "nerve disorders". This flagged up a number of diseases, some of which I recognised, like Alzheimer's and Parkinson's, and others that I had never heard of before, like Lewy body disease. I didn't like the sound of these conditions, but my symptoms didn't seem to fit any of them very well.

November 2014

During a routine walk with Sam, I tripped slightly on the curb of the pavement and only just stopped myself from falling over. A couple of weeks later the same thing happened again. At the end of the month, during a walk into Edinburgh, my leg felt as if it wasn't behaving properly. I was still walking at my normal speed, but my leg simply didn't feel right.

December 2014

After another stumble, I rang my doctor's surgery. My usual GP was not available so I accepted an appointment with a different doctor. I talked through the background to my previous visits and explained that I was still waiting for my nerve conduction test. I described what I had noticed about my left leg. The doctor asked me to do a variety of basic tests, like pushing and pulling my hands against his own, gripping his hand as tightly as possible, and touching the end of my nose with my eyes shut. He also watched me walk and tested my reflexes. The doctor said I should have a CT scan, which he could arrange, but this would probably not happen until the New Year. I asked him what he thought might be wrong with me. He said it could be a number of things but I should try not to worry. Over Christmas, I noticed that I was struggling to wrap and unwrap presents properly. I got very frustrated on Christmas Day when I had to ask Elaine to help me open a gift that was tightly wrapped with tape.

January 2015

I went for my CT scan, and was informed a week later that it was clear. In some ways, of course, I was relieved, because I knew that this ruled out a number of conditions; however, I still knew that there was something seriously wrong with me. A few days later, we went to see the film, 'The Theory of Everything'. As I watched Stephen Hawking, brilliantly portrayed by Eddie Redmayne, struggle to pick up coins that he had dropped on his floor, and stumble as he walked to a tutorial, the similarities with my own symptoms hit me. As the story unfolded I had a horrible feeling that I knew what I was facing.

Over the next two or three days I read more and more about motor neurone disease. I realised that it was a complicated business. There were clearly different types of the disease, and despite Stephen Hawking's story, the prognosis for the most common type, amyotrophic lateral sclerosis (ALS), was very bleak indeed. Despite the fact that my symptoms did match some of those listed on various MND websites, I knew that self-diagnosis was a dangerous game. I tried hard to convince myself that it was highly unlikely that I could have a disease that only effects one or two people in a hundred thousand.

Over the next two weeks I became more aware of my inability to balance properly. One morning, toward the end of the month, I was out walking with Sam. We took our usual route through a little wood at the back of the house and then we walked up to some large trees that stand on a mound, overlooking the sports field. As I followed Sam down the slope, I suddenly lost my balance and fell head over heels. Sam must have thought I was playing some sort of game, because she rushed over to lick my face as I lay on the grass. I knew that I hadn't tripped over anything. My left leg had simply buckled as I stepped down. Elaine was becoming increasingly concerned about me and told me to book another appointment with my GP.

February 2015

Elaine insisted on accompanying me to see my GP. This time he didn't do any tests. He said I needed to see a neurologist and he would contact the hospital. A week later, I received a phone call from a doctor at the Western General. He said he had heard from my GP and he would like to see me as soon as was convenient. We arranged for me to go to the neurology department in three days' time.

Elaine came with me to see the neurologist. After going through the background to my symptoms, he gave me a fairly detailed physical examination, including many of the tests that my GP had performed back in December. He then said he would like me to have an MRI scan on my head and spine to see if there were any signs of nerve damage. I told him about my fears concerning MND. He said that although there were indications of possible upper motor neurone problems, he felt it was very unlikely indeed that I had MND.

For a few days after this appointment I felt a sense of relief, but this soon turned to anxiety about my upcoming MRI scan. I went to the Western General the following Sunday morning, and had my scan in a mobile unit in the car park. I lay as still as possible in the tube that covered the top half of my body, and I could hear lots of whirring noises. On the way back to the hospital building I very nearly fell going down some steps from the car park, but I just managed to grab hold of a railing.

Two days later, I received my long-awaited appointment for my nerve conduction test. I knew that this test could detect indications of lower motor neurone problems, including the presence of muscle twitches, called fasciculations. The neurologist that I had seen earlier in the month had already carefully examined my arms and legs, and he had said that he could see no signs of fasciculations. Recently, in bed, however, I had felt some twitches in my shoulder, like little bubbles under my skin.

2 March 2015

I made my way along the narrow road that runs through Duddingston golf course. As I walked next to the eighth fairway, I looked across to the practice ground, and thought about the many hours I had spent there over the previous six years. At the end of the road, I turned left and caught a bus to the Western General. When I arrived at the outpatients clinic of the neurology department, there were lots of people waiting. A nurse came over to my seat and explained that I would have to wait longer than normal because they were experiencing technical problems, and were having to merge two clinics. An hour later, a doctor came through and called my name. As we walked into a room, he looked harassed and explained that he was having to see double the number of people as normal. He asked me to tell him about my hands. I told him about the weak grip and then started to explain that since the original referral I had experienced other symptoms and been referred to a neurologist. The doctor looked impatient, said he didn't know about any recent referral, and told me to take off my shirt, trousers, and socks, and lie on the bed.

He stood at the foot of the bed and stared intently at my legs and upper-body. I guessed that he was looking for fasciculations. He then attached electrodes to my arms and switched on his machine. I felt little electric shocks, just like the ones I experienced as a boy, when my father gripped my hand as he held the electric fence on the farm. The doctor did the same thing on my leg and then he began sticking a needle into my feet, legs, arms, and hands. The needle was attached to his machine, and whenever I moved my toes or fingers I could feel a pain through the needle. As the doctor looked at the monitor of his machine, he gave a hint of a sympathetic smile. He then said that he wished he had been told about my recent visits to neurology. He asked me to get dressed and said I should go back to the waiting area while he went to speak with another consultant.

As I waited, I became increasingly anxious. Two weeks earlier, I had been told that there were no signs of lower motor neurone problems, but I knew that this doctor had seen something. I looked at the posters on the wall; I looked at patients going into the clinic and others coming back out, but nothing could distract me from the depressing thoughts that were going through my head. Finally, the doctor appeared at the doorway and beckoned me to join him in the corridor outside. He explained that he had not been able to find his colleague, and that I would need to come back in a week or so to see another consultant. I just stood there looking at him, and after a pause, I said that I was fairly sure that I had motor neurone disease. He looked uncomfortable and said, "This isn't the place to discuss a diagnosis, but I think you might well have worked it out for yourself".

He then asked if someone was with me and I told him I was on my own. He shook my hand, said he realised that this was terribly difficult, and said I should try not to worry. He had all but confirmed my worst fears.

As I walked down the long south corridor, which stretches almost the entire length of the hospital, I felt numb. I walked straight out of the hospital and got on the first bus that came along. As soon as I took my seat I realised that it was not going my way, so I jumped off at the first stop and walked along to Stockbridge, a suburb of Edinburgh. When I reached the Stockbridge Tap, I went in and ordered a pint of lager and a packet of crisps. I looked at the tall glass on the table and reached out to hold it with both hands. I removed one hand, and as I felt the glass slip a little between my finger and thumb, just as it had three years earlier, I burst into tears. After apologising to the lady behind the bar, I called Elaine on my mobile and asked her to come and fetch me.

On the way home we said very little, because there was little to say. Elaine wanted to stay with me, but I persuaded her to go back to work. The afternoon passed in a haze. Later that evening, Elaine and I talked about the future. Back in October, Elaine had been appointed as Warden (Head) of Glenalmond College in Perthshire, and was due to start in August. Having both spent most of our teaching careers in boarding schools, we knew the rewards and challenges that a post like this would bring for her. We also knew that my likely journey with MND would make those challenges even harder. We discussed it as logically as we could. Elaine said her instincts were to forget the job, so that she could look after me, but I was adamant that she should go ahead. She had recently completed a very successful eighteen-month stint as acting head teacher of Loretto School, and I knew that this was an outstanding opportunity for her. She was far too young to retire, and I couldn't bear the thought of her losing this chance because of my situation.

3 March 2015

I cried more than I had in the last forty years. Sometimes it was just a few tears that I could quickly brush away, but at other times I found myself sobbing uncontrollably. I knew that I still didn't have a definite diagnosis, and I tried to cling on to the hope that my condition just might be something other than MND. However, I knew that the odds were stacking up against me, and I felt justified in feeling sorry for myself. I didn't want to see anyone (Sam was more than enough company), but I wanted to email certain people before they called me on the phone. I sent emails to my daughters, Lorna and Megan, and to my brother, Peter. The only people I phoned were my sister, Steph, and my mother-in-law, Janette. Neither of them used email, but both of them spoke to me like my mother used to, and if she had been alive, I would have wanted to speak to her. When Elaine came back she said that she had spoken to Cameron on the way home from work, and later that evening she phoned her older son, Tom, who was at Glasgow University.

4 March 2015

I received some lovely messages from Lorna and Megan. Both of them were very upset but they also wanted to be strong for me. Suddenly, I felt more like the child and less like the parent. I also received a very moving email from Peter. Back in 2012, Peter had collapsed after a routine swim and within hours he had been diagnosed with an aggressive and malignant brain tumour. He had surgery but was told that his prognosis was very poor. Against all the odds, Peter had survived longer than anyone had expected. He had experienced some very dark times, but he had also remained incredibly positive. If anyone knew what I was going through, it was him.

His email read:

Dear Richard

I am absolutely devastated for you, Elaine, and the children to hear the news of the diagnosis today of Motor Neurone Disease (or almost certain diagnosis). It won't necessarily help, but I know from a deep place something of what you are going through, and have been going through for some weeks now. That horrible sense of it being something potentially awful but hoping against hope that after the tests or biopsies or whatever it is, that it will turn out to be something else. The feeling of being robbed, while in the prime of life. The grief for oneself, and for those closest to one, for a loss to come at some uncertain time in the future. The fear of death; but more, the fear of the process of death. At least, this is what I remember just before and after my diagnosis in 2012.

It seems a ghastly injustice that you and I should end up with grave conditions that only two in 100,000 and one in 100,000 people get, respectively. It makes me furious at the universe. I have read The Book of Job more than once in recent years, and I share Job's fury at God. What have we done to deserve this?

At the moment I just want to share the sense of shock you might have, and this almost grief-like state you might feel. I just want you to know I am there with you, as your brother in more than one sense. I am available to speak whenever you want. I want to come and see you when I can, and when it is good for you — sometime soon.

But I also want to say, somewhat haltingly since everyone's experience is different, that in my case I have found it helpful, after the initial anger and rage and grief has dissipated a little, to focus on a day at a time. I made many plans to cover various eventualities as you know, but that isn't how I have tried to live since 2012. I have tried to make the most of every moment.

Also, I did discover that it was possible to rethink the kinds of statistics that are given out at initial diagnosis. Why can't I possibly be one of the ones at the tail of the curve who defies the odds? Someone has to be in the one in 20 or one in 100 who does so much better than anyone else? (It doesn't stop one preparing for the worst of course. My oncologist told us to put hand rails in the shower on the first day since I would need them soon — though so far, I haven't needed them.) I found that this sense of overwhelming helplessness at first can evolve into more hopefulness. Yes, some resignation that this thing might devour me suddenly or slowly from any moment, but that while I still had enough cognitive and physical function, or treatment to deal with any cognitive or physical dysfunction, that I would aim to live my life as well as I could.

Our conditions are different and our fears might be different. We have slightly different circumstances. None of this may help or mean anything at the moment. Words with good intentions can sometimes be enraging. But I have always found that some attempt at words, however clumsy, is infinitely better than nothing at all.

All my love,
Peter x

I could hardly read these words for the tears that were pouring down my cheeks. I knew that I could never match the style of his prose (my brother is the English specialist and I am the economist) but I had to reply and thank him.

Dear Peter

Many thanks for your kind, caring, and perceptive message. You have an understanding of my plight that few people could ever imagine.

I am trying hard to be positive. I cling to the possibility that the provisional diagnosis might be false, whilst recognising that I am almost certainly hoping against hope. Feelings of anger, guilt and disbelief come in waves, interspersed with moments of utter desperation. The worst thing at the moment is simply not knowing — living in a state of limbo.

I really appreciate your words - certainly not clumsy, nor enraging! With love to you,
Richard

5 March 2015

I decided that I would do some planning for my death and my funeral. I had been weighed down by thoughts and fears of dying for three days, so I thought it might help if I confronted them in some way. I started writing an email to Elaine titled "When I have died". I was in tears by the time I had written the first line, but I forced myself to carry on. As I wrote my message, I tried to be as practical as possible, and I included a checklist for her to follow. When I had finished this I began another document called "Ideas for my funeral". As I wrote tentative suggestions for words and music, I could clearly see pictures of the funeral service in my mind. It was a very strange experience. When I had saved the documents on my computer, I felt much better. I had finished wallowing in my own death; now it was time to concentrate on living. If only it could have been that easy.

10 March 2015

The neurologist, who had seen me back in February, called and asked if I could come in to see him and a colleague at Edinburgh's Western General hospital. He said he had spoken to the doctor who had done the nerve conduction test and he had the results of my MRI scan. He said I should come straight to the neurology ward and he asked me to confirm that I would have someone with me.

16 March 2015

It seemed strange to go upstairs to the hospital wards rather than downstairs to the outpatients clinic. We were asked to wait in a room that had no beds, and a few minutes later the young neurologist and a lady doctor arrived. She introduced herself and I recognised her name from the list of neurology consultants that I had looked up on the NHS website. After a fairly brief physical examination she told me that the MRI scan had not indicated any other condition, and she confirmed that I had a form of MND. She said that the senior Edinburgh-based consultant for MND was a man called Richard Davenport, and that I would soon get an appointment to see him at his clinic in the Anne Rowling Building at the Royal Infirmary. She said that I would now be allocated a specialist MND nurse who would coordinate my care in the future. The young neurologist was visibly upset. He said he had been sure that my problems were connected to upper motor neurone issues only, and that he was very sorry that this was not the case. I found myself reassuring him that it was all right, and the consultant said that this just highlighted how difficult diagnosis was in this area.

As we walked down the stairs from the ward, I didn't feel the shock that I had experienced a week earlier. This was the news that I had been expecting, and although it was shocking, I almost felt a sense of relief. After all those months of worry, confusion and uncertainty, I finally knew what was wrong with me.

CHAPTER TWO

My Advanced Death Certificate

17 March 2015

I sat with Sam on my lap and wrote emails to my daughters Lorna and Megan, and my brother Peter, confirming the news of my diagnosis. I also called my sister and mother-in-law. As I did this I felt calm and strangely detached. Confirming the news to myself, however, was a different thing altogether. I tried to read a few pages of Michael Palin's diaries, but after five minutes I couldn't remember a word of what I had read. I decided to take Sam out for a walk. We did our usual circuit around the Cavalry Park playing fields, and came back through the little woods behind the house. The rest of the day passed slowly as I tried to distract myself by watching television, listening to music, and reading.

27 March 2015

I had spent days attempting to lose myself in the life of Michael Palin — a life which seemed far more interesting and amusing than mine. Now it was the end of term, however, and that evening Elaine and I talked about the holiday period ahead. We agreed that we would try to carry on with the plans we had. All our immediate family knew the score, but we decided that we would not tell anyone else about my diagnosis until after my appointment with Dr. Davenport.

3 April 2015

At lunchtime on Good Friday we went to pick up Peter and his oldest son, George, from the station. Peter looked very well and you would never have guessed about his condition. He kindly said the same about me and we spent much of the day talking and laughing about things that most people would have cried about. He had a natural feel for what I was going through.

4 April 2015

We took Peter and George up to Tranent, a small town in East Lothian, to see Elaine's family. Elaine had told them how much she liked my brother's voice, and she certainly wasn't the first woman to comment on his dulcet tones. Jim, my father-in-law, said Peter sounded just like a BBC newsreader. We talked about Peter's work at Sotheby's and his holiday plans, but we avoided the subject of terminal illness. Later that day, we went to the local pub to have a meal. As we walked along the road beside the playing fields, I realised that I was struggling to keep up. I wasn't out of breath, but my left leg didn't feel very steady, and I nearly lost my balance as I stepped off the pavement. Elaine noticed, and for the rest of the walk she took my hand.

13 April 2015

Judy Newton, my designated MND nurse, phoned to say hello. She told me that the next appointment with Dr. Davenport would not take place until 19 May that year. I said I had hoped it would be much sooner, but agreed to wait until then instead of seeing anyone else at an earlier time. Judy said that she would like to come out and see me quite soon, so that we could begin the process of getting my future care organised. We agreed on the following week. I was disappointed that I would have to wait another five weeks until I could see Dr. Davenport. I had read all about the Ann Rowling Clinic and I was keen to visit it.

14 April 2015

With another month to go before my appointment with Dr. Davenport, we decided we needed to let certain people know about my diagnosis much sooner. The first person on the list was Lord Menzies, the Chairman of Council at Glenalmond College. We both felt it was important to tell him before he heard from anyone else, and we wanted him to know that my diagnosis had come long after Elaine's appointment as Warden. When Elaine phoned him, he was very understanding and said that he knew the Glenalmond community would be very supportive. They agreed that we would then tell Gordon Woods, the Warden at that time, and his wife, Emma.

16 April 2015

We drove up to Perthshire to see Gordon and Emma. It was strange telling people face to face for the very first time. We couldn't gradually build up to it, because the reply to the usual "How are you?" couldn't really be the usual "Fine". Gordon and Emma were clearly shocked, but Emma said she had wondered about things when I had mentioned to her in February that I was going to see a neurologist. Gordon, just as I would have done, found it hard to express how he felt. Emma showed more emotion and wanted to give me a hug. We all agreed that it would be best if Glenalmond and Loretto staff told their school communities at the same time so that rumours didn't circulate on the grapevine. On the one hand, I didn't want my condition to be the centre of any attention, but on the other, I didn't want to answer lots of individual questions.

20 April 2015

Both schools mentioned my condition at their morning staff meetings. The Loretto staff were also informed that Elaine would be finishing most of her work at half term. This would give the two of us some precious time together before she started her job at Glenalmond in early August.

Judy Newton came to see us in the afternoon. She was very calm and very direct. She did her best to answer all our questions about types of MND, the symptoms that might develop, and the various health professionals and organisations that would be there to support me. I was frightened about asking anything about prognosis, and I knew that it was an unfair question. However, I couldn't stop myself. Judy reminded us that every case of MND was different, and said that she knew several patients who had had the disease for a number of years. And, of course, there was always Stephen Hawking. I said I was unsure whether Stephen Hawking's long life was actually much consolation for people like me. His story was certainly inspiring, but I, and others who had just been diagnosed, knew that our chances of living for very long were very remote indeed.

22 April 2015

I met my daughter Megan for a drink at All Bar One, in George Street, Edinburgh. This was the first time we had met since my diagnosis. When I had caught the bus into town, I had shown the driver my bus pass and then lost my balance as he pulled away. I lurched across the aisle, grabbed hold of the luggage rack and only just made it to a seat at the front. I was sure the other passengers must have thought I was drunk. I spent the rest of the journey worrying about how I would safely get off again. Having got off without mishap, I carefully climbed the steps up to the bar entrance, found Meg, and gave her a hug. I was determined to appear as normal as possible, but I could see the concern on Meg's face as I walked very slowly and unsteadily back from the bar with our drinks. I was concentrating hard on maintaining my balance and not spilling any beer. I did my best to be as positive as I could, and Meg did exactly the same.

23 April 2015

A lady from MND Scotland called to introduce herself. She had been given my name by Judy Newton, and she wanted to tell me about the organisation in general and the support groups that were available. She said the Edinburgh group would be meeting at The Kings Manor Hotel on 18 May. She said there was no pressure to attend. I knew perfectly well that such groups could be very helpful, but I felt relieved that I wasn't expected to go along.

As soon as I put the phone down, it rang again. This time it was Nicola Povey, the welfare advisor from MND Scotland. She wanted to come and see me the next day. Suddenly, after having heard very little, immediately after my diagnosis everyone seemed to want to see me. This was a strange feeling, but it felt good to know that there were people out there who both cared and understood my situation.

24 April 2015

Nicola arrived and told me all about PIP, Personal Independence Payments. PIP was replacing the old Disability Living Allowance. I knew that these payments were not means tested, but having filled in endless forms for DLA on behalf of my stepdaughter Alice, who had epilepsy, I also knew that it could sometimes take months for the Department of Work and Pensions (DWP) to process any claims. Nicola assured me that if I rang DWP and explained my situation, they would act quickly. I was not convinced. Nicola told me about a number of other benefits that were available, but we agreed that the only one I might be entitled to would be a blue disabled badge for my car.

27 April 2015

I rang DWP, expecting to have a long call, and to be taken through hundreds of questions. However, after explaining my situation, a very helpful lady told me that my application for PIP would be fast-tracked as soon as I could get a form called a DS1500 signed by my GP. I asked what this was, and she explained that it was a form that would confirm that I had a terminal illness with a very limited life expectancy. I hid my shock at hearing these words by laughing, and said that it sounded like an advanced death certificate. The lady said she was sorry, and I apologised for making such a stupid comment.

3 May 2015

After much discussion and changes of mind, I decided to accompany Elaine to a drinks reception at Loretto. I was apprehensive about meeting a number of ex-colleagues. I was unsure how I would bear up, and I didn't know how people would react. As it turned out, our closest friends were wonderful — sympathetic, articulate and tactile. Some people avoided me, which was perfectly understandable, and one or two simply avoided the subject and talked about cricket.

7 May 2015

I had a visit from an occupational therapist. She was pleased to see that I was still quite mobile, but quickly recognised that due to my unsteady left leg and poor balance I was nervous going up and down the stairs. I explained that we would be moving in August, and she offered to pass on my details to an OT based in Perth.

As if to underline the concerns of the OT, later that day I very nearly dropped Sam as I carried her down to the ground floor. Due to her very short legs, she was unable to go up or down the open wooden staircase, so we had all got used to carrying her. Going down one step at a time, holding Sam under one arm while gripping the banister with the other was becoming more and more precarious.

Although I had originally resented having to look after Sam all day, I had grown incredibly fond of her. She had been my constant companion for nearly eighteen months, and in recent weeks I had regularly spoken to her about my fears for the future. I realised that I was not going to be able to look after her for much longer, and I knew that I would miss her terribly.

8 May 2015

Elaine came with me to see my GP. I mentioned the dreaded DS1500 and he said that given my diagnosis, he would be happy to sign one for me. I was relieved that he was willing to do this because I had read about cases where doctors had delayed this process by weeks or even months. He gave me a copy of the form and placed the original in my file. I asked him if I should try to find a new doctor in Perth before we moved, and he said this would be a good idea. We shook hands and left.

We were in and out of the surgery in less than ten minutes. The hopeless nature of MND hit me as I drove home. My GP hadn't asked about my condition and he hadn't examined me in any way. He hadn't needed to because he knew that there was nothing that he could do. Instead, he had simply signed a form, which told everyone that I was terminally ill, and said goodbye. I felt sorry for myself, and I wondered how impotent my GP must have felt.

14 May 2015

My PIP arrived, along with my blue badge. Again, as with the DS1500, I felt strangely grateful to have these things. I had been used to seeing Alice's blue badge on the car dashboard, but it seemed very odd to have one with my own photo on it. Later that evening I went to a drinks party in Edinburgh. It was held in a bar near Broughton Street, and there were just a few steps to climb. I looked at the steps and felt angry that there was no handrail. How could such a simple manoeuvre, like going up three steps, have suddenly become so frightening?

18 May 2015

This was the day of the Edinburgh MND support group meeting. In the days leading up to this I had decided that I wouldn't go. I didn't want to confront my condition so publicly, and by seeing other people with more developed symptoms, I didn't want to see what I was going to become. In the end, however, I forced myself to go, and I was very relieved that I did. There were people there with all kinds of symptoms. Some could still walk but couldn't use their hands, some were using a straw to drink with, some were in wheelchairs but otherwise fine, and some were using a synthetic voice to communicate. Everyone made me very welcome and I was amazed how upbeat everyone seemed to be. There was a discussion about mobility aids, and one carer explained how difficult it was becoming to turn her husband around in his wheelchair, now that his legs were rigid and stuck out. A number of possible solutions were discussed and then the man himself typed a message into his mobile phone. In a voice that sounded similar to that of Stephen Hawking, he said, 'You could always cut my legs off'. Everyone laughed.

19 May 2015

Finally, it was time to see Dr. Davenport. The Ann Rowling Clinic at the Edinburgh Royal Infirmary couldn't have been more different than the neurology department at the Western General hospital. There were no dark corridors with peeling paint, and no old black and white photographs of pioneering neurosurgeons. Instead, there was plenty of light, bright colours, high ceilings, and modern furniture. The reception area resembled a hotel more than a medical building. We were shown in to see the young but bald-headed Dr. Davenport, and Judy Newton was also there. Dr. Davenport said that he had read about my case, but he didn't want to make any assumptions about my condition. After a fairly thorough physical examination, including the usual tests to measure the strength of my limbs and the briskness of my reflexes, Dr. Davenport commented on my good muscle strength and announced that if I had had full-blown ALS for over three years, there would be a good chance that I would be dead by now. This blunt statement took me a little by surprise, but I realised that he was actually being positive. He said that he knew about the findings of the nerve conduction test, but he wasn't totally convinced that I had ALS. He said that he was sure that I did have a form of MND, but he would like to review my symptoms in three months' time. I explained that we were moving up to Perthshire before then. He said he would pass my details and his report to a Dr. Morrison at Ninewells Hospital in Dundee.

Immediately after my appointment with Dr. Davenport I was introduced to a researcher based at the clinic to discuss voice banking. We made an appointment for me to return so that I could record as many sentences as possible. This would help with the possible production of a personalised synthetic voice. There was a high probability that my voice would gradually go, and I was keen to learn as much as possible about this research.

20 May 2015

Following my visit to Dr. Davenport, I had very mixed emotions. I had read about primary lateral sclerosis (PLS), a form of MND that mainly effects the upper rather than lower motor neurones, and I knew that although the symptoms of this could be very similar to ALS, the prognosis was better in terms of life expectancy. I knew that this possibility should encourage me, but I felt depressed by the uncertainty of it all. I had spent the last two months trying to come to terms with the fact that I might not live much longer, and frightening as that was, it offered some sort of clarity. Now, suddenly, I was unsure again; I didn't know where I was. I tried to remind myself to concentrate on the here and now, rather than dwell on the more positive past or the bleak future, but that day my attempts at mindfulness failed to lift my spirits.

23 May 2015

Lorna had arrived from Saudi Arabia, where she had been working, the day before. She was very keen to see exactly where I would be living in the future. For all her travelling, she needed to have a reference point for her UK home.

26 May 2015

Lorna and I met Meg for a drink at The Espy, a favourite pub of ours in Portobello. The girls rarely see each other more than once a year, and this was the first time they had met since my diagnosis. Despite the situation, it was wonderful to see them together. Although they looked very similar, I couldn't help thinking how different they were. Lorna was the adventurous, ambitious traveller, and Meg was the more self-contained, conservative, home bird. I felt so proud of both of them, but I couldn't find the words to express my feelings.

30 May 2015

We spent most of the day with my sister, Steph, in Topsham, Devon. Steph had lived in Devon for fifty years before she suddenly went to live in France. She had spent eight years over there, much of it rather unhappy, and had returned to Devon a year after her husband had died. Steph's health had been poor since her return, and her love of tobacco and brandy was not helping. We took her out for lunch, but she ate very little. She was terribly thin, had a smoker's cough, and was very unsteady on her feet. Despite her own poor health, Steph had tried to be very strong for her younger brothers, regularly phoning us to offer support. But I knew she worried terribly. That day, we could all see the deterioration in her condition, and as we said goodbye, I knew that it might be the last time I would ever see her.

4 June 2015

I attended my first physiotherapy appointment. After watching me walk up and down a few times, the physio told me that I needed a stick. Janette had been trying to persuade me to use one of Jim's sticks for a few weeks, ever since I had fallen head first into one of her evergreen bushes, after stumbling down the steps from her front door. So far, I had stubbornly refused her offer of help. The day before my appointment, however, I had over-balanced trying to carry two heavy bags of shopping and fallen into the stairs. I tried out a stick that had a moulded handle to fit my right hand, and after getting hopelessly confused at first, I gradually managed to co-ordinate the movement of my right hand with that of my wonky left leg. The physiotherapist tested my muscle strength and said it was good. That was the one thing that I had been clinging on to, while my hand grip, stiffness, and balance had all continued to worsen. She gave me a series of exercises to do at home and said I should try to do them two or three times a day.

8 June 2015

I did my stretching and balancing exercises in the morning but forgot about them for the rest of the day.

10 June 2015

Elaine was leaving the next day for Kenya to visit some boarding schools on behalf of Glenalmond. I had reluctantly accepted that it would be too dangerous for me to look after Sam on my own. Elaine's brother Ed had kindly offered to take over her care, so he came around that afternoon and took her away. That evening, my stepson Cam and I both found it very strange without her. We knew that we would continue to see Sam, but her absence from my lap during the day, and from the bottom of Cam's bed at night, was going to be hard to get used to.

15 June 2015

I collected Elaine from Edinburgh Airport and we drove straight up to Oban. We were on our way to the Isle of Mull for a short break. After parking on the ferry, I found it difficult to weave through the cars to get to the lift, but I eventually made it to a seat strategically placed between the bar and the toilets. Sitting under a large sign that said, 'Disabled Passengers Only' I felt rather self-conscious. I hadn't adjusted to the fact that I had rapidly become someone who needed to be helped to do even simple things. Half way through the journey I needed to go to the toilet, and I found it hard to keep my balance as the ferry swayed.

19 June 2015

After four lovely days exploring Mull, including a trip to the beautiful Isla, we returned to Oban and drove up to Appin. We were on our way to the little island of Lismore to visit our friends Katherine and Bobby. Katherine had been my deputy at Loretto Junior School, and she was now head teacher at the small, but flourishing, Lismore Primary School. Getting on to the tiny passenger ferry was quite a challenge because the boat was moving around in the swell. I couldn't use my stick so I just had to grab the outstretched hand of the ferryman and hope for the best. Katherine and Bobby were great hosts; we reminisced, and it was great to see them again.

22 June 2015

As we were going away for two weeks in July, we felt we should make a start on packing up some things in preparation for the move to Perthshire. I found the whole exercise incredibly frustrating. I couldn't help get things down from the loft because I couldn't balance on the ladder unless I held on with both hands. I could pack boxes if I knelt on the floor, wedged against the wall, but I couldn't carry them without fear of toppling over. I swore loudly several times to vent my feelings, but Elaine finally persuaded me to concentrate on doing things I could manage and do sitting in a chair.

24 June 2015

After my experience with the packing and my problems with stairs in general, I realised that going through airports and getting on planes might be difficult on our upcoming holiday. I called the airline and explained my situation. They were very helpful and said they would arrange for a wheelchair to be available at both Leeds Bradford and Kefalonia Airports. They also said they would try to allocate me a seat as near the front as possible.

7 July 2015

We went up to Tranent to see Janette and Jim, before driving down to a hotel near Leeds Bradford Airport. Sam often spent time with them when Ed was at his recording studio, and that morning she was curled up on Janette's lap. She looked very content, but I was relieved when she jumped off and ran over to me — at least she hadn't forgotten me. I bent forward from my chair to pick her up, and was amazed at how heavy she felt. I knew that Janette was giving her too many rich tea biscuits, but as I struggled to lift her I suddenly realised that my muscle strength must be deteriorating. As if to underline my increasing dependence on others, Jim came over and helped lift Sam up. Jim and Janette had been incredibly kind to me, and I was very grateful to them, but I couldn't help feeling guilty that two people, both in their late seventies, were doing so many things for me. It really should have been the other way around. Janette was very worried about how I would cope on the plane and how we might be affected by the cash crisis in Greece. We tried to reassure her but we knew that she was always on tender hooks whenever anyone in the family went abroad. She would only stop worrying when we were safely back on Scottish soil.

8 July 2015

We arrived at Leeds Bradford Airport and I decided that I could manage the walk-through security without any assistance. The problem came when they waved Elaine through first, took away my stick, and asked me to take off my shoes. I felt very frustrated as I tried to explain that I would have to sit down to do this, but there were no chairs. In the end one of the staff scanned my shoes, and I limped through the body scanner. When we arrived at Kefalonia, the steps off the aircraft were steep. I should have waited until everyone else was off the plane, but I was keen to get moving. Much to my embarrassment, I ended up holding people up as I went down slowly, one step at a time. As soon as I reached the bottom a man appeared with a wheelchair, but I wanted to walk.

22 July 2015

I felt tired by the time we got home, after the return flight and the drive back to Edinburgh. It had been a lovely holiday, our fifth time to the beautiful and unspoilt fishing village of Katelios. This year, however, things were different. I couldn't walk up the hill to one of our favourite restaurants, and I didn't manage to get to the old village along the valley. The beach was only a few yards from our apartment, but getting up from my sun bed was hard work. In the end I found it best to roll off the bed, get onto my knees, and haul myself up. The sea was shallow so I could walk in fairly easily, and swimming was good. The problem came when I stopped swimming and tried to stand up again. I kept overbalancing, falling head first into the sea, and swallowing lots of salty water. As the fortnight progressed, I became more and more convinced that I would not be able to return to this wonderful place. On our last day we went along the beach and sat in our favourite bar. It is perched just above the water, and in the evenings, if you are lucky, you can catch glimpses of turtles in the blue water. I told Elaine that this was where I would like her to scatter my ashes.

CHAPTER THREE

Tests in Tayside

1 July 2015

We packed up the car, or more accurately, I stood and watched as Elaine carried everything out. We had just enough clothes for the next week, plus a bag of kitchen utensils and the laptop. It felt strange driving away from Edinburgh. There was excitement about starting a new chapter in our lives, but it was tempered by uncertainty about my condition. I was also worried about access to the flat that we would be living in for our first three weeks at Glenalmond. It was right above the main arch, at the top of a spiral stone staircase.

As we drove along the college, we were struck again by the scale of the grounds and by how impressive the buildings were. I walked through the main arch, glanced at Gladstone's statue, and went into the reception area. I collected the keys for the flat, and began my slow and rather perilous accent up the spiral stairs. The flat had been newly decorated and furnished, and there were plenty of pots and pans in the kitchen. After Elaine had carried everything up, we sat on the window seat and admired the beautiful view.

3 August 2015

After a weekend spent exploring the college campus, including the far-from-finished Warden's House and the local area, today was Elaine's first day on the job. Her office was still being refurbished, so she based herself in the Sub Warden's office, which was conveniently located right next to the flat. I worked out the safest way to descend the stairs and went for a short walk around the quad and along the cloisters. Afterwards I sat in the sunshine on a semi-circular wooden bench across from Gladstone, and decided that it was going to be a lovely place to live.

4 August 2015

We drove over to Dundee for my appointment with my new MND consultant, Dr. Morrison. Dee was also there. After a brief chat, Dr. Morrison examined me and did all the old familiar tests. I almost knew the routine by heart, and Dr. Morrison, like others before him, commented on the good strength I had in my muscles. He said that while he could confirm that I had a form of MND, he would like me to have CAT and MRI scans again and repeat my nerve conduction test and electromyography. He apologised for asking me to go through all this again, but said it should help him give me a more precise and definite diagnosis. The thought of going through all these tests again, particularly the one that involved having needles pushed into me, was very depressing.

5 August 2015

I spent ages trying to get through to the right department in John Lewis so that I could confirm payment and delivery for various items of furniture and household goods. It seemed that there were problems with my delivery address being different from my billing address, so I couldn't finalise things online. When I tried to call on my mobile, the only way I could get a signal was to stand with my arm stretched up against the window. Having spent ten minutes going through my details with someone, I bent down to get a piece of paper and lost the signal. I cursed, and was about to try again when I realised that my arm was really aching. I had noticed the same thing the previous week when I had been talking on the phone to my sister. On that occasion, I ended up supporting my arm with my other hand. I sat down and tried to work out what was happening. Only yesterday I had resisted Dr. Morrison's attempts to push my arm up or down, so how could it suddenly feel so weak? I didn't know the answer but I did know it was certainly linked to my MND. For several minutes I sat in a panic, convinced that my condition was about to worsen rapidly. I could see myself quickly going through the stages of decline: walking with a frame, sitting permanently in a wheelchair, losing the ability to speak and swallow, and then becoming totally paralysed. Eventually I pulled myself together, managed to get through to someone on the phone and, after repeating all the details I had already gone through once before, I finalised the transaction.

13 August 2015

Dawn Hamilton from MND Scotland emailed to check that I had moved and let me know that there would soon be a Tayside MND support meeting at St. Johnstone's football ground. It struck me as ironic that a meeting for people with severe mobility problems would be held at a venue that was all about fitness and agility.

14 August 2015

An MND nurse called Dee emailed me to say that she had now referred me to a dietician, a speech therapist, and a physiotherapist. She said appointments should arrive soon. She also said that she would arrange for the council to contact me about getting an alarm so that I could contact someone if I fell when alone. I was impressed by the speed with which my new care was being arranged, but it reminded how much care I needed already. And this was only the start.

21 August 2015

The removal men had packed up the house the day before, and they arrived at the Warden's House by late morning. I had been in the house the day before, and there was still an army of painters, carpet fitters, and joiners working inside. The house was not ready to move into but we really didn't have any option. My stepsons Tom and Cam and my brother-in-law Ed arrived in advance of the removal van, and I was told to stay out of the way. I felt frustrated and fairly useless, but agreed to stay in the flat and watch cricket on my laptop. That evening I went over to the house and had a look around. There were several rolls of carpet lying around but I was impressed by how much of our furniture was already in place.

24 August 2015

I was determined to make some sort of contribution to the unpacking, so while Elaine worked away in her office upstairs, I decided to carry crockery from the kitchen and put it into a cabinet in the dining room. On each journey I was worried about falling over a roll of carpet that still lay across the dining room, and almost inevitably, on my final trip I caught my lazy left foot on the carpet and did what my father-in-law would call a 'header' into the open cabinet door. I took the door straight off the top hinge, crashed into the wall, and ended up in a heap on the floor. I lay there, feeling a little dazed and very pathetic. Less than a year before, I could have hopped over the carpet without even thinking about it, but now my balance was becoming a really serious matter. I made a promise to myself to use my stick in future, but I knew that I probably wouldn't do so. As I pulled myself up using the radiator for leverage, I felt a dull ache in my shoulder where it had hit the wall, and I noticed blood dripping from my forehead.

2 September 2015

Last night we had over a hundred teaching and support staff in the house for drinks. I could hardly believe the sitting and dining rooms were ready, but over the last two days Ed, Jim, and Janette had helped Elaine move furniture into place, fix lampshades, and put up pictures. I had sat in the middle of the rooms making suggestions and telling Ed the exact height to hang the paintings. I think everyone had been fed up with my interference, but they had all remained very patient. Anyway, I knew that I couldn't trust myself to walk around with a glass in my hand, so I positioned myself on the window seat. During the evening, lots of people came over to say hello, and I was very touched by the warmth of their welcome.

3 September 2015

This was the first day of the new term, and a number of parents came in for drinks after they had dropped off their children at their boarding houses. This time, I managed to welcome people into the house, and my only problem occurred when a lady shook my hand so firmly that I nearly fell over. Luckily I managed to grab the newly repaired cabinet that I had head-butted the week before, and I regained my balance. I kept my glass safely on a side table because I knew that if I coughed my hand would suddenly jerk. I didn't want to spoil the evening by throwing red wine all over one of our guests.

4 September 2015

A joiner fitted an additional banister on our staircase to match the rail that he had put up on the wall below. The wood was great to look at and it was shaped to maximise my grip. It made a huge difference to my ability to climb the stairs, and even more importantly, it made it far easier for me to come back down again. Before the banister was in place, I kept on freezing at the top, worrying just how I would get down without falling.

13 September 2015

This was the day of Elaine's Installation as Warden of Glenalmond. The chapel service was taken by the school chaplain, Fr. Giles, and the Bishop of St Andrews, Dunked and Dunblane, who looked magnificent in his robes and mitre. Some leading Council members attended, along with a large number of other guests from the wider Glenalmond community. Janette, Ed, Tom, and Cam came, but sadly Jim was still recovering from his knee operation. The ceremony included a sequence when Lord Menzies, Chairman of Council, escorted Elaine from her seat, next to me, and led her down the aisle to the altar. She had to kneel before the Bishop and make a number of vows in connection with her leadership of the college, and she was then 'installed' in a throne-like seat, next to the alter. It almost felt as if Elaine was being taken away from me, so that she could marry the college. The singing during the service was wonderful, as it had been the week before, and afterwards many of the guests came over to the house for a buffet lunch. I had some food in the kitchen before the guests arrived, and then did my best to talk to as many people as possible. By using my stick like the third leg of a tripod, I managed to remain on my feet for well over an hour, and I realised just how foolish I had been to try to get by without it on previous social occasions.

28 September 2015

My brother Peter arrived in the afternoon. He had taken his bike on the train in London, travelled up to Edinburgh, and then on to Perth. I had been shopping in town, and was returning home when I spotted Peter peddling away on the final stretch of road leading up to the college. I overtook him and waited by the entrance to the front avenue. As I watched my brother coming towards me I felt very emotional. It seemed surreal that he was cycling along the road, over 400 miles from his home. I embraced him through the car window, and then he followed me back to the house.

29 September 2015

This was my sixty-second birthday. Elaine had been away overnight at a conference, and over breakfast Peter wanted to do as much for me as possible. I tried to reassure him that I could still fetch and carry things around the kitchen, but my little brother was determined to look after me. We talked and laughed for a long time, and then I took Peter to see some very old books in the college. Peter has spent his whole career working with books, most of it with Sotheby's. He has travelled all over the world valuing private collections, and has acted as auctioneer for the sale of some very rare manuscripts. My father had been very proud of his son's achievements, and until he was well into his eighties, he had regularly travelled up to London to see Peter in action.

When Elaine returned in the evening we went out for a birthday dinner at the Huntingtower Hotel, and Peter allowed himself to drink a little more than normal. I also enjoyed my wine, and when I got up from the table, I felt more unsteady than usual. I knew that alcohol made my poor balance even worse, but I was unwilling to stop doing something that I really enjoyed.

30 September 2015

I felt sad as I watched Peter ride away from the house and up the drive, on the first leg of his long journey home. As always, we had greatly enjoyed each other's company, and although our respective health issues did cast a shadow, we certainly felt all the closer for it. After Peter had gone, I sat quietly in the kitchen and reflected on our situations.

8 October 2015

Judith, whose husband, Tim, is the Director of Music at Glenalmond, collected me and took me to my first Glenalmond lunchtime recital. Apart from chapel every Sunday, this was one of my first outings to a school event. A number of different pupils performed and I was very impressed by the standard. I was tempted to have some biscuits at the end, but a few days before I had choked on a piece of shortbread, and I didn't want to cause any embarrassment. After the recital, Tim and Judith gave me a quick tour of the music school. The atmosphere was bright, busy, and friendly. There were lots of smiling pupils and a real sense of enjoyment. Judith dropped me off at home, and I readily accepted her offer to make this a regular event.

14 October 2015

I went for my first physiotherapy appointment at Perth Royal Infirmary. My new physiotherapist is called Louise, and after carefully observing me walking a few times, she suggested that we spend that first appointment simply talking through my situation. Louise clearly has an excellent understanding of MND, and I felt very relaxed talking to her. She has a good sense of humour, but she quickly detected that I had not been following the exercise programme given out by my previous physiotherapist. At the end of our session I asked Louise how many sessions I would have. She said that she would be there for me, for the whole journey. I was so touched to hear this that I nearly began to cry. Louise walked back to reception with me and we made another appointment for the following week.

16 October 2015

I choked at breakfast time, trying to swallow four pills at once. I knew that problems with swallowing were very likely to occur at some point, but I found the whole idea of not being able to eat properly very frightening. Elaine told me that I was silly to try to take so many pills at once, and I would have to be more careful. Later, I made a conscious effort to chew my food more before swallowing, but the next morning, I was back to taking pills four at a time.

27 October 2015

Elaine had left for the Far East a few days earlier, and I was staying with her parents Janette and Jim in their house in Tranent. I had tried to argue that I would have been fine on my own, but everyone decided that it would be best if I had company. I suppose I could have insisted, but part of me was very happy to have been over-ruled. Ever since my fall in September, Elaine had been nervous about leaving me for long periods, and my alarm had still not arrived. I knew that Janette also worried about me. Throughout my stay she made sure that I was as comfortable as possible; she wouldn't let me do anything to help, and she generally spoiled me. The one thing she didn't do was talk about my condition. I suspect that would have been too upsetting. Jim told me stories about his cycling trips as a boy, and Janette reminded him that he had told me the same stories many times before. Jim also entertained me by playing his beloved piano. He could easily have played for hours, but Janette didn't find it as relaxing as he did.

Ed spent quite a time with us and I made an extra effort to lift Sam on to my lap without any help. We joked about her weight, but Janette declared that she was now only giving her a corner of a rich tea biscuit. I went down to Musselburgh to get my hair cut, and as I passed the racecourse, Loretto School, and Luca's ice cream shop and then drove over the bridge, I thought of all the years I had spent living there.

The four of us plus Sam drove up to Glenalmond and Ed spent a couple of hours hanging more of our pictures and putting up light shades on the top floor. Apart from an early exploration back in September, I had hardly been up to the top floor since we moved into the house. The stairs were fine but the banister was fairly low, and the drop to the bottom looked frightening. Once again I felt pretty useless and sat downstairs in front of the television.

28 October 2015

Janette and Jim took me to Perth Royal Infirmary for my next physiotherapy appointment. I left them in the WRVS café while I went down in the lift. It was good to see Louise again, and this time I was taken through a number of physical tests, some whilst lying on a mat and others when I was standing up. My left shoulder was still painful so Louise said she thought some cortisone might help. She said she would book me in for the injection clinic. She also told me that I should go to an orthotics clinic so that they could look at my left leg. Again, she would arrange this. Louise told me she would like to concentrate on a few stretching and balancing exercises; things that would be of practical help with basic daily activities. I thought this made absolute sense and I promised to follow the programme.

1 November 2015

Giles, the school chaplain, came in for a chat, and he arrived with a bottle of red wine. When I suggested that we open one of my own bottles instead, he politely informed me that he was rather fussy about wine, and thought we should drink his. We did, and it was very good. Giles, like all good boarding school chaplains, sees himself as a pastor for the whole school community, and he takes his role very seriously. He asked me direct questions about my MND, including my prognosis. I told him that I would have a better idea about that when I saw my consultant in three days' time. I also said that I was fully expecting to be told that I had ALS, the form of MND with the shortest life expectancy.

3 November 2015

The lady at Ninewells Hospital who carried out the Electromyogram (EMG) and Nerve Conduction Test was a more sympathetic person than the man who did the same tests back in March. She explained clearly what she was doing, apologised for having to put me through it all again, and was very thorough. Having a needle inserted into my feet, legs, arms, hands and neck was hardly relaxing, but after the initial shock, I found it uncomfortable rather than painful. I knew that these tests were important in terms of confirming the type of MND that I had, and I hoped I might be told there and then. However, at the end of the tests, the lady said she wouldn't give me any feedback, because I would get that from Dr. Morrison the next day. When I got back to Glenalmond, Elaine was waiting for me. She had just returned from Edinburgh Airport, after two long flights from Singapore. She, like me, had hoped that I might have heard something straight away, but we accepted that we would have to wait until the next day.

4 November 2015

On the drive up to Dundee that morning we both knew that the most likely outcome of this appointment would be a confirmation of ALS, so it came as no surprise when Dr. Morrison told us just that an hour later. He also said he thought it would be a good idea to have a feeding tube inserted in the near future. He explained that although I didn't need to use one yet, it would be better to have the procedure done whilst I was still relatively strong. I told him that we were planning to go to New York for a short break, just before Christmas. He said we should do this first and asked Dee to arrange for me to have the procedure early in the New Year. I asked Dr. Morrison how often I would see him in the future. He said he would need to see me after my feeding tube was fitted, but after that I could have an open appointment. He assured me that he would be very happy to see me again if I wanted, but Dee would now be my main point of contact. This was a very polite way of saying that there was nothing more he could do for me – that with no cure or treatment available, palliative care was the only thing on offer.

As soon as we left his office, Dee took us to the room next door to meet Laura Stephenson, an MND research nurse, who was based at the Euan Macdonald Centre at Edinburgh. Laura said she knew that I had just had my diagnosis of ALS confirmed, and that she was very sorry. I had managed to remain calm up to this point, but as soon as Laura said this I lost control, and the tears flowed.

5 November 2015

Judith emailed to say that she would be happy to collect me for the lunchtime recital. We laughed about her becoming my 'escort' and this made it easier for me to tell her about getting my confirmation of ALS. Once again, I was very impressed by the quality of the performances, and the range of pupils and staff who attended.

12 November 2015

My dietician explained how important it was for me to maintain my weight. I had always associated dieticians with very clear rules about keeping to a healthy diet, so I was amused to hear her say that I should basically eat whatever I liked. We talked about supplementary milkshakes that I could have, but we agreed that for the time being, I would try to manage without them.

14 November 2015

Meg and her boyfriend, Euan, drove up to see me. This was the first time that Meg had been up to my new home, and I hadn't seen her since she had introduced me to Euan, back in August. When Meg had attended her interview for a place at Moray House in March, she had not been confident of gaining a place, but she had been successful, and she was now about to go on another primary teaching placement. It was great to see her enthusiasm, and I was very pleased that she had chosen a similar career path to me. We talked about football, and I told Euan how amazed I was to learn that my daughter, who had never particularly enjoyed sport as a girl, was now a season ticket holder at Hibs. Meg looked very happy, and as her father, that was all I wanted to see.

CHAPTER FOUR

Saying Goodbye to My Sister

19 November 2015

At my physiotherapy appointment Louise gave me a couple of new exercises, and then explained why she thought it would be a good idea for me to get a wheelchair. This suggestion, coming so soon after the recommendation for a feeding tube, took me by surprise. Louise could clearly see my anxiety, but she calmly explained how a wheelchair would benefit me and Elaine. She asked me what plans I had for Christmas, and when I told her about our upcoming trip to New York, she suggested that a wheelchair would make it far easier to get around. We discussed the best places to visit, and Louise told me where she had been during her own visits. At the end of our session, I agreed that I would get a wheelchair and Louise said she would make the arrangements.

24 November 2015

The Orthotic department at Perth Royal Infirmary was not very accessible. There was very limited parking close to the entrance, and there was quite a steep path up to the front door. As most people who go there are disabled in some way, this was not ideal. As I went up the slope to the door I knew that going back down was going to be difficult, but I tried to put it out of my mind. The people inside the building were very helpful, and after watching me walk up and down, they said I needed something to help with my drop foot. For some months I had been aware that my left toe was occasionally catching on the ground as I walked, and that I was throwing that leg rather than lifting it up. The ever-observant Louise had spotted this at my first visit, and she had made this appointment. I was shown how to put on a contraption that would pull my left foot upwards. It involved a cuff above my left ankle, which had a loop attached to a hook that sat under the laces of my left shoe. As soon as I made a few steps with this in place, I could feel the difference it made to my walk, and when I left the building, I felt a little less nervous as I went down the slope.

When I got home, I decided that I would practise putting the thing on. Before I could do that, of course, I had to get it off. My thumbs and forefingers were so weak that it took me five minutes to get the elasticated loop from under the hook on my shoe; then I couldn't unfasten the Velcro that held the cuff in place. I got very angry with the Velcro and even more annoyed with my inability to do such a simple task.

26 November 2015

Peter called me in the morning to say that Steph had died during the night. Lizzie, my niece, had called me a few days before to say that her mum was in hospital, but at that point she didn't think that it was too serious. However, it transpired that a number of Steph's organs, including her very abused lungs and liver, were seriously failing. I was just so relieved that she had not been in pain, and had died peacefully with her three children at her bedside.

I was due to go for my cortisone injection that morning, and part of me felt that I should cancel it. I hate having needles stuck into me, and I had a perfectly good reason to avoid such an experience. I knew, however, that my sister, of all people, would have told me not to be so stupid, so reluctantly I made my way to Perth Royal Infirmary for the fifth time that month. Whilst the nurse examined my shoulder, I had a strong urge to tell him that my sister had just died. I knew this would be very unfair on him, but I also thought Steph's death should be noted in some way. In the end I kept my news to myself, and just thanked him for giving me an injection that I hardly felt at all.

3 December 2015

I had been agonising over whether I should go down to Steph's funeral. I certainly wanted to go, but I was really worried about the journey to Devon. The date had been set for December 11. That was the last day of the Glenalmond term, and there were two carol services that evening. Elaine had to be there for the services and there were no flights that would have got us back in time. In the end I decided that getting on and off a plane, or travelling for eight hours on a train on my own, would be too much. I called Peter and apologised for not going. He understood, told me to stop worrying about it, and said he would include some words from me in his eulogy.

4 December 2015

I got straight down to writing about my big sister. I wanted to keep my piece fairly short, partly because I knew that Peter would not have a great deal of time to speak, and also because I knew my brother would have written more than me. Our sister had left fairly detailed instructions about hymns, readings, and music, but she hadn't included much space for anything else. I sat for a while, looking at a blank document on my mac, and then decided to write something about my sister's childhood. Steph was thirteen when Peter was born, so his memories of her would be more as an adult. Once I got started, all sorts of stories came into my head, and the challenge quickly became one of editing rather than finding material. By lunchtime, I had written something that I hoped captured my sister's direct approach to life, her extraordinary popularity, and some of her insecurities. I sent my words to Peter, and then felt anxious for several hours, until I received a very kind and positive reply that evening.

5 December 2015

I went to do some shopping. My weekly trips to Tesco supermarket had become an important symbol of my independence. I enjoyed the drive into Perth because, apart from the awkwardness of getting in and out of the car, it was one of the few things that I could do as confidently as ever. There are plenty of disabled parking slots near the entrance to the store, and once I had a trolley I could use it like a Zimmer frame on wheels. That morning, as I slowly collected my groceries, I thought about my father. Dad had died two years earlier and that would have been his 90th birthday. He had been terribly upset about Peter's brain tumour, and although we all missed him very much, I was relieved that he had not lived to see his daughter die before him. My diagnosis would also have been very difficult for him to take.

When I got home, I lifted the boot too quickly, lost my balance, and fell backwards. Fortunately, there was still snow lying on the ground, so I had a fairly soft landing. I lay on my back for several seconds and began to panic about getting up. I knew that it would be very difficult to get up on my own, but I didn't really want to wait until someone came by. I had no doubt that a passing pupil would have come to my rescue, but the idea of being hauled to my feet by a fourth former would have been a dent to my pride. I managed to roll over, and crawl to the side of the car. I grabbed a door handle with freezing hands, and, after slipping around, I managed to pull myself up.

11 December 2015

This was the day of Steph's funeral, so at the time of her service, I read through the words that I had written about her.

My earliest memory of my sister is my earliest memory of anything. We were sitting in a red paddling pool on the lawn, at the front of the cottage where we lived, just outside Witheridge, in North Devon. Steph was cutting up pieces of card with a pair of scissors and our mother was sitting on a rug, laid on the grass. Steph

53

suddenly jabbed at a large piece of card and the scissors went straight through the side of the pool. The air came out, the paddling pool deflated, I burst into tears, and Mum was not amused.

On a Sunday morning a year or so later, after we had moved to the farm in the village, Steph helped me up a ladder in the yard, and we climbed to the top of the hayloft. By looking through a little hole in the wooden wall, we could see through the window of the Methodist chapel next door. We looked at all the people singing. Steph encouraged me to make faces and pretend to sing, knowing that no one could see us. When my mother saw me trying to get down the ladder, she told off Steph for taking me up there.

In many ways these incidents were typical of the way Steph approached things for much of her early life. She tackled everything head on, she did most things quickly and she showed little fear. This was how she rode her pony as a girl when out hunting, raced her Morris Minor against local teenagers on the road to Barnstaple, ran the beach shop at Putsborough, and drank with her friends in bars all over Devon. In some ways it was also typical of the rather strained relationship that she had with our mother. It would be fair to say that Mum and Steph often came at things from very different angles. Although Dad also lost patience with his daughter on occasion, he and Steph always had more in common, such as their shared passion for horse racing.

Sometimes people assumed that Steph was very confident, particularly when she expressed her strong views on politics and wrote letters to the Daily Mail. But Steph, like most of us, had many insecurities and she worried about things far more than most people realised. Whatever else was happening in her life, however, she was always there for me. She sat with me at the top of the stairs when I cried about going back to boarding school, she visited me in hospital when I had meningitis, and she hid me in the back of her car and took me to Barnstaple Fair when I was supposed to be at school.

Steph's driving frightened me back then, and I was still terrified 40 years later when, during a visit to see her in France, she insisted on driving me from Popiniere to the airport at Potiers. On that occasion, she was convinced that there was a mouse under her seat, and as we careered along narrow roads at high speed, she kept bending down to look for the imaginary creature. It was both a funny and dangerous journey, and I didn't know whether to laugh or cry. In some ways it summed up Steph' s time in France. There were some happy times at Popiniere, but they were difficult years for her.

When Steph returned to Devon in 2009, she was in a very fragile state, and we all feared that she might not get her life back together again. But despite the odd mishap, she established a new life for herself in Topsham. Most of Steph's motivation came from her desire to see her family and friends, and it was her daughter, Lizzie, who convinced her of the need for some self-control. Steph loved her time with her grandchildren, and she often called me to tell me about their cake-making sessions and shopping trips. Her second home was, unsurprisingly, the local pub. I remember speaking to one of her fellow drinkers, and he described the enigma that was my sister.

"Your sister is an amazing woman. She knows everyone, she watches Manchester United on the telly, she knows more about horse-racing than any bloke in here, she does that long crossword in the Telegraph, and she can drink most people under the table!"

A few years ago, Steph managed to get herself all the way to Edinburgh on the train, and she was a witness for Elaine and me at our wedding. She was in great form during her stay, and Elaine's family has never forgotten her. But then, who wouldn't remember my sister?

Later, in the afternoon, Peter called me to say that the chapel at the crematorium had been packed with people, and many of them had had to stand at the back. He said people came from all over Devon, including many who had known Steph when she lived near Barnstaple, but hadn't seen her for years. Peter said there was just enough time for him to include his and my words. After the service, everyone had gone back to Steph's favourite pub in Clyst St. Mary, where there had been plenty of tears, but lots of laughter. I still felt very guilty that I had not been there, but I was glad so many people had been. In the evening I went to the second of the carol services. It was a beautiful occasion, with some wonderful singing. I was frustrated, however, that I couldn't hold a candle in one hand and turn over my service sheet with the other.

15 December 2015

A few weeks earlier I had ordered a second-hand electric golf buggy, and it arrived that morning. Although I could still drive, I wanted a means of getting around the college grounds and playing fields. This would allow me to get some fresh air and watch some of the school matches. As 1st X1 coach at Loretto I had spent many hours umpiring cricket matches at Glenalmond, and everyone agreed that it was the most beautiful ground on the school circuit. The old wooden pavilion is a lovely building, and the view across the pitch and over to the mountains is simply stunning. After a brief lesson from the deliveryman on how to charge the batteries, I went for my first drive.

There was something missing of course: my golf bag. One of my deepest regrets about my condition has been that I will never play golf again. I had managed to play a few pitch shots on the practice area at Duddingston, just before we moved up to Glenalmond, but as soon as I attempted anything like a full swing, I fell over in a heap. By December, however, I had come to terms with this particular loss, and as I drove up the slopes that morning, I felt a great sense of freedom.

In the afternoon I had another delivery. This time it was my wheelchair. The man who brought it showed me how to fold it up, and how to put on the footplate, but after he had left, I sat in the chair and felt very sorry for myself. Of all the mobility aids I had been given, this was the one I had dreaded. Lots of people use grab-handles and walking sticks, but a wheelchair is a much stronger statement in terms of disability. I decided to see if I could do a circuit of the ground floor, and after a few collisions with furniture and some bangs on my knuckles, I managed to get all around the house. I was amazed how tired I felt after this short trip, and I found the whole experience very depressing.

17 December 2015

At Edinburgh Airport, we parked near the walkway that leads straight from the multi-story car park into the airport itself. This was my first outing in my wheelchair, and I suddenly realised what Louise had meant when she said that the wheelchair would actually make life much easier when we were travelling. When we got to the United Airlines desk the lady checked our passports and then asked for our visa waivers. I told her that I had looked this up on the internet and had read that UK passengers didn't need a visa. The lady explained that we still needed a visa waiver, and that we wouldn't be allowed on the plane without one. She told Elaine that there should be enough time to get electronic waivers downloaded online. Elaine initially tried to do this on her mobile, but when that didn't work, she had to move to a bank of laptops.

I was left beside the check-in desk, sitting in my wheelchair, feeling very frustrated and rather exposed. I had applied for visa waivers before other trips to America, and I couldn't understand how I could have been so stupid. I tried to wheel myself forward so that I could see around the corner, but I couldn't see the bank of laptops. I tried to turn around but I knocked into someone's case. Twenty minutes later, the staff began moving the posts that led to the desk, so I wheeled over to ask if the check-in was closing. I was told that there was still a little more time, and that one of their staff was helping Elaine. By this time, I was convinced that we would not make the flight. I knew that it was my fault, and I couldn't blame it on my MND.

Suddenly, Elaine came running around the corner with one of the airport staff. They quickly handed over our case, and then the member of staff grabbed the handles of my wheelchair. We raced through to the security area and went straight to the front. Someone removed my shoes and another man scanned me, and the wheelchair. I was told there wasn't time to put my shoes back on, so I held them in my lap as I was pushed along to the gate and out to the plane. Elaine helped me to my feet, my wheelchair was taken away and we sat in our seats right by the door. I laughed nervously, but Elaine looked exhausted.

22 December 2015

We were on the flight back to Edinburgh. We had had a wonderful time in New York, and I had become totally sold on the benefits of the wheelchair. The only place I didn't use it was at the theatre on Broadway, but it enabled me to go to Fifth Avenue, Ellis Island, St Patrick's Cathedral, Macy's, Little Italy, and the Metropolitan Museum. All the airport staff had been extremely helpful, and when we landed at Edinburgh someone wheeled me all the way back to our car.

24 December 2015

I was back at Edinburgh Airport, this time to collect Lorna, who was coming over for Christmas. As soon as I went through the barrier to the drop off zone, I saw my petite daughter pulling an over-sized suitcase. This was something I had seen many times over the years, as Lorna had returned home from her frequent travels. Before her current job in Saudi Arabia, she had already lived in Denmark, Germany, Australia, America, and Spain. Lorna had developed the travel bug ever since the two us had spent a month travelling around India when she was only ten. I got out of the car, and desperately wanted to help her with her case, but there was no way that I could help lift it. I stood there, feeling helpless and hopeless, as she struggled to get it into the boot.

Later, my mulled wine was only just ready when a group of teachers and children arrived at the house. Elaine and Lorna passed around drinks and sausage rolls, and everyone sang carols. Our house was the first stop on a well-worn circuit that would take the singers all around the Glenalmond campus. I was surprised that Fr. Giles declined the mulled wine, but he reminded me that he had to take midnight mass later in the evening

25 December 2015

A number of people had told us that the Christmas Day Service at Glenalmond was rather special, and they were certainly right. I was amazed to see nearly two hundred people in the chapel. In addition to teaching and support staff, there were local parents and pupils, and several families from the local community. Some of the little children walked up and down the aisle whilst their parents sang carols, and there was a lovely sense of inclusiveness and celebration.

Soon after the three of us got back to the house, Elaine's parents and her brother arrived, along with Sam, and they were soon followed by Tom, Cameron, and Alice. Alice was very excited. As always, she had been talking about Christmas for several weeks, and she was desperate to open her presents. Her severe learning disabilities are tragic, but her belief in Father Christmas is as strong as ever. Watching her delight in opening her presents that morning was wonderful to see. Once all the wrapping paper had been collected up, attention turned to lunch. Only a year before I had played a full part in preparing, cooking, and serving the food, but on this Christmas Day I was forced to sit by the fire, while Elaine and Janette were busy in the kitchen.

At the end of a long and very enjoyable lunch, Cam came up to my end of the table and poured me a glass of wine. I thanked him, but I was immediately suspicious. Cam rarely does such things unless there is an ulterior motive. Right on cue, he asked if he could try out my golf buggy. It was getting dark but he was desperate to have a go. I tried to explain a few basic points about starting and driving the machine, but in typical fashion, Cam said he knew all about how to drive one. By the time Cam and Tom returned from their drive, it was dark. They had clearly had some fun and I was looking forward to going out myself in the coming days.

27 December 2015

Lorna and I drove to Perth station to collect Meg, and we went for lunch in Mill Street. This was the first time that the three of us had been out on our own for over two years. Meg had always been old for her years, but she had been very much the younger sister. Now, however, I suddenly had two grown up daughters. As I listened to them talking about their lives, their friends, and their work, I felt grateful that I had seen them both reach adulthood. Whatever happened to me in the near future, no one could take that away.

28 December 2015

Lorna had a very early flight the next morning, so she was staying at a hotel near Edinburgh Airport. We had a final meal with her at the hotel, and said goodbye. Lorna had already travelled the world far more than me, and she had done most of it on her own, but I still felt anxious as I watched her go.

CHAPTER FIVE

Tears and Laughter at the Hospice

30 December 2015

I had not been looking forward to this day. Some weeks before, Dee had told me about the Cornhill Macmillan Centre at Perth Royal Infirmary, and she had strongly recommended that I go there on one of their Wednesday drop-in days. The idea of visiting a place that specialised in end-of-life care seemed very depressing, and I had originally decided that I was not ready for this. I knew that my illness was terminal, and I knew that I would probably need to go into a hospice at some point, but I didn't want to face this prospect so soon. However, after I received a friendly phone call from one of the staff at Cornhill, I decided to give it a try. Elaine and I drove up the hill behind the hospital and parked outside the centre. As soon as I stepped into the building, I felt calm and secure. The staff members were extremely friendly, and the whole atmosphere was completely different from what I had expected. There were lots of smiling faces and plenty of laughter, and I felt very much at home.

Caroline, a very bubbly and welcoming nurse, told us all about the activities and therapies that were available at the centre. She also made it clear that it was a place where people should feel safe to express themselves. As she put it, "Here, you can laugh or cry, and nobody will mind." I signed up for some sessions of reflexology, and as we drove home we both agreed that, despite my misgivings, it had been a very uplifting experience.

31 December 2015

If Cornhill had been a very pleasant surprise, New Year's Eve brought me down to earth. Hogmanay has never been my favourite time. Whilst many people see it as an exciting sign for the future, I tend to view it at as a reminder of how quickly the years pass by. That evening I was very aware of a sense of loss, and I certainly wasn't in the mood for parties or fireworks. In the end, we drank too much Champagne watching 'Still Game' and I kept falling backwards on the bed as I struggled to take my socks off. Lying there, unable to get up, like an upturned turtle, I didn't know whether to laugh or cry.

1 January 2016

We drove down to East Lothian for Jim's eightieth birthday lunch at Craigielaw. As always, all of Elaine's family was there, including Jim's children and grandchildren, and his two sisters and their husbands. I decided to have liver because I thought it would be easier to cut and swallow than beef. Due to the stiffness in my wrists, I was finding it increasingly difficult to use cutlery properly. Once or twice, I had been forced to ask Elaine to help me cut up meat, and I didn't want her to have to do it in front of everyone. At the end of lunch, Jim decided that he wanted to read out a poem that he had written for the occasion. Janette was embarrassed by the prospect of him doing this in the busy restaurant, so reluctantly Jim agreed to move into the foyer area. We all sat in chairs whilst Jim delivered his birthday poem. It was full of puns and reminiscences, but Janette seemed relieved when it was all over.

In the evening we went to Carberry to see Steve and Jean. They were some of the first people we told about my diagnosis and they had both been very supportive. Most bursars spend quite a bit of their time saying "no" to people who want their school to spend more money on a particular area. Being impartial and growing a fairly thick skin are essential requirements for the job, and Steve certainly appears to have both. He is, however, far more sensitive than most people know, and he has a great sense of humour. That evening, as always, they were direct, practical, but very caring, and we laughed a great deal.

3 January 2016

We went to see the film *Danish Girl*. Eddie Redmayne's portrayal of transgender pioneer Lili Elbe was astonishing. Throughout the film, however, I was reminded of his role as Stephen Hawking in The Theory of Everything, and how that film, one year earlier, had convinced me that I too had MND. The walk back to the car along Mill Street seemed longer than usual, and I realised that I should have listened to Elaine when she had suggested taking my wheel chair. Although I had been fine about using it in New York, I was finding it hard to accept the need for it at home, where we might meet people we knew.

5 January 2016

After phoning Ninewells Hospital to check that they had a bed for me, we left for Dundee. I was still slightly unsure about the exact procedure that I would be having, but I knew that it was called a gastrostomy. I settled into my single room, which had its own en suite bathroom, and spent most of the day reading. In the afternoon, an anaesthetist came to see me and he explained how the procedure would be carried out the next morning. Dee also popped in to make sure that I fully understood what would be happening.

6 January 2016

By nine thirty in the morning I was in the theatre, surrounded by nurses and doctors. I was more concerned about a tube that had to go down my nose than anything else, but a little anaesthetic made that experience mildly uncomfortable rather than painful. I remember the anaesthetist telling me that I would feel a little woozy, but the next thing I knew, the whole procedure was over. I was taken along to a large open ward, which seemed to be filling up with other people who had just had operations. A nurse told me she would be staying with me for a period of observation, and she said I must tell her if I needed painkillers. At first, I couldn't feel anything, but gradually a sharp pain developed in my stomach. I told the nurse that it felt as if I had been stabbed. She smiled, said that was very close to the truth, and gave me some morphine.

After half an hour, I was wheeled back to my room on the ward, and a nurse showed me how to use the remote control to adjust my bed. I spent a long time trying to make myself comfortable and finally settled on a half sitting-up position. I tried to look at my stomach, but the tube was covered with dressings. The slightest movement was very painful so I spent the rest of the day lying as still as possible, staring at the clock in front of me, and drifting in and out of sleep.

7 January 2016

I continued to lie as still as I could. Tea, meals, and blood pressure checks punctuated the day along with regular requests from me for water bottles. The dressing on my stomach had been changed in the morning and the nurse had told me that the site was still bleeding a little, so I would not be allowed to get up to go to the loo. Simply manoeuvring the water bottle into place was painful enough, so I couldn't imagine what getting out of bed would feel like. By the time Elaine arrived in the evening, I was feeling pretty sorry for myself, but, as always, she managed to cheer me up.

8 January 2016

At six in the morning, a nurse came and removed my dressings. Seeing the tube sticking out of my stomach for the first time made me feel a little nauseous. The nurse said the best thing would be for me to get used to touching it as soon as I could. She showed me how to fix a syringe to the end of the tube, and then she pushed the water into the tube. I felt a cold sensation as the water went into my stomach, but there was no pain. Within half an hour I was out of bed and having a shower. My arms and legs felt very stiff, and for the first time in my life I used a seat in the shower. I sat there, holding the tube from my stomach, and looked at the emergency cord that the nurse had told me to pull if I needed help. I was briefly overwhelmed by my loss of independence, and I shed a few tears of self-pity. I took hold of the cord, but I couldn't bring myself to pull it. I let go, hauled myself up, dried myself, and managed to get into a fresh pair of pyjamas. As I walked slowly back to my room, I passed another patient who was slumped on a chair in the corridor. He was singing *Flower of Scotland* with considerable passion, and I suddenly felt very English.

11 January 2016

I had spent most of the weekend sitting on the sofa at home. For some reason my cough, which I had had for two weeks, did not trouble me in hospital, but at home it had returned. The area where the tube came out of my stomach was still very sore, and it hurt badly whenever I coughed. I rang the district nurse number that I had been given at Ninewells, but I was told that I had got through to Perth city by mistake. I was given another number, and I spoke to one of the nurses based at Stanley. She told me that she would be out to see me the next day. I was relieved to hear this, and feeling more positive, I decided to write a belated email to our friend Emma Woods, in reply to her letter at Christmas. I didn't want to moan on about my condition, but I wanted to give her a fair picture of my life at Glenalmond:

Dear Emma,

This is a belated reply to your letter — sorry for the delay.

Well, we have survived our first term and Coll feels more and more like home. Elaine has been incredibly busy dealing with "matters of state" and I have remained below stairs in my supporting role! You said it was a special community and you were quite right. I have really enjoyed the chapel services and the lunchtime recitals — the singing is very beautiful and the music in general is very strong. I have managed to get to most of the Old Glenalmonder dinners, including the London one, and I have bought myself a second-hand electric golf buggy so that I can drive around the campus and watch matches. We had a wonderful few days in New York just before Christmas, and Elaine got very fit pushing me up and down 5th Avenue in my new wheelchair!

I have just got back after a few days in Ninewells. They decided to fit a feeding tube whilst I am still strong enough to have the procedure. Fortunately, I can still eat and drink fairly normally, but at least it is there for the future. The MND is relatively stable at the moment, although my balance is gradually deteriorating. Someone compared the disease to living in a room where the walls close in by an inch each day. My world, in terms of mobility, dexterity, and energy levels, is gradually shrinking, but despite that I feel positive about life on a daily basis, and I am very happy living here. I am looking out to the slopes, the sun is shining (just), I can see snow on the hills to the north, and the school bell has just struck twelve.

Elaine joins me in wishing you both a very Happy New Year!
With love,
Richard

12 January 2016

The district nurse had a good look at my tube and she cleaned the area under the plastic disk that keeps it in place next to my skin. She said everything was looking fine. We sat and talked about my MND and my care for the future. She explained that her team of nurses would be there to help whenever I needed them, and I felt extremely grateful for this reassurance. I knew that as time went by, I would become increasingly dependent on them, and although that was depressing, it was a great comfort to know that they would be there for me.

13 January 2016

This was my first outing since getting home. I was nervous about moving around with my tube, but I was determined to make it to my physiotherapy appointment. My regular sessions with Louise had become important to me, and I wanted to tell her about our trip to New York. Louise decided that it was too soon after the gastrostomy procedure to do any exercises, so after a chat about New York and her new puppy, called Luna, we talked about the best ways of managing my needs for the future. We agreed that I would go back in a month.

15 January 2016

Elaine Mundill came to see me in the afternoon. Elaine is one of the librarians at the college, and her library is one of the most beautiful buildings in the school. It sits in the middle of the main quad opposite the magnificent chapel, and it is a wonderful facility for the boys and girls. Very sadly, Elaine's husband, Robin, had died in the summer, after a battle with cancer. Robin was Head of History at Glenalmond, and he was much loved by his colleagues and his pupils. Elaine understands loss better than most, but she is determined to remain strong. Hearing her talk about Robin's work at the school, I couldn't help wonder how my Elaine would speak about me when I am gone.

16 January 2016

I decided it was time to see if my buggy would still work. It had been sitting outside the house for nearly three weeks since it was last used. Cam and Tom had charged it briefly after their drive on Christmas Day, but I knew that being uncharged in freezing temperatures was unlikely to have done it much good. I had plugged it in the day before, but even after 16 hours on charge, I was doubtful if it would start. I switched on the key, put the switch into forward, and pressed the accelerator. Nothing happened. I put the switch into reverse, and the warning sound immediately came on. This suggested that there was charge in the battery, so I turned the ignition key again and gently depressed the accelerator. This time, to my amazement and relief, the buggy moved. I felt a huge sense of relief as I made my way up the front avenue. I completed a full circuit of the college grounds and then decided to see if I could get the buggy into the main quad. There was a post in front of the main arch, but I just managed to squeeze between that and the wall. Aware that the post was obviously positioned to stop vehicles from entering, I had a look around to see if the coast was clear, did a quick spin around the library, and drove out again. As I went back to the house, I felt the same sort of mild exhilaration that I had experienced as a boy when I had broken bounds at school and not been caught.

20 January 2016

It was time for me to visit Cornhill on my own. As I walked down the passage and looked through the glass in the door to the main day room, I felt a little anxious. When we had gone there before Christmas it had been very quiet, but this time I could see that the room was very busy. It was a little like going to a new school or golf club for the first time. I was convinced that everyone would know each other, and that I would be left standing on my own. My fears were to prove totally unfounded. As soon as I was in the room, Caroline, the nurse I had met before, immediately came over and welcomed me like a long-lost friend. Within minutes, I was sitting alongside outpatients, carers, and volunteer helpers, with a cup of coffee. One of the volunteers asked me where I lived, and it turned out that a close friend of hers had a child at Glenalmond. She then asked me if I would like a hand massage. I said I had never had a hand massage, except as part of a whole-body massage. She said it was about time I tried it. I couldn't believe how relaxing it was, not just for my hands, but for my entire body. As I left the building later, I knew that this place was going to be very important to me, both for the immediate future, and for the rest of my life.

27 January 2016

For the first time since Christmas, I settled into a routine of writing in the mornings and watching TV or reading in the afternoons, As I did so, I found myself looking forward to my next visit to Cornhill. That day, Hazel, my dietician, was at the centre, so she took the opportunity to check my tube. After pulling the plastic disc a little further from my skin, she turned the tube through 360 degrees. It wasn't painful, but feeling the balloon inside my stomach moving around was a strange sensation. She told me that I should do this regularly to make sure that the tube didn't get stuck to my skin. I nodded, but I wasn't sure that I was ready to do this yet. Over coffee that morning I met Bob, who had also been diagnosed with MND earlier in the year. We chatted about our experiences and compared notes. Although we were both suffering from the same disease, it was clear that our symptoms were quite different. Bob had stiffness and some muscle wastage in his arms, and he talked about fasciculations. He said they were like bubbles that moved under his skin. In other ways, Bob was much more mobile than I was. He said he had walked all the way up the hill to the centre. I knew that a year ago I would have been able to do the same, but now I needed to drive up to my disabled parking space, walk with my stick, and take the lift up to the first floor. We talked about the way diagnosis had affected us, and we agreed that it had been, and in many ways remained, a very difficult thing to accept. Bob said that he thought he needed to become more positive about things, and I tried to explain how mindfulness had helped me in recent months.

As we sat and talked, I found it impossible not to think about which one of us was more or less fortunate than the other. I knew this was a pointless exercise; we were both in the same boat, and hardly in competition with each other, but it was difficult not to measure my situation against his. As I drove home, I realised that one of the reasons I wanted to help Bob come to terms with his condition was that it would help me do the same.

28 January 2016

I was in Dundee by 9.30 am for my second meeting with Moira Moulton, my neuropsychologist. This time, when we talked about mindfulness, I was able to tell her about my attempts to discuss it with Bob. Moira thought this could be a very positive experience for me, and she suggested that I should now be given an open appointment. I wouldn't have a specific date to see her, but I could ring to arrange one if I needed it. As I drove home, I tried to work out if I had been entirely honest with Moira, or myself. The fact that I knew quite a bit about the theory behind mindfulness didn't necessarily mean that I was actually putting it into practice. Perhaps I was simply hiding my anger and despair behind a facade of cheerfulness.

I got back just in time to go to the weekly recital. Afterwards, Judith came in for a cup of tea and we talked for over an hour. Judith practices psychotherapy, and she is refreshingly direct. She also fully understands the way that humour can help us cope with difficult situations. We laughed about a number of things but talked about sad things too. I had found that tears and laughter were increasingly going together, and it happened again that afternoon. Judith was not embarrassed by my outburst of emotion, and said she would pick me up again the following week.

31 January 2016

We drove into Perth and picked up my uncle Gerald and his wife Gill, who had travelled up from Devon by train to see us. Gerald has always been more like a big brother than an uncle, and some of my most vivid memories of childhood are the times we shared at family events in Devon. I used to spend part of my holidays on his farm, and he would take me rafting in the river that ran through a valley on their land. We stopped off at

Huntingtower for Sunday lunch and then came back to the house. Gerald has been writing about his childhood memories of growing up in North Devon. He told us some fascinating tales about that, and then we reminisced about the many people from our village that we had loved and lost over the years. This included Gerald's parents (my grandparents), his sister and brother-in-law (my parents) and most recently of course, Steph, his niece and my sister. After Elaine had shown them around the school, we took them to Evensong in the chapel, which they thoroughly enjoyed.

CHAPTER SIX

What's Happening to my Voice?

1 February 2016

Jenny, my speech therapist, came to visit me in the morning. Since her last visit in November, I had become more and more concerned about my voice. I could still speak fairly normally, but I had noticed that words sometimes didn't come out as clearly or as quickly as before, and that my voice seemed to get tired as the day went on. Many people had tried to reassure me that they couldn't tell much difference, but Elaine was certainly aware of it, and she knew just how much it frightened me. I know, with growing certainty, that MND will continue to take away my mobility, my dexterity, my ability to swallow, and my power of speech. Of all these functions, I think it is the loss of the ability to talk that worries me the most. A recent television documentary called *Simon's Choice* vividly described how a man with MND recently made the decision to opt for assisted suicide. Even at the end, his mobility and dexterity were better than mine, but he couldn't bear the fact that he was rapidly losing his faculties in general, and his voice in particular. Whilst a visit to Dignitas is certainly not on my wish list, I can fully understand why Simon made the choice he did.

Jenny and I talked about various apps that are available for use on an iPad. My preference was to wait until a synthesised voice, based on my voice banking, might be ready, but Jenny thought it would be best to get an app that could be used with certain commercially produced voices. One such voice, called Oliver, is described as "Standard English", and it is probably as close to my own voice as I am likely to find. Back in May, Ed had helped me to record hundreds of sentences that were then used by an American company online to produce a digital voice based on my own. Ed set up a grid system on my computer, which allows me to type in various sentences, and then play them back by simply hitting a single key. This voice is more like my own, but it tends to make me sound very impatient. At least I now have two voices that I can use to communicate with, when my own voice disappears.

2 February 2016

I had an appointment with an occupational therapist, who specialises in conditions like mine. This was another referral that had been made by Louise, who was determined that I should get all the help that was available. Sheena's room was full of all sorts of aids for people with limited dexterity. She had a close look at my hands, and after completing some basic tests, I realised that the fingers on my left hand would not straighten as well as those on my right. Several months before, at an MND support group meeting in Edinburgh, I had seen a man whose fingers were almost closed into fists. I remembered how difficult it was for him to grip anything, and how his wife had had to hold his cup of tea to his lips. Sheena brought out a spoon with a large, round, and spongy handle. I immediately said that I didn't fancy the look of this thing, but she persuaded me to try it. Of course, it was much easier to use than a normal spoon, and reluctantly I agreed to take it home, along with a similarly odd-looking looking knife and fork.

3 February 2016

That morning, I found it hard to find my positive self. The previous two days had clearly confirmed that my condition was continuing to decline, not necessarily more quickly (although I feared that was actually the case), but inexorably. I knew from past experience that if I allowed myself to dwell on the journey ahead, I risked becoming very angry, very depressed, and very frightened, so I struggled into my coat, took the little ignition key off the hall table, and went outside. After wiping down the seat with an old towel, I started my buggy and drove up the slopes in front of the house. The ground was very wet, and as I did a slow circle, I could see heavy tracks in the grass, but the sun was out and the views over the distant hills were beautiful. I tried to find the best way to get up to the main cricket pitch, but after discovering that this wasn't going to be possible, at least until the track was drier, I set off on a circuit right around the college grounds. By the time I reached home I felt a little better about the world.

An hour later, I was eating sandwiches at Cornhill, waiting for a hair appointment. Moira, a local stylist, has her own little salon on the premises, and it was such a relief to be able to have a haircut in familiar surroundings, without the problems of parking and walking to somewhere in Perth. After a break of only five minutes, Ann collected me for my first session of reflexology. I felt a little self-conscious as I sat on the treatment bed, and Ann started to untie the laces of my shoes. I offered to do it myself, but she said it was part of the service, and all I needed to do was lie back and admire the beautiful view out of the huge window in front of me. Ann carefully removed my shoes and socks, and then put oil on her hands. I had never had a foot massage before, except as part of a full-body treatment, so I wasn't quite sure what to expect. As Ann began to massage my feet, I quickly became very relaxed, and within ten minutes I could feel myself drifting off to sleep. The experience was really enjoyable, and I could feel the tension leaving me, not only from my feet, but from my whole body.

As soon as I had finished the session, I went straight into a relaxation class, and I slept through some of that too. By the time I left the building, I was feeling tension-free and the negative thoughts that had plagued me in the morning were well and truly gone.

5 February 2016

In the afternoon I drove down to Tranent. I was attending the annual dinner for Old Lorettonians in the painted gallery at Pinkie House at Loretto School, and I was going to stay with Janette and Jim. I felt embarrassed as I watched my eighty-year-old father-in-law carrying my overnight bag, but I felt even worse when he took it into his own downstairs bedroom. I tried to object, but Janette would have none of it. I was informed that they would be fine in an upstairs room, and told to sit down and have a cup of tea! Later, I tried my best to get into my clothes for the evening, but my fingers were too weak to do up the top button of my shirt. In the end I was forced to ask for help. The collar was a fraction too tight, and Jim had quite a job doing it up, not helped by our inability to stop laughing at the situation. After Jim had fastened my bow tie and Janette had helped me into my dinner jacket, I drove down to Loretto.

My next challenge was to get up the two sets of stairs in Pinkie House that would get me to the pre-dinner drinks on the first floor and the actual dinner on the second. Ben, one of my ex-pupils, and a fellow member of the OL Executive Committee, had arranged for me to be carried up the stairs in my wheelchair. Stubbornly, and probably ungraciously, I refused, and said I would manage with my stick. With Ben immediately in front and someone else behind me, I made it to the old library, collapsed into a chair with a glass of Champagne, and chatted to many old faces. One of these was Justin, who had been my Head of House back in the mid-nineteen eighties, and I had only seen him once since he left school. He was still as charming as ever, and he decided that it would be his mission to get me up the narrow winding staircase to the gallery. He hauled me to my feet, gripped me firmly under the arm, waved people aside, and proceeded to help me (in a frog-march sort of way) up to the floor above. Safely deposited at a table, I was delighted to find myself surrounded by a group of old boys and girls who had attended my Economics classes in the eighties and nineties. Some of the most precious rewards of a career in teaching can come to you when men and women, who you remember as boys and girls, make the effort to thank you for helping them when they were at school. That evening we reminisced and shared memories of times we had spent together in the classroom, in the boarding house, and on the cricket pitch. I thoroughly enjoyed their company, and I left them drinking merrily when Jim came to collect me at the stroke of midnight. When we got back to the house, Janette was surprised to discover that I was still relatively sober. This was due less to abstinence, and more to my growing inability to drink large quantities of liquid.

6 February 2016

I slept well in my borrowed bedroom, and got back home in time to watch the rugby. Supporting England in sporting fixtures, when you live in Scotland, can be a tricky business, particularly when it comes to football or rugby. I have learnt to keep quiet if England win, because even mild acts of celebration can easily cause offence. Of course, if England lose, I am expected to take the taunts that follow with good humour. I have tried hard to convince Cam that people in England tend to support Scotland on most occasions, but he refuses to believe me. During the last football world cup, I had to laugh when he asked me to wash a tee shirt he had been wearing at his Dad's house. When I opened it up it had "Anyone but England" emblazoned on the back. Anyway, that afternoon, England won the Calcutta Cup, and in the privacy of my own home, I felt free to cheer loudly when they scored.

9 February 2016

Elaine is off to visit prep schools in the north of England, so she dropped me off at Tranent on the way. As always, Janette and Jim looked after me very well. One of the only things I can do to delay the progression of my MND, apart from my exercises, is to maintain my weight. Janette certainly does her best to help me on this score, and after a second breakfast of fruit loaf, I worked my way through a three-course lunch, afternoon tea, and another meal in the evening. Once again, I felt guilty for using their bedroom, but I knew better than to argue. In the afternoon, Ed came up with Sam, and to my surprise, she actually looked slightly thinner. Ed had been to the vet with her and he had been given instructions to reduce her food and cut out all snacks. As we enjoyed tea and cakes, Sam begged on her hind legs, and Ed shouted at Jim when he tried to give her a corner of his biscuit.

10 February 2016

We packed our bags and left for Perth. Janette and Jim had kindly offered to take me to Cornhill for my usual Wednesday visit. When we arrived, they were a little unsure about joining me in the day room, but I managed to persuade them that everyone would be delighted to see them. I can perfectly understand why people are nervous about going into a hospice environment, but within minutes of going in, we were all sitting with the staff, enjoying tea and biscuits, and admiring the beautiful view. When I returned from another very relaxing reflexology session, Janette and Jim were chatting to some of the regular visitors, and they looked very comfortable. I was pleased that they had visited Cornhill; it was rapidly becoming a very important part of my life, and I wanted to share that with my family.

That evening, we watched a cup match between West Bromwich Albion and Peterborough. The team from the lower league played really well, and in some ways, they were unlucky to go out on penalties. Jim loves his football, and he is very knowledgeable about the game. However, he also loves to talk while he watches, and this habit tends to irritate Janette. The game was punctuated by several of her requests to "Shush, Jim!"

14 February 2016

Although half-term had officially started two days earlier, Elaine was kept very busy over the weekend, reading and sending emails, and finishing off her paperwork. Finally, late on that Sunday afternoon, she closed the study door, and we caught up with missed episodes of *War and Peace*.

17 February 2016

We spent two lovely days at Balathie House. This was our fourth stay at this very friendly hotel, but it was the first time I had used my wheelchair since our trip to New York. I felt very self-conscious as Elaine pushed me into the reception area, but when we found our suite, which is adapted for disabled guests, I felt much happier. The suite had a large bathroom, including a very accessible walk-in shower, a sitting room with French doors to the front lawn, and its own back door with a parking space immediately outside.

There are some very comfortable sitting areas in the hotel, and my favourite is a chair in front of the roaring fire in the hallway. In our previous visits, we had enjoyed some wonderful walks along the wooded paths that lead away from the hotel, next to the river. As I sat by the window in the sitting room during our first afternoon there and watched Elaine walk across the lawn, I had a strong sense of loss. Balathie, along with Kefalonia, is a very special place for us, and part of me hated the fact that we could no longer enjoy all of it together. When Elaine returned from her walk, she said she had found it very difficult, too. I didn't help the situation by joking about the need for her to find new friends to do things with.

On our way back home, we called in to Cornhill, and we both went to the relaxation class. Elaine enjoyed it as much as I did, and I just wished that she could come with me every week.

18 February 2016

At my physio appointment, Elaine finally got the chance to meet Louise. The two of them conspired to persuade me to try a triangular walker. The fact that I had started to use my wheelchair a little more seemed to convince both of them of the need for me to have more support than just my stick. When Louise fetched a three-wheeled walker, complete with a little pouch for carrying things, she laughed as she saw my face. "I knew you wouldn't like it" she said, but after trying a few trips up and around the gym, I think I surprised them by agreeing to give it a go.

19 February 2016

We had lunch at the Sheep Heid, with a group of old friends from Loretto. We have known Paul, Simon, Dan, and his wife Jasmine for years, and it was really good to catch up with them. While Elaine and the boys tried hard not to talk too much about school, Jasmine and I chatted about the challenges of life-threatening illnesses. She has had her own battles with cancer, so she understood much of what I have been through, as well as my fears for the future. As we talked for longer, I could feel my voice getting tired. As I opened my mouth to speak, the words didn't come out as quickly or as clearly as I expected.

22 February 2016

Some prep school girls arrived in the morning with their overnight bags. They were going to stay with us for three days while they took scholarship papers. It was good to hear young voices during the afternoon and evening, as the girls came and went. At bedtime, Elaine made the girls hot chocolate and they drank it as they studied for their exam papers the next day.

25 February 2016

I thought of my sister, Steph, and my daughter, Meg, on their shared birthday. Steph would have been 65 and Meg was 23. I hadn't organised myself properly in terms of buying a card, so I had sent Meg an e-card the night before. It involved singing penguins, and despite my in-built suspicion of such things, I found it very amusing. I also realised that it might not be long before I would have to use such things more often. After our weekly trip to the lunchtime concert, Judith invited me back to her house for coffee. We sat by the fire and talked about the appropriateness of the term "mental illness". At one point, I was trying to recall a story about something that had happened to me, when I found myself unable to speak. This time, it wasn't my voice that was failing me, but my inability to stop laughing. I had read that some people with MND experience "emotional lability", where they have uncontrolled bouts of laughter or tears, often at inappropriate moments. A few times recently, I had felt an involuntary grin forming on my lips, when listening to someone talk, and Elaine had noticed this too. However, that afternoon, for a couple of minutes, every time I tried to speak, the more I started to laugh. The more I tried to control myself (and the more Judith laughed too), the worse it got. After gaining a little more control of myself, I remembered that I needed to go for some shopping. Judith asked if I would get her a couple of things, so I headed off to Tesco. On the way home, I tooted the horn outside Judith's house, and she came out and took her shopping off the back seat. It was such a simple thing, but it felt really good to have done something for someone else. I was increasingly dependent on other people, but I wasn't useless, at least, not yet.

26 February 2016

Another trip in my wheelchair, this time to Perth Concert Hall to watch Glenalmond musicians, and those from a number of other local schools, perform at a Perth and Kinross charity concert to celebrate the Queen's ninetieth birthday. There was a wealth of talent on show, and the Glenalmond fusion band, along with the pipers and drummers, certainly played their part. Before the concert, we attended a reception in the art gallery next door. I was surprised how different the whole experience was in a wheelchair. As I sat there, surrounded by standing people, I experienced a range of emotions, including feeling small, detached, and slightly freakish. People responded in very different ways when they saw me. One or two glanced down and moved away, one woman just stared, and some smiled in sympathy. Fortunately, most people came straight over, shook my hand, and carried on as normal. Elaine didn't want to leave my side, but I reminded her that she was the person these people expected to see. I also knew that I had to get used to being in my chair on my own.

28 February 2016

At chapel, the choir sang an anthem called *O Nata Lux*. The sound of the unaccompanied singing was beautiful and very moving. This was the first time I had heard this piece, and I instantly added it to my mental list of "probables" to be played at my funeral. Up until then my front-runner had been "Blessed be God and Father" but I was beginning to have second thoughts. We then had to go down to Edinburgh for the Glenalmond music scholars' concert in St Giles' Cathedral, so we decided to have a late lunch on the way. We both ate steak in brandy sauce in a very friendly Italian restaurant on Queensferry Street, called Quattro Zero. Much as we love living in the beautiful surroundings at Glenalmond, it was good to spend a little time in our favourite city.

We arrived early at St Giles, and Elaine wheeled me to a good position near the front. There was soon a very good crowd of people, including Jim and Janette, and the concert that followed was simply outstanding. I have been listening to young musicians perform for over 40 years, both in England and in Scotland, but I have never heard a group of school pupils perform to such a consistently high level. At the end, Tim Ridley, the Director of Music, amazed many of the audience when he announced that several of the performers were only fourteen or fifteen. We went to a reception at the Radisson Blue after the concert, and I felt incredibly proud of the fact that Elaine is the Warden of the college.

1 March 2016

I kept writing for as long as possible in the morning, determined to cover as many blog entries as I could. As I write about more recent events, the facts are fresh in my mind, so the temptation is there to write in more detail. I took a look back over the entries for the last month, and this confirmed that the entries were, on average, getting longer. Just as I was about to leave for a yoga class at Cornhill, a series of sonar-like bleeps told me that someone was calling me on Skype. Seconds later, I could see and hear Lorna on the screen. I still find it slightly amazing that this is possible, when I am sitting in Scotland and she is in Saudi Arabia. It was good to speak to her, and I was also able to see her new dog, Lucy. She looked beautiful, if a little unusual, with a long and bushy tail. Apparently she is part desert dog. I said I wanted to get the blog up and running, so that it could go "live". Lorna told me to send her the rest of my entries, plus some photos, and promised she would work on it over the next two weeks.

I thoroughly enjoyed my yoga class. Initially, I felt a little self-conscious sitting in a chair when everyone else was on the floor, but the lady taking the class, and the other participants, made me feel very welcome. Throughout the class, instructions were repeated for "those who are sitting" and I was surprised how easy it was to copy most of the exercises. At the end, we did a winding down session, and the instructor gave out blankets to ensure that we felt warm. This was very relaxing, even sitting up, but it felt a little strange to be surrounded by eight women lying on the floor, looking as if they were all tucked up for the night.

In the evening, Giles came around for a chat. This time, I insisted we tried some of my own wine. I told him that following his slightly disparaging, but very accurate, assessment of my previous collection, I had arranged for some better wines to be delivered. I asked Giles to make the selection, and he chose one from the "old world". A little nervously, I asked Giles about types of funerals that could be held in the college chapel. To my relief, he was perfectly happy to talk about this, and he encouraged me to continue to write down my ideas and preferences. Talking about such things can obviously be difficult, but Giles' direct approach made it easier, and we both managed to find plenty of humour in the situation.

2 March 2016

At Cornhill, I enjoyed having my hands massaged by Elma. Both hands are now very stiff, and the fingers of my left hand are beginning to curl in. None of this is painful, but the massage relaxed my fingers, and indeed, my whole body. By the end, I could easily have let my head drop onto the table and slept. Caroline, however, was as lively as ever. A keen snowboarder, she made us laugh by leaping about on the floor, trying to demonstrate how she achieved 180 degree turns during her latest visit to the slopes.

In the evening, we went to McDiarmid Park to watch St Johnstone play Patrick Thistle. John Wright, a veteran Head of Classics at Glenalmond, has been an avid Saints supporter for 27 years and he is a long-standing season-ticket holder. John had arranged for a group of us from the college, along with the head teachers of Ardvreck and Craigclowan, to join him for dinner in one of the club's suites before the match. We had a good meal, and then the Glenalmond pipe band played before the game started. John insisted on wheeling me down to the disabled viewing area, where he sat next to me for the entire match. Unfortunately, Saints got off to a poor start, conceding two goals in the first fifteen minutes. After half time, they managed to pull one back, but they couldn't find an equaliser. This was the first live professional game that I have seen for a very long time, and the atmosphere was terrific. The whole experience, including the cheers and moans of the crowd and the pies at half time, took me straight back to my childhood, when I used to watch Exeter City with my dad.

3 March 2016

Judith emailed in the morning to ask if I would like to go for a walk (or a wheel) in Macrosty Park, after the weekly recital. I readily agreed, so after the concert we drove to Crieff. The district nurse had been in earlier to change the water in the balloon that sits in my stomach, and that holds my feeding tube in place. During the recital, the tube had felt very loose, so I explained to

Judith that I would have to adjust it. I mentioned that if anyone saw me sitting in her car with my tee shirt pulled up, fiddling with my stomach, they might wonder what was going on. We laughed at the prospect, but Judith found a discrete parking place where no-one was likely to see me.

I thoroughly enjoyed seeing the river and all the trees as Judith pushed me around and her Westie terrier ran behind us. I talked about my frustration that I will never again be able to do such things independently. As usual, Judith countered this with humour, and said if I wasn't careful, I might end up in the river. After we abandoned an attempt to go up a very steep path to the teashop, we drove into Crieff and had coffee by the fire, in a café called *The Red Squirrel.* Just as we were about to drive back, Judith remembered that she had a picture to pick up from a framer. By the time we had wound around the streets, I had no idea where we were, but Judith emerged from a shop carrying quite a big package. Getting it into the back of the car without damaging either the picture or the dog proved difficult. In the end a man who was passing came to her assistance. As I sat there, unable to help in any way, I felt like shouting, "I'm not being lazy, I'm disabled!" but I kept quiet.

5 March 2016

Meg and Euan arrived in the morning. Meg has enjoyed her teaching placement, but as always, there have been challenging moments. People are often quick to criticise teachers, but the vast majority of them have never actually stood in front of a class and taught all day. They have no idea how daunting that experience can be.

Fortunately, Meg is very child-centred, and she has a calm disposition, which are very useful traits in the classroom. I was keen to show Meg that despite my lack of physical mobility, I can still be independent, so I drove us into Crieff to get some shopping. The disabled parking spots at the supermarket were all full, so I had to park in a fairly narrow space. Trying to squeeze myself out of, and back into, the car, without knocking the door against the next car, proved very frustrating. Jumping in and out of a car is something I have done all my life without thinking, but suddenly, the whole process has become such an effort. My head and shoulders will not bend over as they used to do, my knees won't lift very easily, and my ability to balance on one leg unaided has totally gone. My instinct in such situations is to swear at myself, and that is precisely what I did that morning. On the way home, I took a short drive up the Sma' Glen. The sky was blue, the sun was shining, and the views of the snow-capped mountains were beautiful. Meg said I was very lucky to live where I do, and she was right. Mobility problems were quickly forgotten.

Late in the afternoon, Steve and Jean arrived. They had been collecting a tandem from Callander, and had taken a detour to see us. What started as a chat over a cup of tea rapidly became a whole evening, as we caught up on each other's news. While Elaine and Steve collected an Indian takeaway from Methven, I offered Jean a glass of wine. To my annoyance, I couldn't find the strength in my fingers to twist off the cap, so Jean had to do the honours. Having poured the wine, we clinked glasses, but in the process, I managed to throw wine all over my trousers and on to the carpet. Jean sponged off the wine with a kitchen towel, and we had a good laugh at the situation. I tried in vain to work the bellows so that the fire would take, but Jean had to take over. Quite rightly, she refused to allow me to feel sorry for myself, and told me to get out of the way before I fell headfirst into the flames. The curry was very good, and there was enough left over for me to have some for tea the next day.

CHAPTER SEVEN

My Blog Goes Live

I spent much of the morning writing entries for the blog. I am getting close to the point where my writing will be "live" rather than retrospective. I have sent all my material, plus some photos, to Lorna, and she is creating the actual blog site. In the afternoon, I drove up to Dundee for an appointment with Dr Morrison. He wanted to check that I was coping with my feeding tube, which had been inserted exactly two months ago. I reported that I was getting used to having it sticking out of my stomach. We talked about the unpredictability of MND, and the importance of living in the present. I said I tried to resist the temptation to either look back at what I used to be able to do, or look forward to what I might become. I described how I used to see life like a tunnel, that led from the past, into the present, and through to the future, but now I try to focus only on the cross-section of the tunnel that represents "today". I said that while I fully understood the bleak outlook that faces all of us with this disease, I was disappointed by the way the progression of MND was sometimes portrayed in the media. I mentioned two television documentaries in the last six months that had strongly implied that, for all MND sufferers, the road to paralysis was always rapid, and life expectancy was very short and predictable. We agreed that neither assertion was necessarily correct, and that while such programmes did much to raise awareness of, and money for, MND, they were not always helpful for newly diagnosed patients. Before I left, I mentioned that I was writing a blog, and that I had tried to trace the progression of my symptoms over a three-year period. Dr Morrison said he would like to read it, and suggested I contact MND Scotland to see if they might publicise it.

9 March 2016

After another session of 'seated' yoga the day before, I was back at Cornhill for my drop-in session and relaxation class. I took in some sandwiches and chatted to Margaret, who I had first met a few weeks earlier. Margaret is from South Africa, but now she lives in Perth. We talked a little about our conditions, and Margaret explained how determined she is to remain in the present. We then had a brief discussion about the apartheid system that had existed in her home country. Margaret told me how awful life had been for her mother at that time. She said her mother had to step off the narrow pavement in her own street, whenever a white man or woman came towards her. I found this a very touching example of the appalling way the old, racist governments of South Africa behaved. Caroline joined us for a while at our table, and we soon found ourselves laughing again. Margaret went off for her aromatherapy and I joined Caroline for my relaxation class. This week, the sound track consisted mainly of waves gently lapping onto a beach, and in no time at all I was fast asleep.

In the afternoon, I re-read a section of my blog entries and found a number of spelling and grammar mistakes. I knew that my eagle-eyed daughter would spot them in Saudi Arabia, but I noted them down and emailed them to her. I then started to play around with different fonts to see which one might be best to use for the blog. I googled "fonts for blogs" and was surprised by the number of different websites that are dedicated to this topic. I was quite confused by all the different types of script families, such as serif, sans serif, cursive, and fantasy. One website suggested that I should avoid serif scripts like Times New Roman and Garamond, because they have little hooks on the end of each letter, and this can cause the type to look blurred. I had a little laugh at this, because it reminded me of a headmaster I worked for, who insisted that the only font that was appropriate for his school was Times New Roman. I liked the look of a font that I had never heard of before called Lucida Sans, but I wonder what Lorna will come up with?

10 March 2016

Our alarm went off at 4.15 a.m. Elaine had to get to London for a meeting, and she wanted to avoid the daily traffic jam at the Forth Road Bridge on her way to Edinburgh Airport. I tried to get back to sleep by using the relaxation techniques I had learnt at Cornhill, but there were too many things going around in my head. After writing an entry in the blog, it was still only 9.30, and for the first time in many weeks, I couldn't decide on what to do next. I read for a while, checked my emails, and then just sat and looked out of the window. I knew that this was dangerous territory, because, as my mother used to say, "It doesn't do to dwell on things". I settled back to my book but It seemed like a long day. In the afternoon, Judith emailed to suggest that I drive up in my buggy to join her and Lottie for a walk. I did my best to go at walking pace, and Judith showed me some new paths that were suitable for the buggy. After our drive/walk we came back to the house for a quick cup of tea, and Lottie slept peacefully on the carpet. Elaine got back at 7.30, but after a brief catch up, she had to go and prepare her notes for a series of meetings that were taking place early the next morning. She has been working very long hours, seven days a week, and I am relieved that the Easter holiday will soon be here.

12 March 2016

I spent much of the morning looking at holiday ideas for the summer. With the beautiful but mountainous Kefalonia sadly ruled out, I looked at hotels that were described as "wheelchair friendly". This, however, was often misleading. Many of them only had two or three rooms with wheel-in showers, some had very limited wheelchair access to other facilities, and some were situated on steep ground, which made it almost impossible to get out of the hotel. In the end, I concentrated on specific websites for "accessible holidays", and I was pleasantly surprised by how helpful these were. In the afternoon, just as I was about to settle down to watch the England vs. Wales game, Jim, Janette and Ed arrived.

They had been visiting friends in Comrie, and had decided to call in for tea. I quickly pressed the "record" button on my remote. We had a good catch up about family affairs. The night before, they had watched Cam perform in a musical revue at the Loretto theatre, and as usual, he had been one of the star turns. Cam is totally set on a career in drama, and although he knows all the statistics about out-of-work actors, I believe he has the confidence and talent to pull it off. At the moment, however, Elaine's main concern is that Cam buckles down to some revision over the Easter holiday, in preparation for his AS level exams in the summer.

In the evening we watched a recorded episode of *Happy Valley*, one of the stand-out dramas of the year, and then we caught the end of *Casualty*. The main storyline concerned a lady suffering from Huntington's disease, a neurological condition, for which there is no cure. The parallels with MND made it frightening, and compelling viewing. After the programme was over, I looked up the condition online, and I couldn't stop myself following a web link to MND. I had resisted doing this for many months, and I immediately regretted doing so. I already knew all about the progression of MND symptoms, and the statistics on prognosis, but reading them again made me aware that I had already lived longer with this disease than many of my less fortunate fellow sufferers. I had a picture in my mind of a fourth official holding up a display with the amount of extra time I still had left. How many months or years will I get until my game is over? I tried to use my relaxation techniques to get myself off to sleep, but for the first time in many weeks, I spent part of the night thinking about the uncertain future rather than the present.

13 March 2016

Lorna rang me and talked me through the address for my blog. She had been working on it for a few days, and was confident that it would be live within a week. It was strange to read my own words on what is effectively a website. We talked about the technicalities of editing the blog, and Lorna, quite rightly, suggested that I continue to send her the blog posts, and she will publish them in WordPress.

15 March 2016

It seems strange to be writing about the present, after months of writing about events in the past. Well, yesterday I went back to Crieff to see if it might be a good shopping venue. The scenery on the back road is certainly more spectacular than the road to Perth, and the town itself has more character, but things went downhill as soon as I reached the supermarket. I found a disabled parking bay, but when I reached the trolley park, I realised that I hadn't brought a pound coin to "release" a trolley from the pack. I went into the store, waited for five minutes to get some change, and promptly dropped some coins on the floor. When I finally had a trolley, I discovered that its wheels were almost as unsteady as my legs. Instead of providing me with some stability, it made my progress around the store very unpredictable, so I simply grabbed a few essentials, plus some "good quality mince" for Judith, and headed home. I had a busy afternoon sending and reading emails to and from Lorna. She was working on the layout for the blog and she wanted me to log on to the site and see what she was doing. Watching the layout of the headings and photos take shape, literally as I watched, was very exciting, and I realised that I couldn't have done it on my own. I am very lucky to have had Lorna's help.

In the evening, Janette phoned. She knew that Elaine was away for two days, and she wanted to know if I was coping on my own. I said I was doing fine and we had a brief chat. I know that my voice has gradually been deteriorating for months now, but last night, during that call, I really struggled to speak with any fluency. Janette must have heard how hesitant I was, and how slow and slurred my voice sounded, but she would never have said anything. I knew then, for certain, that it was time to find a new voice. As soon as I put the phone down, I picked up my iPad and purchased the *Predictable* app that my speech therapist had recommended. As I watched the little "download" circle gradually fill on the screen, I knew that the loss of my voice was going to be one my biggest challenges yet.

16 March 2016

My drive to Cornhill took longer than usual because they were re-surfacing the main road between Crieff and Perth. I joined a long queue before being "escorted" through an assortment of lorries, tar spreading machines, and steamrollers, although I doubt if they run on steam these days. When I arrived, someone had parked right in front of the main door, an area that is supposed to be kept clear for ambulances. I felt compelled to tell the lady at the desk, and she promised to find the owner. Once upstairs, I was joined for coffee by a lady who is fighting a battle with lung cancer. She appeared to be very positive, despite having had one lung removed, and after comparing medical notes we talked about smoking, drinking, and God. After I had eaten my sandwiches, Hazel showed me how I could change my feeding tube, should it ever fall out and I can't find a nurse or doctor. I had told her that I was nervous about travelling abroad with the tube, but she said there was no reason why I shouldn't learn how to do the procedure myself. She gave me a demonstration tube and balloon to take home. Sheena then came over and asked me some questions about how I am coping with basic tasks at home, such as getting up and down the stairs, cooking, and washing up. She suggested that I try a perch stool, and said this would stop me getting so tired. Before going to my relaxation class, I collected a number of email addresses from staff and volunteers, and said I would send them a link to my blog later in the day.

As soon as I got home, I called Lorna. This was the day my blog was to go live, exactly a year on from my confirmed diagnosis. We spent an hour going through final edits, section headings, and photos, and then Lorna sent me the link to the blog. I had drafted group emails and Facebook messages earlier in the week, so all I had to do was copy and paste the link, and send them off. I told Lorna that I was relieved that it was going out at last, but she reminded me that I would have to keep on writing. I tried to forget the blog during dinner, but there were several pings on my iPad. When I checked my inbox, I was surprised to find several emails from people who had already looked at it, and this continued throughout the evening. I had no idea how people would react, so I was delighted to get so many messages of support. I was very touched by some of the comments, and they made me laugh and cry, in equal measure.

17 March 2016

At breakfast this morning, I couldn't peel my banana. I tried to grip the stalk between my right hand thumb and forefinger, but when I pulled, it kept slipping out of my hand. I tried with my left hand, but the result was the same. I looked at Elaine, shook my head, and gave it to her. She casually peeled it and handed it back with a smile. I remember getting help like this from my mother when I was a young child. It was easy then, because she was doing things that I had never managed myself. Now, however, I am increasingly having to watch Elaine, and others, do things for me that I have done for most of my life: simple things like opening a packet of crisps, taking the lid off the butter, or lifting off the seal that hides underneath the cap of the milk carton.

Judith emailed to ask if I wanted to go to Perth to watch some of the Glenalmond pupils compete in a local music competition. I asked if I needed to dress up, and when she replied that "smart casual" would be fine, I went and changed out of my jeans. We called into Tesco on our way and I took charge of the trolley, partly to help, but mostly to give myself support. After some prompting from Judith, I bought an Easter egg for Elaine. At the checkout I tried to take a single £10 note from my wallet, but my silly fingers pulled the rest of my money out too. I tried to put the notes back neatly, but ended up scrunching them into an untidy ball.

When we arrived at the church, I reminded Judith that we could park virtually anywhere with my blue badge, so we stopped right outside. Judith's husband, Tim, is the college Director of Music, and he was inside with a number of his pupils. As always, they sang beautifully, both in the small choir and solo sections. Some of them wanted to get back to school rather than wait for those who were performing later, so they squeezed into the back of the car and we drove back. As I sat in the front, I smiled as I listened to the young and excited voices behind me, joking about the heat of the Scottish sun coming through the windows, and talking about their plans for the Easter holidays. They were so full of life.

18 March 2016

First thing in the morning, I had a look on Facebook to see if there had been any response to a group message that I had sent out about the blog two days earlier. I am still a novice at social media, so I wasn't at all confident that my message had actually reached anyone. To my surprise, however, there were several comments and messages, and they were all very supportive. I realised that I was becoming distracted by my desire to get positive feedback, so I settled down to some reading instead. In the evening we drove down to see Elaine's daughter, Alice, who has a supported-living flat in Edinburgh. Alice had a stroke before she was born, and a combination of epilepsy, severe learning difficulties, and autism mean that she needs one-to-one care, twenty-four hours a day. Her condition can also seriously affect her behaviour, so these visits can be unpredictable. That night, however, Alice was in a very positive mood, and she was happy to talk about her plans for the Easter break. A couple of months ago, she had been given a CD of traditional Scottish dance band songs that Jim and a friend had recorded a few years before. Jim sang the songs and played the piano, and his friend played the accordion. Alice has taken a real liking to these songs, and she plays them continuously on a loop. That evening we heard them all three times over.

19 March 2016

It was a beautiful morning so I got into my buggy and went for a drive. I had been told that there were some good paths to explore near the college golf course, but in order to get to them I had to cross the road near the end of the drive. The pavement was just wide enough to take the buggy, but just before the dropped curb, there was a signpost, which blocked my way. I thought of trying to reverse all the way back, but I couldn't twist my neck far enough to see behind me. I couldn't contact Elaine, or anyone else, because there was no mobile reception, and I didn't want to sit there, waiting for a passing pupil or car. In the end I simply turned off the pavement with a bump and headed across the road. The woods on the other side are ideal for children to play in, and in addition to the beautiful golf course, there is a wonderful outdoor classroom. I went a little way into the woods but I didn't want to risk getting bogged down in the wet ground. I will retrace my tracks in the summer.

20 March 2016

Palm Sunday, and there was a donkey in chapel, ridden by the daughter of one of the staff. Child and beast behaved beautifully and all members of the congregation were given palm crosses. As soon as we got back to the house, Elaine organised laundry and then got to work on her report writing. Doing 400 individual reports is quite an undertaking, but she is determined to finish them by the end of term, on Wednesday. I know from experience that writing reports after the children have gone can be more peaceful, but less purposeful. In the evening we went to the Spring Concert. The hall was packed with staff, parents, and guests, and we were all enthralled by the outstanding quality of the programme. From soloists to quartets, and from the string orchestra to the concert band, the standard of the performances was consistently high, and served to underline the extraordinary musical talent that exists at Glenalmond. At a reception afterwards I met up with an old friend that I hadn't seen for over 25 years. Alwyn was a housemaster here and he was my opposite number when I ran the cricket at Loretto. Alwyn had a stroke 20 years ago, and this left him with serious mobility and communications problems. Neither of us knew about each other's health issues, so it was an emotional reunion. Alwyn gripped my hands in his, and we cried a little and laughed a lot more. We reminisced about the times we had spent umpiring, and talked of our determination to enjoy life to the end.

March 22 2016

I met a new MND sufferer at the support group meeting, which was held at St Johnstone FC. Ian lives in Comrie and he has had the disease for a few years. Over soup, pies, and chicken drumsticks, Dawn Hamilton from MND Scotland gave us an update on research, funding, and therapies. Apparently, someone is about to be appointed as an MND therapist for my area. Dawn said I should hear quite soon which type of therapy I will be offered. I really don't mind; reflexology, aromatherapy, and therapeutic touch — they all sound very relaxing. Dawn explained that the original promise by the Holyrood government to double the number of MND nurses in Scotland has not been kept. Nicola Sturgeon has argued that the delay is due to recruitment problems, but others say that some health boards have spent the money that was allocated for MND on other things. We agreed that a combination of the two claims was the most likely story.

Before I left, I told Ian all about Cornhill, and I said I hoped that he would come along on a Wednesday. His wife, Shirley, gave me his email address, and I promised to send him a link to my blog.

On the way home, I thought about what I should have said at the meeting — that there simply aren't enough of us with MND to make it worthwhile for governments or drug companies to invest heavily in MND research. The sad fact is that drug companies are more likely to make a return by developing yet another pill for headaches than they are by investing in research to find a possible cure for a deadly, but very rare disease, like MND.

Giles came around for a chat later in the afternoon. We briefly resumed our previous discussion about my funeral options. Giles, quite rightly, suggested that it would be unfair of anyone, including me, to try and lay down exactly how their funeral should be arranged. He said partners, children, and loved-ones should never be put in a position whereby they may feel guilty for not having carried out someone's wishes exactly to the letter. I completely agreed with him and promised to allow for plenty of discretion. After that we covered more immediate and positive matters, like where we were planning to go on holiday.

23 March 2016

I had a busy time at Cornhill. I arrived with my sandwiches and spent some time battling to open the cardboard box that contained them. I tried with my hands, then with my teeth, but I had to admit defeat, and ask one of the volunteers for help. Several visitors and staff members came over to talk about the blog, and I collected seven more email addresses. Moira collected me for my hair appointment, and this time I asked her to cut off as much as she liked. She said she was not allowed to use electric clippers but she quickly got to work with her scissors. Moira knew that I was keen to make the relaxation class, and she delivered me back to the dayroom just in time. I now know most of the words that accompany the various CDs, and as I lay back in my zero-gravity chair I found myself anticipating the instructions. The chair, the music, and the calming voice combine to create the perfect environment for relaxation, and the only thing that disturbed the peace for the next 30 minutes was the rhythmic snoring of one of the participants. When the lady snorer woke up, we all politely lied and pretended we hadn't heard a thing.

As soon as I got home, I saw an email from MND Scotland. Niamh had written an intro for me to accompany a link for my blog that she was happy to put on their website. She also asked for a photo. I spent several minutes trying to find a decent photo, and then emailed her back to say I was happy with what she had written. Within five minutes she emailed to say that it was all up on the website, under *MND Information - Personal Stories*. I checked the site, and there it was — the wonder of modern technology.

CHAPTER EIGHT

I Shouldn't Look at Statistics

25 March 2016

As the day before had been very quiet, I decided not to write a post. At first I was relieved, because I could spend the morning doing other things. But relief quickly turned to frustration. Writing every morning has become such an important part of my routine that when I don't do it, I feel lost. Ever since I retired, I have struggled at times with the freedom that comes with not working. At first, having a choice over how to spend my time and having few deadlines sounded wonderful, but I quickly found that I imposed deadlines and routines on myself. I broke up my housework into different categories, and then allocated them to different days of the week: bathroom cleaning on Wednesdays, dusting and ironing on Thursdays; hoovering on Fridays. I even had a timetable for my golf practice. If I got out of sync with these activities, I became frustrated, and had to quickly catch up with my routine. Over the last six months, my ability to help with the housework has gradually diminished. Last September, I was still hanging up washing on the pulley, hoovering the carpet, and ironing my shirts, but now, even folding a large towel can seem daunting. Getting hold of the corners without losing my grip can take several attempts, and lifting the towel above my shoulders can cause me to lose my balance and stumble backwards. Writing, on the other hand, poses fewer problems.

Elaine finished her end-of-term newsletter by lunchtime, and we went to Tesco in the afternoon. We needed to stock up on food because my brother and his two sons are coming to stay at the weekend, and Tom and Cam are also coming up to celebrate Tom's twenty-first birthday. I would like to have helped, but I knew from experience that one of Elaine's "big shops" would take well over an hour. I stayed in the car and listened to commentary of a rugby league game between Wigan and St. Helens.

26 March 2016

Peter and his sons George and Max arrived. I collected them from Perth station, and we had a very noisy journey home as we cheered and groaned during the last few overs of England's T20 World Cup game with Sri Lanka. Eight-year-old Max was the only one who never wavered in his belief that his team would win — his optimism remains undented by years of expectation and disappointment. It was great to see them all again. Peter has been a huge support to me since my diagnosis, and this was the third time he had made the long train journey up from London. George is really enjoying his work at an Art College in London and he is rapidly becoming a very accomplished photographer. Max is as bright as a button, exhausting, and very entertaining. We hoped the rain would stop and allow us to get outside but it continued to pour, so we settled in for an evening by the fire, and caught up on all the family news.

27 March 2016

Easter Day, and after a few false starts, we all made it to chapel. Regular staff families were joined by people from the local community, and Fr. Giles led a very inclusive and friendly service, including some wonderful humour in his sermon. Afterwards, most of the congregation collected in the Senior Common Room and enjoyed coffee and chocolate cakes. Max certainly tucked into the chocolate, but as soon as we got back to the house he was keen to get outside and play football. I am no longer bitter about my inability to run around, and at my age, my pace would be rather slow, but as I looked out of the window and watched Peter and his two sons run across the slopes, I did feel a little jealous. Later, however, I was able to join them in my buggy. Max sat in the middle, between Peter and me, and George jogged alongside. I didn't let Max steer, but he enjoyed pressing the accelerator to the floor. We did a circuit of the school grounds and just got back before the rain started again. Elaine then arrived with Cam and Tom, and for the first time since Christmas, the house felt full. Tom opened his birthday presents, Cam spent an hour doing his hair, and then Elaine drove them off for a celebratory dinner.

Peter helped me download my *Model Talker* synthetic voice to my iPad and install it on my *Predictable* app. The app is very clever, and as its name suggests, it has the capacity to predict text and turn it into speech. There are several categories of phrases that can be pre-loaded, and there is even an emote button to simulate the sound of a sigh, a yawn, or a laugh. At the moment, the thought of relying on this type of communication is very depressing and frightening. I also know, however, that I probably won't have any choice but to embrace the technology and simply get on with it. I typed in various words and phrases, and my text was translated into speech. It sounded rather electronic, but it was definitely based on my own voice. George reckoned it sounded like a mixture of myself and Stephen Hawking.

28 March 2016
While Peter and George dashed around the house getting Max organised for the journey back to London, I put on my shoes. I am getting quicker at attaching the cuff that goes around my ankle and the loop that attaches it to my laces, so I was ready to go before the others. I went to the loo, but discovered that the metal pull of my zip had got stuck between the bottom of the zip and the fabric of my trousers. This is something that has happened many times over the years, and I have always simply prised the pull back up with one of my fore fingers. This time, however, I could not grip the end of the pull. I tried again, but with no success, and by that time everyone was ready to leave. I went to the front door, asked Elaine to do the zip, and we left for the station. When I returned to the house, Tom and Cam had surfaced, and we all had a brunch of bacon, eggs, and toast. The boys had things to do, so we took another trip to the station, where Tom found a train for Glasgow and Cam headed off to Edinburgh. Back at the house, it all seemed very quiet.

29 March 2016

A letter arrived from MND Scotland with information about their manifesto for the upcoming elections. The manifesto calls for action on a number of issues, including the level of financial support for MND sufferers and their carers, the number of MND clinics, and the level of MND training for health and social care professionals. Some of these problems are linked to the lack of knowledge about MND. Given that the average GP is only likely to come across one, or possibly two, cases of MND in his or her entire career, it is hardly surprising that there is a lack of understanding of the symptoms and the effects of the disease. I am incredibly lucky to live where I do. The staff and volunteers at the Macmillan Cornhill Centre in Perth are excellent, I have the opportunity to see my dietician or my OT on a weekly basis, and I can call the local district nurses whenever I need advice. I also have regular contact with my specialist MND nurse and my physiotherapist, and I have an open appointment with both my consultant and my neuropsychologist. This level of service is not available to everyone.

The manifesto "ask" that interested me the most, however, was the one calling for more money to be spent on research, including the funding of three PhD studentships, and the setting up of a Scottish base for MND clinical trials. Treating the symptoms of MND by providing more care and support for those who suffer from it is a wonderful thing to do, but if governments are really serious about tackling this disease then research is the answer, and that brings us back to economics.

31 March 2016

The first thing I looked at in the morning was a Facebook message from a former pupil who had been reading the blog. He wanted to know if I thought my brain had compensated for other parts of my body that had declined, and if this had enabled me to feel more positive. Not an easy question to answer at 8.00 a.m., but I replied as follows:

Good question, Tom!

I don't think my brain works any better since the loss of other faculties and the terrible shock of diagnosis. It is more that my attitude and approach to life has adapted to my situation. I now live very much in the present, and rarely waste precious time, either thinking about what I used to be able to do, or worrying about the further "losses" that will happen in the near future. By enjoying everything I see, feel, and do "today", I find that I am more at ease with life and with myself than I was for much of the time before this happened. I am also lucky that I really enjoyed my career, that my daughters are now independent, that I live in a beautiful part of the world, and that I have Elaine.

I was quite happy with my reply, and it made me feel good about the day ahead. Unfortunately, my mood rapidly became less positive when I looked at the back of an MND manifesto card that I had been reading the day before. A number of statements were written in large dramatic print. These included information on the nature, the symptoms, and the incidence of the disease, but it was the final statement that jumped off the page:

'From diagnosis, average life expectancy with MND is just 14 months.'

I had read similar information about the prognosis for MND sufferers before, so I knew this fact already, but seeing it there in bold print gave me a shock, particularly as it is almost exactly 13 months since my own diagnosis came through. A number of ridiculous questions came into my head. 'Do I only have a month left? Will I be Mr. Average when it comes to MND? How does Stephen Hawking fit into all of this?' After ten minutes of reflection, I was saved from further torment by the arrival of Linda, the district nurse. It was time to change the water in my feeding tube balloon. Linda talked me through the procedure and let me use the syringe to take out the old water and then replace it with fresh water. After we had finished, we chatted for a few minutes about the timings for future procedures, and then Linda gave me her email address so that I could send her the blog. When she had gone, I put the MND manifesto in the back of a drawer and cheered myself up by re-watching the highlights of England's victory over New Zealand in the semi-final of the T20 World Cup.

2 April 2016

Emma spent the day with us. She has known Elaine since she was a girl at Dollar Academy, and she is currently working at the University of Warwick. Emma is a very bright lady, and when I saw her briefly after my diagnosis, she gave me some very direct, slightly unpalatable, but excellent advice. She told me that, difficult as it was going to be, I was on a new journey, and although it was not the one that I would have chosen, I had to try and enjoy it. At the time I could not square the fact that I had MND with the concept of enjoyment, but one year on, not only do I understand what she meant, I know that she was right.

After a late breakfast, Emma and I sat in the buggy and Elaine walked alongside, as we went on a tour of the college. With all the pupils on holiday, I squeezed into the main quad, and as I sat in the buggy, while Elaine and Emma went into the dining hall and chapel, I chatted to Dougie, one of the college janitors. Dougie asked how I was managing with the buggy. I told him that I could charge it easily enough, but I might need help checking the batteries for distilled water. Dougie said if I gave him a call he would be happy to come up and do this for me. Another act of kindness and another problem solved. We drove all around the college buildings and grounds. Emma, like most first-time visitors, was amazed by the beauty and size of the campus.

In the afternoon, I had an email from Judith saying that Lottie had been injured after being attacked by another dog. She was having surgery at the vet's. Fortunately, a couple of hours later, I heard that Lottie was out of surgery and out of danger. I was so relieved. We get so attached to our pets, and dogs in particular tend to reward us so much with their affection and loyalty. I vividly remember my first dog. Pip was a border collie, and he was supposed to be a sheep dog for our farm in Devon. My dad brought him home on my eighth birthday, and for the next three years, we were pretty inseparable. We walked all over the village together, we raced in the fields, and we tumbled around in the farmyard. My only regret was that Pip was not allowed to come into the house. I had watched a film about a dog called Lassie who slept at the foot of his master's bed, but dad insisted that Pip was supposed to be a farm dog, so he had to stay in the stable, next to my sister's pony. When I went off to boarding school I missed Pip terribly, and I was always surprised that he remembered me when I saw him in the holidays. Dad tried to train him to round up sheep, but Pip never really got the hang of it. Dad said I had spoilt him too much as a puppy, and I am sure he was right.

3 April 2016

A group of friends from Loretto came up for lunch. With eight of us, it was a good opportunity to use the dining room, but my feelings of guilt and uselessness re-surfaced as I sat there in the morning and watched Elaine prepare all the food and lay the table. We enjoyed seeing everyone and catching up on their news. Having spent so many years working with them as colleagues, it was strange to be out of the loop with regard to their daily lives. They were keen to see around the school in the afternoon, but I took the opportunity to have a rest instead. Admitting that lunch had tired me out was rather embarrassing. All I had done was sit in a chair, eat and talk — what could be tiring about that? The truth is that constantly lifting a fork to my mouth makes my arm ache and the more I talk the more effort it takes to speak. While everyone else walked around the college grounds I put my feet up and watched football on my laptop.

4 April 2016

Before we could leave for our short break at Ballathie, Elaine had to finish some schoolwork before putting her "out of office" message on her email. I foolishly decided to wear a different pair of shoes because I thought they might go better with some of the clothes I was taking. These shoes were much newer and much stiffer than my normal ones. I sat on a chair and swore as I repeatedly tried to loosen the laces enough to squeeze my left foot into the shoe. I simply couldn't do it so, for the first time, Elaine put my shoes on for me. I know that this will become a daily occurrence in the future, but I don't want it to start now.

As soon as we drove up to the hotel, we both felt more relaxed. It was great to be back in one of our favourite places. The fire in the hall was still roaring, the view over the river Tay was just as beautiful, and the food that evening was as lovely as ever.

5-6 April 2016

Despite the poor weather forecast, our first two days at Ballathie were sunnier than we expected. Having to use the "disabled room" is sad but it certainly has its compensations. It is far bigger than the normal rooms and has its own lounge, overlooking the lawns and the river Tay. I spent several hours sitting inside and outside the French windows, reading my first "Jo Nesbo" thriller and looking at the beautiful view. A line of daffodils created a yellow ribbon that stretched away from the lawn and down the slope to the water. A blackbird was busily collecting twigs for nest building, and the willow trees arched gracefully over the river. Across the valley I could see a herd of cows grazing and later, in the evening sunshine, the whole scene was bathed in gold.

The location of our room is somewhat unusual, situated at the end of a passageway that includes various entrances to, and exits from, the kitchen area. On our way up this passage, as we head for breakfast and dinner, we usually meet a number of staff carrying trays of food to and from the dining room. And what a dining room it is. Facing the river, with large bay windows, the interconnecting rooms are furnished with lovely round tables, ornate wall panels, and beautiful drapes, and, best of all, the food is stunning.

After dinner, we took coffee in the bar, next to the fire. There is a large illustrated book about the distilleries of Scotland on the shelf under our table, so following some research each day, I tried a different malt whisky each evening. On our second evening a man came in as we and another couple were enjoying our drinks. The man ordered whisky and, when asked if he wanted any ice, he announced in a very loud, and rather pompous voice, "That's the way to ruin it!" The man across from me smiled as he raised his arm and rattled the ice in his glass.

8 April 2016

I had that sinking feeling when I woke up and realised that our holiday was virtually over; that we would soon have to pack up our bags and carry everything out to the car, or, in our case, poor Elaine would have to do all that while I sat idly by. There was still breakfast to enjoy, though. Our fellow guests were used to seeing me being pushed around the hotel, but as I wheeled into the dining room and transferred myself from the wheelchair into a "normal" chair, several of them stole a glance in my direction, and one or two gave me that sad smile that says, "You poor chap". The Maître d' immediately appeared and took the wheelchair to its parking spot, just around the corner. He, and all the other hotel staff, have been incredibly kind throughout our stay. Unlike some people, who see the wheelchair but not the person in it, they have looked me in the eye, talked directly at me, and treated me just like anyone else. I wonder if they get training in this sort of thing?

I had my usual bowl of porridge, served with cream, followed by scrambled eggs, bacon, sausage, mushrooms, and tomatoes. The need for me to keep my weight up is of considerable importance, but after breakfasts like these, I don't think there is much danger of me returning home any lighter than when I left. After "we" had finished the packing, we spent a final half hour reading the newspapers in the hotel lounge, and then left for home. We were sad to go but I was looking forward to seeing Lorna, who had arrived in Scotland on Monday. She has been staying in Edinburgh, catching up with her sister and friends, and Ed is driving her up to Glenalmond on Sunday. As always, it will be wonderful to see her.

9 April 2016

After a good sleep and a long lie in, getting myself up this morning was very frustrating. As I stood up, I could really feel the stiffness in my legs. This, like so many things to do with the MND, has gradually been getting worse for a long time. The trouble with such a slow deterioration (and I am grateful that it has been slow) is that it creeps up on you and then you suddenly realise that things have changed. It is rather like looking at the hour hand on a clock; it is moving inexorably around, but you don't actually see the movement. I walked to the bathroom, feeling like the tin man from *The Wizard of Oz*. I then very nearly lost my balance as I bent down to take a towel off the heated rail, but just managed to grab the sink and prevent myself from falling straight into the shower screen. Once in the shower, I sprayed very hot water on to my legs and felt the stiffness gradually begin to ease.

I could see the sun streaming in through a gap in the bathroom curtains, so I decided it was time for jeans instead of cords. I grabbed a pair off a hanger in the wardrobe and took them over to the low chair, which I use as a prop for getting into trousers. I sat on the chair and worked one foot into one of the legs of the jeans. I then stood up, grabbed the top of the chair with one hand and, whilst balancing on the one leg that was already in the jeans, and tried to get my other leg in. Because the jeans had not been worn since they were washed last summer, they were rather stiff, and I had to lift my leg higher than normal in order to get my foot into them. I tried several times but I couldn't do it without falling over, and after each attempt I felt so tired that I had to sit down for a few moments to recover my strength. Refusing Elaine's repeated offers to help, I sat back in the chair and very gradually worked my toes into the open leg of the jeans, and then pushed my leg inside. I carefully stood up, and finally managed to get them pulled up. The simple process of putting on my trousers, something that I used to perform in about three seconds, had just taken me five minutes — and then it took me two more to fasten them.

10 April 2016

I spent a lazy morning reading and watching a recording of *Match of the Day* while Elaine went to collect Lorna. With the school empty, it was very quiet, but the peace was eventually shattered by the familiar sound of Sam's barking. Lorna had decided to bring my old friend with her for a few days. I had wanted to greet Lorna on my feet, looking as normal as possible, but after standing unsteadily in the hall for a minute or two, I realised that this would be a pointless exercise, and rather ridiculous. Part of me, like most parents, will always see my daughter as a child, but she is an adult in her mid-thirties, so trying to protect her from reality would be silly. I took hold of my three-wheeled walker and made my way to the back door. Of course, Lorna didn't look at me, or the walker, in horror — she simply came over, gave me a big hug, and made a joke about how many wine gums I could put in the basket!

The afternoon was taken up with exchanging news. I found it difficult to give Lorna an accurate picture of how the MND had progressed since I had seen her at Christmas. "Oh, very much the same, but worse" sounds both uninformative and ambiguous, but it was all I could come up with at first. I then admitted that my mobility had declined due to the increased stiffness in my legs; that my dexterity was worse because my fingers were less flexible, and my tiredness in general was greater. When put like that it sounded more alarming, but we did our best to skate over the implications. I was more interested in hearing about her life in Saudi Arabia, and I was pleased that her job with Aramco seems to be going really well.

Later on, I joined Lorna for a walk with Sam — well, they walked as I drove the buggy alongside. Triathlon Scotland were holding a training event at the college, and competitors kept running out of the quad, grabbing their bikes and peddling away. Sam, in typical dachshund style, decided that we needed protection from these strange creatures, so she barked fiercely as they raced by. We kept to the slopes and didn't risk letting Sam off her lead, in case she caused a pile up on the front drive. Having got to the top of the slope, we stopped for a quick photo and then Lorna and Sam jumped into the buggy for the ride back down.

12 April 2016

As mentioned before, my brother, Peter, was diagnosed with a brain tumour in 2012, and he is currently in remission. Despite having a terminal illness of his own, Peter has been a tower of strength for me since my own diagnosis. On 4-5 June he will be raising money for MND by taking part in a sponsored night cycle ride all around London. This is the email he sent to all his friends yesterday:

Dear friends and family — apologies for the group email —

Last year my brother Richard (62 years old, ten years older than me) was formally diagnosed with Motor Neurone Disease, after a slow onset of symptoms, which began some three years ago. This diagnosis came three years after I had also been diagnosed with my terminal illness, from which as many of you know, I am currently in remission. The two illnesses are normally found in around 1/100,000 people (there is no genetic link between them); both suffer from poor funding for research, and both are currently incurable.

Richard is remaining as upbeat as possible despite the onset of this terrible disease. He is sharing his experiences on his moving blog, which he is sharing and asking others to share if people are interested:

https://momentswithmndblog.wordpress.com/

He is receiving wonderful support from MND Scotland. But funds for more research into this horrific disease are urgently required, as are funds for care of those suffering from it. I know some of you will have relatives or friends or friends of friends who are suffering or who have suffered from MND.

Despite the fatigue and myalgia I encounter myself, I am determined to do my bit to raise awareness and raise some more funds for MND research. Please support me for this London Night Cycle Ride taking place on 4-5 June for this important cause close to my heart.

Today I have created a fundraising page on Virgin Money Giving.

Thank you for any degree of sponsorship — at whatever level — you can offer.

Yours,
Peter

This morning, I checked the link to Peter's virgin money giving page, and discovered that his target of £1,000 has already been exceeded in less than 24 hours — 53 days before he takes to the saddle. For anyone involved with MND, this is very good news.

13 April 2016

Lorna and I have just got back from Cornhill, where we have spent much of the day. I was very keen for her to see the centre and meet as many of the staff and volunteers as possible. As I drove into Perth, I talked a little about end of life issues — it seemed appropriate to do so as we were heading for a place that specialises in palliative care. Lorna was quiet in the passenger seat but also brave. She said her main worry was that when the time comes, she wants to be able to get back from Saudi Arabia to say goodbye.

As soon as we walked through the door, coffee and biscuits were brought over and lots of the staff introduced themselves to Lorna. I had told her that it was a happy place, but Lorna was still surprised by the warmth of the welcome, the amount of laughter, and the very positive atmosphere. We sat and talked to lots of different people for well over an hour, and Elma gave me a hand massage. By the time we went to have our lunch, Lorna was totally won over by the people and the place. It means a huge amount to me that she has been there, and that she can now picture me there when she is back in Saudi Arabia.

After lunch we went back for the relaxation class, and Lorna joined the rest of us on our zero gravity chairs. Today it was my favourite storyline about a visit to the beach, and we both drifted off to sleep during the session. When we came through the front door at home, we met three members of the college support staff. One of them asked if we had had a good day, and I said, "Yes, we've had a fun time at the hospice". The lady looked a little taken aback.

14 April 2016

Another plane journey with "wheelchair assistance" — this time from Edinburgh to London City. I began the day by saying another farewell to my daughter, although this time it was me leaving her rather than the other way around. Lorna was staying in Edinburgh for a few more days before flying back to Saudi Arabia, but she will be gone before we get back on Sunday. They say it is easier to leave someone than to be left, but I still felt the same old feelings of regret and even abandonment as we hugged each other goodbye. She made me promise to get in touch if anything "serious" happened, and said she would fly back immediately.

Everything at Edinburgh went smoothly. I was given priority through security, and allowed to keep my shoes on and remain in my chair. A man spent a few minutes running his hands over me, and a portable scanner over every inch of the chair. The only awkward moment came when he felt my feeding tube through my sweater. I explained what it was but he looked a little uncertain. I was tempted to reassure him that the tube was not filled with liquid explosive but decided that might cause a panic. When we reached the gate, I was quickly scooped up by one of the airport staff and taken down to the ground floor. I was wheeled across to the back of the plane and we were placed on a mobile lift, which took us up to the aircraft door. I only had to walk a couple of steps to cross the threshold and three more to get to my seat. We sat in the otherwise empty plane for a few minutes and then everyone else came on board.

For some reason, we came into London via Clacton-on-Sea, but this long and slightly delayed approach gave us a wonderful view of the city. Half an hour later, we were in

the Caledonian Club where Elaine has honorary
membership through her job. She had to attend a
function at The Gherkin in the evening, but I was feeling
very tired after all the travelling so I stayed behind and ate
in the club's impressive dining room. The club, as its
name suggests, is very Scottish. There are plenty of
highland landscapes on the walls, along with tartan
carpeting and upholstery. There is also a huge selection of
malt whisky behind the bar, and a stag's head on the wall.
The dinner menu included several Scottish favourites,
such as haggis and cranachan, but I chose beef wellington.

16 April 2016

After a filling "full" breakfast, Elaine wheeled me
around the beautiful square next to the club. A very
friendly taxi driver pushed me up a ramp into his vehicle,
and ten minutes later he pushed me back down, next to
the entrance to the National Gallery. The whole gallery
was wheelchair friendly and we worked our way steadily
through the centuries, beginning with the 15th and ending
with the 20th. So many wonderful paintings to see,
including works by Rembrandt, Monet, Botticelli, and
Stubbs, but my favourites were a group called Marriage à-
la-mode, a series of six pictures painted by William
Hogarth. After all those religious paintings from the
centuries before, it was a relief to see some of the humour
and satire of the 18th century.

17 April 2016

So much of what I saw today reminded me of the late
Princess Diana. First of all, there was the story from the
morning news about William and Kate sitting on "her

bench" in front of the Taj Mahal, then we walked past her memorial fountain in Hyde Park, and finally we passed Harrods, which always makes me think of her. In the middle of all this, Elaine pushed me along the edge of the serpentine and we watched children trying to feed the swans. Few of the swans actually got any of the bread intended for them because the pigeons, gulls, and geese stole most of it before it reached their beaks, despite their outstretched necks.

At London City Airport things were chaotic. The belt to carry luggage at the bag drop area was broken, so there was a very long wait for Elaine before she could hand over our luggage. I sat in a crowded corridor, getting rather irritated as people bumped into my wheelchair with their over-sized cases. Most were very apologetic, but one or two showed no concern whatsoever as they knocked me into the wall. Despite their frustration, everyone formed an orderly queue, and we got to security in plenty of time. A rather harassed young lady with a scanner in her hand waved Elaine through, and then told me that I would have to get out of my wheelchair and remove my jacket and shoes. I explained that with no stick (that had already disappeared on the belt) and with no Elaine, that would be very difficult. Her response was a terse, "Why?" I said, "I have MND", but she looked at me as if I was mad. Fortunately, an older, and more helpful colleague, heard this, and came to my rescue. He carefully scanned me and my wheelchair and reunited me with my stick. At the gate, another assistant took me on a journey that included some industrial-sized lifts and a very long "behind the scenes" corridor. We finally emerged on to the tarmac, where I was transferred to a very narrow seat, strapped in, and carried backwards up the front steps of the aircraft. Until very recently, I could have walked up on my own, but those days are gone forever.

CHAPTER NINE
Falling Over Again

18 April 2016

Alison, my speech therapist, came to see me in the morning. I have been quietly (and sometimes not so quietly) fretting about my voice for several months now, and whenever Alison visits, I become more anxious about it. This is unfair on Alison because she, like all the health professionals, is positive and very supportive. We had a chat about how my voice can get tired, just like most other parts of my body. Talking is such a natural thing to do, and something that, until very recently, I have taken completely for granted. As a teacher, I spent hours speaking every day, and only in early September each year, after the long summer holiday, did I ever feel my voice begin to struggle. Alison reminded me that the muscles in my mouth, including my tongue, are getting weaker and that I must rest my voice, particularly after prolonged use. I fully understand the logic behind this advice, but I find it difficult to put into practice.

I showed Alison the *Predictable* app that I had recently downloaded on my iPad. This was the app that Alison had recommended to me during her last visit. I would like to have been able to demonstrate my competence in using this device, but I had to admit that I had hardly ever played with it. Over the last month I have opened the app several times, but after a minute or so of typing in words and hearing my slurred synthetic voice speak the text, I have usually felt so depressed by the experience that I have quickly switched it off. I apologised for this, but Alison told me not to worry. She said the app was there for the future, and I should communicate with my own voice for as long as possible. I stopped myself from asking how long that might be because I knew that it was an unfair question. Instead, I simply said, "It must vary a huge amount, I imagine". Alison said people ask her this question all the time, but there really isn't a definitive answer.

After Alison had gone, I sat and spoke to myself for a little while. I tried to pronounce each word slowly and deliberately, rather as if I was talking to someone who understood very little English. I tried a few simple words like "no" and "go" and they didn't sound too bad. I had noticed before that when giving my name on the phone, I often had to repeat it several times before the person on the other end got it. I said, "Richard Selley" as clearly as I could, but I found it hard to get my tongue into the right position, and both words still sounded slurred. In my frustration I said, "bugger!" — that came out more easily and much clearer.

20 April 2016

I have always found the beginning of the summer term to be so much better than the other ones. Even as a boy returning rather reluctantly to boarding school, I felt excited by the prospect of better weather and the beginning of the cricket season. Yesterday I watched groups of boys and girls coming down the slopes in the morning sunshine. Some were deep in conversation, presumably catching up on news from the holiday; some were busy on their mobile phones, taking advantage of the sudden improvement in signal strength due to a newly installed mast, and a few were kicking a rugby ball around. They looked very happy and relaxed, and there were no signs of the stresses that exams will bring in the coming weeks.

At Cornhill Caroline was back from her holidays. She looked very tanned, except for white, panda-like rings around her eyes, due to wearing goggles. She told me all about her snowboarding exploits in Austria and France, and explained that she will only be based in the day unit for another month or so. She will then return to the in-patient section, which is on the ground floor of the building. Working in palliative care is certainly not for everyone, but Caroline, like so many of the staff at Cornhill, has the essential qualities of compassion and empathy, combined with a very positive attitude, and a great sense of humour. Their priority, by necessity, is to provide those in their care with quality, rather than quantity of life.

I talked to Hazel about my feeding tube. She had brought a different system for me to look at. This one has a balloon on the inside, just like mine, but the ports for filling the balloon and for feeding are on the outside of a button that sits flush with the skin. The thought of not having a tube dangling from my stomach was good, so I decided to have it changed over the next couple of weeks. In the middle of our talk, Margaret came and sat next to me. She asked if we minded her joining us, and I said, "Not at all Margaret, I shan't be getting my tube out". Hazel and Margaret couldn't stop laughing, and I blushed like a little boy! After regaining my composure, I ate my sandwiches, enjoyed a hand massage from Elma, and went off for my relaxation class.

22 April 2016

A year after I retired, I began writing about my childhood memories in general, and my days at boarding school in particular. I think I was trying to make sense of the fact that although my own experience at boarding school was less than positive, I had just spent my entire career working in that environment. When I began, I had no idea how much I would write, but I got into a rhythm of writing about 500 words each weekday morning. After a few months, I suddenly realised that I had written over 40,000 words. Lorna, who was staying with us at this point, read what I had written. She told me that I needed to do a great deal of editing, but pointed out that I had already written the equivalent of half a novel. She suggested that I should re-write it in the first person, so that my voice as a child could be heard. I was daunted by this prospect, but after a few weeks of uncertainty, I started writing again. At the time of my MND diagnosis, I had written over 80,000 words, but there was still some editing to do. As I tried to come to terms with what was happening to me, my motivation to keep writing deserted me. Logic dictated that with time running out, I should press on and try to finish the project, but part of me simply couldn't see the point.

Yesterday morning, as I was trying to find something on my laptop, I came across a file called "Memories". I opened it, started reading, and within minutes, I was absorbed in the process of editing. I decided that I would start working on the project again. My first session, however, was cut short by a ring on the doorbell. Elizabeth Peters is a community OT, and she was visiting me to advise on accessibility issues in general, and the prospects of having a wet room installed in the future. Lynn Peebles, the College Facilities and Maintenance Manager, joined us, and she and Elizabeth discussed building regulations, timings and grants. Elizabeth fully understood the progressive nature of MND, and although she shared my desire to be as positive as possible, she calmly and sensitively reminded me of the need to plan for the future. We talked about ramps, an electric wheelchair, a seat for the shower, and a hands-free toilet. The latter certainly conjured up a very different picture of a "wash and blow dry" than the one I normally have in my head.

24 April 2016

I lay in bed and tried to decide whether I would go to chapel. I really enjoy the services, particularly the singing, and although Elaine is away on school business, I knew I would have been very welcome. My main worry was that I wouldn't be able to wear a tie. I can still do the knot, but I can't do up the top button of a shirt or fold down the collar. I told myself that this was ridiculous — God, (whoever or whatever He may be) would surely not judge me by my appearance. No, my problem is simply that I am still too proud to ignore certain conventions. Fairly soon, I am going to have to swallow my pride or face the prospect of becoming a recluse, but yesterday was just too soon.

Having made my decision, I stayed in bed and switched on the radio. There were some beautiful love songs being played on Steve Wright's show, but there were only so many happy requests and stories that I could take. I was genuinely pleased for all those people who were celebrating their 50th wedding anniversaries or their 80th birthdays, but after a while their longevity only served to put my own situation into sharp contrast. Telling myself that I was being selfish, I switched it off and got up.

I spent much of the morning watching the London marathon. As aerial pictures of the course were shown, it was strange to think that I was there, exactly a week ago. As usual, the elite men's and women's races were dominated by very thin athletes from Kenya and Ethiopia — they seemed to glide effortlessly along the roads. The cameras kept finding runners from Britain; they looked bigger and stronger, but their progress looked rather laboured in comparison. In years gone by I would probably not have watched for much longer, but this year the most interesting part of the programme was the mass race. Thousands of men and women of all ages, shapes, and sizes were running for charity and raising millions of pounds. Some of these people were running for MND, and this made me feel very grateful to them — and very guilty for not having run for charity when I was fit enough to do so.

Tim and Judith came to collect me after lunch for my first wheelchair outing around the college grounds. We went straight up the front avenue, and after a trip around the edge of one the boarding houses, Tim pushed me up to the cricket pitch. We were soon joined by Judith's neighbour, Corinne, and we settled down to watch the game. I can think of no better way to spend a Sunday afternoon than sitting in the sunshine with a bottle of beer, and watching cricket in such a beautiful setting. To my surprise, I didn't feel self-conscious about my wheelchair. We met a number of boys and girls during the afternoon, as well as several members of staff. They were all as friendly as ever — I was simply a disabled person, like hundreds they had seen taking part in the London marathon, and they treated me just like anyone else.

26 April 2016

Today I fell over in Morrisons car park. Judith was taking me to a Macmillan tearoom on the outskirts of Perth, and she needed some shopping on the way. She suggested that I might like to wait in the car, but I said I would be fine as long as I had a trolley to hold onto. I was slowly wheeling the trolley across the car park, with Judith holding the side, when I went over a small ridge on the ground. The jolt, as the wheels stopped turning, was not sharp, but it was enough to throw me off balance. Before I knew what was happening, I was falling backwards onto the tarmac. Luckily, I managed to break my fall with my bottom and my shoulders, and I didn't bang my head too hard. I tried to turn over and get onto my knees, but lost my balance again, and rolled back again. As I lay there, I knew that I didn't have the strength to get up on my own.

Judith and a passing shopper immediately grabbed me under each arm and hauled me to my feet. Once I was up, I quickly said, "I'm fine", but I knew that I was shaken. I sat in the shop café while Judith did her shopping, and I thought about how unsteady I have become on my feet. It's no good pretending; the stiffness in my legs is getting worse, and my balance is deteriorating. On the way back from the tearoom, which is lovely, I said what I have been thinking for some time — I will have to use my wheelchair far more.

27 April 2016

It's time for my monthly physio appointment. Finding a disabled parking space at the hospital was a nightmare. I drove up to the main entrance but they were all taken. I hovered around the area, which also includes the A&E entrance, and waited along with another car. An ambulance arrived, so we both circled around the car park to allow it in. A couple came out of the hospital entrance, got into one of the parked cars, and drove off. We both went for the vacated space, and it ended up in a dead heat. With the noses of our cars almost touching, we looked at each other, and waited to see who would surrender. Fortunately, at that point another car left. I gracefully gave way, and we exchanged smiles as we hobbled towards the entrance.

Louise had a trainee with her and she asked him to observe me walking with my stick. It is strange how self-conscious we become when someone watches us intently, even when we are doing a basic task. Of course, walking is no longer such a simple matter, and as I went up and down the small gym, I was acutely aware of my slightly dropped left foot. I felt as if I was completing some sort of test, instead of simply demonstrating how things are. Louise decided that the brace on my left ankle was sufficient for the time being, and that I didn't need a splint. After the knock to my confidence following my recent fall, this felt re-assuring; however, we agreed that I would need to use a wheelchair far more often. Louise, like Elizabeth a few days earlier, suggested that an electric chair would be the logical way forward.

At Cornhill I had a great time with the volunteers. They sympathised with me when I told them about my fall in the car park, but there was lots of laughter at the thought of me lying on the ground and having to be picked up. One suggested that I may have had too much to drink, and another said it proved the lengths I would go to get two women to lift me in their arms. This dark humour is so important, both as a means of coping, and as a way of keeping things in perspective. After trying out a perch stool with Sheena, I went with Hazel to have my feeding tube changed. She used a syringe to take the water out of the balloon inside my stomach, and then pulled the tube out. When I glanced down, I was able to see the actual hole in my abdomen for the first time. It looked red but not too large. Sheena pushed another type of tube into my stomach, measured the depth of the hole, then removed it and replaced it with a normal one. She said that she would replace the tube with a button system in two weeks' time.

In the evening I watched snooker for almost three hours. It was one of the most exiting matches that I have ever seen. I found myself shouting at the television as both players produced some amazing snooker, under enormous pressure. In the excitement, I drank most of a bottle of wine, and when I went up to bed, my balance was worse than ever. I went up the stairs very slowly, one step at a time, and realised why Elaine worries so much when she is away.

29 April 2016

After a successful trip to Tesco, with no mishaps with trolleys, I returned to the house. As I crossed the hall, I turned a fraction too quickly, lost my balance, and fell over. I had my stick in my right hand, so I fell towards the left, where a heavy glass container was in my path. I tried to twist away from it, but my left side, just above my hip, hit the edge. I finished face down on the floor, with no chance of getting up. Fortunately, three members of the college management team had just arrived for a meeting in the dining room, and they heard me crash to the ground. Two of them lifted me to my feet and the third took me to the sitting room and helped me into my seat. I knew that I had hit my side, but in the absence of much pain, I assumed it must have been a glancing blow. During the next ten minutes, however, my side felt increasingly sore, and I when I put my hand on it I could feel that it was swollen and bruised. A little later, I heard someone in the kitchen. I went out and found Rachel, Elaine's PA, making tea for everyone in the meeting. I told her what had happened and she immediately went to get Elaine. After a look at my side, Elaine grabbed a freezer bag, filled it with ice, and wrapped it in a tea towel. She then wedged the ice pack between my side and the corner of my chair. I spent the next hour alternating between 15 minutes with ice and 15 minutes without. I then went to the cloakroom, lifted up my jumper, turned away from the mirror, and looked over my shoulder. I could see a dark bruise, about the size of an orange.

That is two falls in the space of only three days, and worryingly, this one happened when I was using my stick. On the bright side, this is the first time that I have injured myself since I fell headfirst into the sideboard in September. The pattern, however, is clear, and I know that I'm going to have to be much more careful. No more stupidly moving around the house by holding on to pieces of furniture; no more trying to get to the bathroom in the dark without my stick, and no more trying to get my coat on by letting go of my stick, leaning against the wall, twisting my arm behind my back, and trying to get my hand into the sleeve. Completing these simple tasks, things that most four-year-olds can easily perform, will either involve me in taking more time, or asking for more help. Whilst the former is mildly irritating, the latter serves to underline my increasing loss of competence and independence. This does not feel like a form of second childhood — it feels as if I am sliding rapidly back into infancy.

1 May 2016

I spent the day resting at home, still rather sore after my fall. This meant that I missed chapel for the second week running, and that I couldn't go to the Choral Society Concert at Greyfriars Kirk in Edinburgh. I was particularly sorry to miss this event — a major highlight of Glenalmond's musical year — but delighted to hear that it was an outstanding success. While I relaxed in front of the television watching the World Snooker Championship final, Elaine rushed from one Edinburgh hospital to another. Her mother is still in HDU at the Western General, following surgery last week. She now has an infection and a partially collapsed lung, so her recovery is likely to take some time. On Friday evening Elaine's daughter, Alice, fell during a seizure and broke her ankle in three places. She needed surgery, but this had to be delayed due to another cluster of seizures. At the Royal Infirmary they finally brought the seizures under control on Saturday night and she had her operation on Sunday morning. With all these things going on in their lives, many people would struggle to cope, but Elaine somehow manages to remain strong and calm, and in addition to supporting her family, she continues to do a very demanding job.

3 May 2016

Today, my brother is travelling up by train from London. I wanted to collect him from Perth station this evening, but he has insisted on bring his bike so that he can continue his training for his 60 km all-night sponsored bike ride across London. When I checked online this morning, I saw that he has already raised £2,800.

As always, I am very much looking forward to seeing my brother. Peter was born more than ten years after me, and by the time he was eighteen months old, I was away at boarding school. Apart from school and university holidays, we never really lived in the same house. Despite this, we have always been close, and apart from brotherly arguments about rival football teams, we have hardly ever had a harsh word. In recent years, events have conspired to bring us closer than ever. First came Peter's brain tumour, and soon after that our father died; next came my diagnosis with MND, and then we lost our sister – all within the space of three and a half years. By facing these challenges together, however, we have drawn great strength from each other.

4 May 2016

Peter arrived last night, tired after an uphill bike ride from Perth station, but certainly looking the part in his lycra and helmet. We ate curry, didn't fall out about football, and caught up on each other's news. This morning we both went with Lynn to meet Elizabeth and two of her colleagues from Perth and Kinross council to discuss plans for installing a wet room when we move house in the summer. It is Field Day at Glenalmond, so we had to get up the main drive before it became blocked by the pipe band. Elizabeth and her colleagues were very thorough, and they had an excellent understanding of the support that someone with MND would need. Peter and I left the specialists to discuss things in more detail, and we drove to Cornhill.

Ever since he was diagnosed as being terminally ill himself, Peter has been going to a hospice in London, so unlike most people, he had a good idea what to expect. I had told the staff at Cornhill all about Peter, including the fact that many people find it hard to believe that he is ten years my junior. When we arrived, everyone welcomed him warmly and teased him about being "Richard's older brother!" Peter took it all in good heart and we spent an hour laughing and joking with patients, medical staff, and volunteers. Caroline talked to me about using a powder to slightly thicken liquids. I choked earlier this morning, trying to swallow too much water, and Caroline was sure that the powder would help. We also talked about the advantages of having a riser/recliner chair that I could use for resting during the day. I practised on one of the chairs in the centre, and I was surprised how much easier it was to get to my feet. The chair literally tipped me right into a standing position. While I enjoyed a hand massage, Peter collected some sandwiches for lunch, and then he joined the rest of us for our weekly relaxation class.

5 May 2016

By the time I was dressed and down for breakfast, Peter had gone. He was already well on his way to Perth station. We had had less than two days together, and the time had flown by. When I looked out of the window and glanced over to where his bike had been parked, I could hardly believe that he had been here at all. I am finding separation more difficult as my time with MND goes on, particularly when it involves saying goodbye to family and friends that I don't see very often. When people I love go away, I try hard to remain outwardly positive and talk enthusiastically about how soon I will see them again, but inside I find it hard not to dwell on the possibility that I might only see them a few more times. This is not the sort of thinking that my psychologist would recommend, but I suppose emotions, rather than thoughts, are rarely logical.

Fortunately, I did not have long to feel sorry for myself. Judith emailed to ask if I would like to go into Crieff, have a wheel around the park and then go for lunch at a café in the town. I gratefully accepted, and within half an hour I was enjoying the fresh air, the daffodils, and the views of the mountains in the distance. Judith was determined that

I would experience a sense of speed, so after pushing me all the way up to the play area, at the top of the park, she pushed me down towards the river as fast as possible. We had soup and rolls at *Café Rhubarb* and then discovered that we didn't have time to get back to the college for the lunchtime recital. This was almost entirely my fault. It now takes me so much longer to eat, and if I try to talk at the same time, it makes things worse.

CHAPTER TEN

A Nurse Takes My Arm

6 May 2016

This afternoon the plans came back from Bert, who on Wednesday had looked at the house we are moving to. I was amazed that he had managed to draw up plans for the proposed wet room so quickly, but there they were, complete with details of new walls, a wheel-in shower, a Clos-O-Mat WC, and all the hand rails that I would need. The drawings looked very impressive, and although they serve to underline the growing extent of my disability, they are also a testament to amount of help that I am getting from the Strathearn and Kinross Care and Repair team.

7-8 May 2016

A weekend leave out, so a chance for Elaine to get a little rest. On Saturday she spent much of the day in her office, but she caught up with her work by late afternoon. At lunchtime on Sunday we went for drinks at Dawn's house in Methven, and met lots of her friends. Her house is on an elevated position to the south of the village, and it enjoys extensive views across the Perthshire countryside. The weather was glorious, so everyone gathered on the decking that overlooks Dawn's beautiful garden. I found a seat in the shade and spent a very enjoyable two hours talking to people, drinking sparkling wine, and tucking into some of the best canapés that I have ever tasted. The contrast with the cold, wet, and windy days that we experienced only a few days ago was quite remarkable — or perhaps not, as this is Scotland in the spring.

We arrived at Edinburgh Royal Infirmary by mid-afternoon, and while I had a rest in the car, Elaine went to see her daughter. Alice is making good progress but she is finding it difficult to understand why she can't walk on her broken leg. Her carers from Garvald are doing a great job in terms of supporting her, and they have an accessibility plan in place for when she leaves hospital.

Our final stop was at the Western General hospital, and this time I got in my wheelchair and accompanied Elaine up to the ward to see her mother. Janette has had a tough two weeks since her operation, and it has also been a very worrying time for Jim, Ed, and Elaine. Yesterday, however, there were definite signs of recovery, and her sense of humour certainly appears to be back. Everyone was trying to persuade Janette that she must eat more in order to regain her strength, but for the moment she is resistant to our suggestions. Knowing Janette, she will take action when, and only when, she wants to.

10 May 2016
The warm weather has continued since the weekend, and yesterday I ventured out in my wheelchair with

Judith, and joined her for a walk with Lottie. I say I joined them, but all I did was to sit in my chair and let Judith push me around the college grounds. We went through the main quad, passed the music school and theatre, and went up towards the cricket pitch. We then went along the edge of the ground and stopped to look at the lovely view across the playing fields and over towards the mountains. Sitting there, feeling the warmth of the sun and the breeze on my face, I realised, once again, how lucky I am to live in such a beautiful place. Lottie lay down among the daffodils and I tried to take a photo of her with my mobile phone. Judith decided that it might be fun to push me down a rough track towards the main drive. We bumped over tree roots but made it safely to the bottom.

Today part of my time has been taken up with concerns over disability equipment. It is a week since Caroline at Cornhill advised me that I really should consider getting a riser/recliner chair. During that time, I have been delaying doing anything about it. On "good" days I can get myself to my feet from the sofa by leaning forward as far as possible, and using the arm of the sofa for leverage. When I'm tired, however, this process is more difficult. I have to push down on the sofa seat with both arms and then throw myself forwards. After a few attempts this usually gets me onto my feet, but the momentum sometimes causes me to lose my balance and I end up toppling over. So far, I have managed to save myself by grabbing hold of the coffee table, but I know that this is not a long-term solution.

11 May 2016

At Cornhill, Bob came over for a chat. Bob is now coming more regularly, and every now and then we catch up about our condition and how things are progressing. We have a connection, because we are the only people with MND who attend the drop-in days; the vast majority of people are suffering from, or in remission from, cancer. While I told him about the increased stiffness and weakness in my legs, Bob described how his arms are suffering in the same way. We talked about our efforts to remain positive but realistic, and we agreed that this was a very difficult balancing act. Bob said that he finds it hard when people inadvertently make light of his situation by saying things like, "Oh well, none of us know what lies around the corner, I could go under a bus tomorrow!" Of course, this is true, but Bob's situation is different. The vast majority of people are so busy living their lives that they hardly ever think about the proverbial "bus". Bob, however, is reminded of the terminal nature of his condition on a daily basis. To use the bus analogy, he can see the bus coming, and he knows it's coming for him. Bob and I were not feeling sorry for ourselves; we were simply acknowledging how difficult it is for people to find the right words.

12 May 2016

Jeremy from the Electronic Assistive Technology Service came to visit me. Jeremy is working with Elizabeth on the plans for the new house, and he wanted to talk to me about other electronic aids that I might need in the future. I showed Jeremy the synthetic voice that I have installed on my iPad, and then we discussed alternative ways for me to use my laptop. The technology available is amazing, but talking to Jeremy, I quickly realised that finding the right type of equipment to suit a person's needs can be difficult. It is also necessary to look at different scenarios for the future. Talking about how I might cope if I cannot speak, move, or use my hands was quite daunting, and knowing that my mobility is deteriorating and my voice is going meant that the discussion was far from hypothetical. Jeremy, however, was very enthusiastic about the assistance that is available, and when we talked about the latest electronic wheelchairs and the different gadgets they include, I found myself getting quite excited by the thought.

After lunch Tim delivered Lottie to my car and she settled down on the floor, in front of the passenger seat. We drove to the Macmillan café near Scone Palace, and met Judith from her work. The paths around the river at the back are marked as wheelchair accessible, but they are neither smooth nor flat. Judith managed to push me up the bumpy slopes and delighted in telling me that she was going to let me free-wheel back down. She didn't let go of course, but it was an exhilarating journey to the bottom. The weather was beautiful, so we sat in the shade, under a tree, and had an ice cream while Lottie drank from her bowl.

13 May 2016

Yesterday morning I had another appointment at Perth Royal Infirmary. I parked in a disabled space next to the A&E department, and walked across to the main entrance. Normally I simply go straight into the lift, which takes me to the physiotherapy department, but this time I had to go down the main corridor, turn right, check in at reception, and then continue to the waiting area. By the time I sat down I was feeling very tired, and I was relieved that the clinic was running a little late. When a nurse called my name, it took me two attempts to get to my feet, and I felt embarrassed by how slowly I was walking with my stick. As I reached the nurse, she pointed down another corridor and said, "I'm sorry, but we're right down at the end." I looked down the corridor, glanced back at the nurse and said, "It looks quite a way." I was suddenly frightened that I might not be able to make it on my own. Half way along the corridor I stopped for a breather, and the nurse then took my left arm for the rest of the journey.

At the end of my appointment, the doctor asked me how far I had to go to get to my car. When I told him, he immediately told me to sit down outside his office, and he said he would get a nurse to wheel me back in a chair. I wanted to say, "No, I'll be fine", but I knew that wouldn't be true. As I sat down, I felt very emotional. I simply didn't have the energy to fight this one anymore, and although I felt sad about that, I also felt incredibly relieved. A nurse arrived with a wheelchair and took me straight to my car door. She helped me to my feet, made sure I got into the driver's seat, gave me a lovely smile, and said goodbye. I sat there for a minute or two, and the tears welled up in my eyes; I couldn't work out if they were due to my feelings of dependence or my sense of gratitude.

14 May 2016

In the morning I watched a recording of the final day of the Invictus games. Awareness and understanding of disability has grown considerably in recent years, and events like the Paralympics have played a huge part in this process. In the past, there was a reluctance by many people to watch disabled people in sporting activities. Watching people who have arms or legs missing perform can be a very uncomfortable experience. I have to admit that I found this to be the case when I first watched the Paralympics in 2012. I greatly admired their courage, but I did not find it easy to watch. As I watched more, however, any feelings of embarrassment were quickly replaced by sheer admiration. The competitive nature of the events also made for exciting viewing.

Watching the games this year, however, was a very different experience. Now I am not only disabled myself, but my disabilities are greater than the majority of the competitors. I still have my legs, but they don't function anymore. Even if I did get artificial legs, my muscles are far too weak to make them work, and no matter how much training I might do, there would never be any improvement. In 2012 I did what many people do when they look at someone with only one arm or one leg — I tried to imagine how I would cope with that situation myself. I can vividly remember thinking that I couldn't bear it, because I wouldn't be able to play golf. That was because I was playing the game several times a week, and despite my high handicap, it was my passion. Now, however, everything has changed, and as I watched the final of the basketball, I knew that I would happily swap places with any of the competitors. I envy their ability to race around the court, and, most of all, I envy the way they talk with such confidence about the future.

15 May 2016

Yesterday I went to chapel for the first time this term. I knew that the walk was going to tire me, but I was determined to get there. When we arrived at the chapel doors, I did not want to go in on my own. My fear of falling, as I hobbled up the aisle, was suddenly much stronger, so I readily agreed to Elaine's suggestion that she should take me to my seat. As we walked in, the members of the choir were already in their seats, and several of them smiled and said good morning. Elaine put me in my seat and then went back to welcome visiting parents and guests. During the service I felt very tired, and for the first time, I sat out some of the hymns, preferring to just sit and listen. At the end of the service, Elaine processed out with Fr. Giles, and I remained in my seat until she had finished saying her goodbyes to the visitors. I listened to Tim play the organ voluntary as the duty pupils collected up all the orders of service, and then Elaine reappeared to help me out. As we walked home, we agreed that it was time for me to use my wheelchair for chapel.

In the afternoon I parked my buggy on the path between the two main cricket pitches and watched young players from prep schools and local clubs compete in the annual Glenalmond Sixes tournament. The weather was lovely, and there were crowds of people watching from the boundary edge. I caught up with two ex-pupils of mine. They had both been at Loretto with me in the mid-1980s, and now they have teenage sons of their own.

15-16 May 2016

Over the last two days I have spent much of my time on the laptop, either writing or dealing with emails. I have also spoken to a number of people on the phone. I am very fortunate to have the support of so many health professionals, but rather like buses, I sometimes don't see or hear from them for a while and then suddenly they all appear at once. This week I have heard from Dee, my specialist MND nurse, Dawn from MND Scotland, Jeremy from the Electronic Assistive Technology Service, and Hazel, my dietician. The wonderful thing about Tayside NHS seems to be the integration between the different services. A good example of this has been my request for a riser/recliner chair. I phoned MND Scotland last week and spoke to Dawn. She said I would need to contact Dee, and as soon as I did so, the whole operation swung into action. Dee obviously spoke to Jeremy, who in turn contacted MND Scotland to check that the chair was compatible with the electronic equipment that he wants installed. This all happened within two days. To know that everyone talks to each other is very reassuring, and it greatly reduces the risk of feeling isolated. This is particularly important when you lose your independence and become more reliant on other people for assistance.

I have spent some time researching travel insurance for our holiday in July. If you type "Travel insurance for MND" into a search engine, lots of different sites come up, all claiming to provide cover for MND sufferers. Most of them promise that an online questionnaire will lead to an "instant quote". I tried this with three different companies, but each time, having filled in the questionnaire, I was faced with the same message: "We are unable to provide you with a quote at this time". I phoned one of the companies, and I was asked to go through exactly the same questions as I had done online. I asked why I needed to do this if they already had the information, but was told that telephone enquiries had to be done on the phone and could not rely on information that had been collected online. After I had answered all the questions, I was told to hold while the sales person checked everything. When she came back on the line, she said she needed to know the prognosis for my MND. "Can I ask if it is more than a year?", she asked. This is one hell of a question to ask anybody, but I did appreciate that the lady was simply doing her job. Her company needed to assess the risk of me dying while on holiday, and obviously, the higher the risk, the higher the premium. There was no point in me getting angry or upset, so I laughed and said, "How long is a piece of string?" I then said that my consultant would not, and could not give a clear prognosis, because every case of MND was different. I added, however, that no one had told me that I would definitely die within the year. The lady said she would put down, "More than a year" and get back to me with a quote.

18 May 2016

On Wednesday I went to Cornhill a little later than usual. After my recent struggles with walking, I decided against going into Tesco to buy sandwiches. Instead I had a very early lunch at home, and then drove in. Most of the morning visitors had left by the time I arrived, so I spent an hour chatting to Margaret and the volunteers. Elma arrived with her pillow, towel, and hand cream, and we talked about football while she massaged my hands. This was Caroline's last day before she returns to her job in the in-patient section. I, like everyone else, will miss her. Caroline was the first person I met at Cornhill back in December, and it was her bubbly personality and wicked sense of humour that swept away my nerves and anxieties about visiting a hospice. I asked one of the volunteers to take a photo of Caroline with me, and then she helped me walk through for our relaxation class. I have noticed that ever since my fall a couple of weeks ago, most of the staff at Cornhill have been reluctant to let me walk on my own. They know (and so do I, when I am honest with myself) that the risks of me falling are increasing. This week I found it harder to let my mind go blank during relaxation, but I still enjoyed the peace and calm. After the class Caroline insisted on helping me down to my car. On the way out I told her that she had been a wonderful help to me. Once I was in the car, she lent through the open window and gave me a big hug. As I waved goodbye I felt very tearful.

19 May 2016

Jeremy came back to see me yesterday. He brought a black, round camera, about the size of a table tennis ball, which had a USB attached to it on a lead. Jeremy placed a silver reflective dot on the bridge of my glasses, plugged the USB into the laptop, and placed the camera in front of the keyboard. He then asked me to move my head up and down to see if the cursor would move across the screen. The cursor moved, but it required me to move my head too far to achieve any results. Jeremy stuck a reflective dot on his forehead and tried it himself, but the results were much the same. Jeremy explained that the camera works very well with a normal laptop but the technology struggles with a Mac. He said that the next time he was passing he would bring his own laptop and give me a demonstration. I am very grateful to Jeremy and many others who are planning for my future, but I do hope that I will be able to continue typing with my fingers for a while yet.

CHAPTER ELEVEN

One Walking Stick to Two

20 May 2016

This morning I was frightened to step out of the shower. I stood there, frozen to the spot, and waited for Elaine to help me step forward. The edge of the shower tray is only an inch high, but I didn't feel confident about lifting my left foot over it; certainly not whilst standing on the wet surface. Even when I held Elaine's hands, I was nervous about falling. As I safely reached the bath mat on the other side, I felt incredibly relieved.

How can I have been reduced to a situation where I am afraid of a one-inch barrier? Of course, the calm and logical answer is simple. I am what I am because of this disease; I have known for some time that my mobility would steadily decline, and there is no point getting angry about it. But, as I stood there, paralysed, I wasn't feeling calm or logical in the slightest; I was feeling angry and frustrated. As I write now, I have calmed down. Sitting in my chair, typing away on my computer, I feel the stiffness, but no pain. I can reach the remote controls for the television and the iPod, I can read my book and answer my emails, and, as long as I don't try to stand up, I almost feel normal.

23 May 2016

A delivery service contacted the college to say that they would be delivering a riser/recliner chair from MND Scotland the next day. I spent a while trying to decide where would be the best place to position the chair. It sounds like an easy decision, but when you need to factor in such things as room for the chair to fully recline without hitting walls, and the need for easy access to phones, chargers, remote controls, and wine gums, it becomes a little more difficult. Having decided on the best position, I had the frustration of sitting idly by while Elaine moved the other furniture around the room.

24 May 2016

In the morning I had a call from the firm I had contacted about a lightweight wheelchair. They said the one I had asked for was out of stock, but they would be willing to deliver a different model the next day. The alternative didn't have the "racing blue" colour scheme that I had fancied, but it did come in a two-tone fabric and, perhaps more importantly, it was even lighter. When I was told that the new chair was £30 more expensive but they would do it for the same price as my original choice, I decided to go for it.

As soon as this deal was confirmed by email, I left for my MND support group meeting in Dundee. Finding the hotel was easy, but finding the right entrance proved more difficult. I parked in the only available space and walked across the car park to what looked like the main entrance. When I went in, however, I was told that I needed to go back to another entrance on the other side. By the time I made it into the correct room I was very tired, and more convinced than ever that my days of walking with one stick will soon be over. I looked around at my fellow MND sufferers. As usual, we were a motley crew — all at different stages of the condition, and all affected in different ways. I have been proud of the fact that I have been able to attend these meetings on my own, but I realise now that I will have to have a 'carer' with me in the future. I sat next to Niamh, the MND Communications Officer, and we chatted about my blog and how it might be publicised during MND Awareness Week in June. When it was time to go, I knew that I was going to struggle with the sloping ramp down to the car park. I asked Niamh if she would mind helping me to my car.

25 May 2016

I was the first person to arrive at Cornhill, and Morag told me off for walking up from my car on my own. We had agreed last week that I would ring her when I arrived and she, or one of the other staff, would come down and help me up. Susie came and collected me for my aromatherapy session. Last week I had found it very difficult to lie face down on the bed. My balance was so poor and my arms were so weak that I could only get onto my side from a sitting position. Susie still managed to massage my back, one half at a time. This week I started on my back and Susie began by doing the front of my legs. It is my legs that have become very stiff over the last

12 months, so it was wonderful to feel them loosen up as the oils were rubbed in. By the time Susie had finished massaging the back of my legs, I was so relaxed that I could have fallen sound asleep. I got up a little too quickly and felt rather faint, so Susie helped me get my clothes on and took my arm as we walked back to the day room. Margaret and Elma met us and I told them that I felt exhausted after my massage. They laughed, and said I needed to sit down and recover.

Not long after this, Judith arrived. She was going to escort me to a concert that the Glenalmond fourth-form pupils were doing at St John's Kirk in Perth, and I had suggested that she come up to meet everyone at the hospice. Everyone made her very welcome and they told her that they had read about her in my blog.

When we arrived at St John's, there was already a good crowd of people, but Judith managed to get my wheelchair into a spot near the front, and I had a wonderful view. The four pupils, all music scholars, but all only fifteen years old, played a variety of pieces on piano, organ, harpsichord, violin, recorder, trombone, and electric guitar. The standard of playing was extraordinary, and I can't imagine how good these pupils will be by the time they leave school in three years' time.

26 May 2016

At 8 a.m. Lorna rang to say that the immigration check at Heathrow had taken so long that she and Nick had missed their connecting flight to Edinburgh. I was disappointed that I would have to wait longer before I would see her, but I said I would meet them at Perth station in the afternoon. I tried do to some writing but found it hard to concentrate. My daughter is a very independent and well-travelled woman, but I am always relieved to see her safely home. This time, I was also looking forward to meeting her new boyfriend. A few hours later, from my parking space, I saw her emerge from the station exit. She looked straight over to where I was and waved. The two of them put their luggage in the boot and then Lorna introduced me to her new man.

While Lorna prepared tea, Nick came to see me. He said he had known Lorna for eighteen months, he was very much in love with her, and he wanted to ask for her hand in marriage. I had an inkling that something like this might happen, but I was still very touched by this formal request. I told him that I was delighted to give my consent, and that all I wanted was for the two of them to make each other happy. Elaine had been down to Holyrood to watch the Glenalmond pipe band take part in the beating retreat ceremony, but as soon as she returned we opened some Champagne and drank a toast to the happy couple.

27 May 2016

I drove Lorna and Nick along to the Sma' Glen. Nick was very impressed by the beautiful scenery, and they both said how wonderful it was to see so much greenery after living in Saudi Arabia. We went to the café at Gloagburn Farm for lunch, and despite having to wait fifteen minutes for a table, we enjoyed some excellent food. Lorna and Nick looked very at ease and happy together. Later, they told Elaine and me all about their planned wedding in the Seychelles, and their extended honeymoon in Tuscany. It sounded idyllic and very expensive. My only question for Lorna, which I asked her when we were alone, was that I didn't want her rushing into things because of my condition. I told her that I really wanted her to be happy, but I wanted her to be sure. She said she had never felt so sure about anything.

28 May 2016

Elaine was taking Lorna and Nick down to Edinburgh where they would stay in our house before flying back to Saudi Arabia the next morning. We took some photos in front of the slopes, and then I said goodbye. It had been a flying visit, and although I was so pleased to see my daughter looking so happy, I was sad to see her go so quickly. I waved from the window and smiled, but some tears followed.

The house seemed very quiet, and with the pupils away for half-term, the grounds were empty. Elaine was going to see Janette in hospital so I knew I had a long day ahead of me. I planned my time around various sporting events and did some writing. Later in the morning, Patrick came around in a borrowed open-top car. He is in the process of building a house a couple of miles north of the college, and he wanted to show me the site. I had to fall into the passenger seat because it was so low, but once inside I enjoyed the ride. The site has a wonderful view across the glen, and Patrick told me that he was keen to have a croquet lawn laid. The highlight of the trip, however, was the sight of an oyster catcher sitting in her nest, very close to the ground with her chick, whilst her mate ran up and down the building site to ward off any predators.

29 May 2016

A rare day off for Elaine, so we enjoyed a late and leisurely breakfast. The weather was warm and sunny, so I took the buggy for a spin while Elaine walked alongside. We stopped at the top of the slopes and took some photos of the college buildings from the side of the rhododendron bushes that are now in flower. We then went up to the new house and sat in the garden for an hour. The house doesn't share the spectacular view of the slopes, but it is surrounded by trees, and the garden is very private. After returning for lunch, Elaine sat on a rug on the lawn and read; a pleasure she rarely has time for these days, while I watched England beat Wales in the rugby. We enjoyed a lovely meal in the evening and then rounded off an ideal day by watching an episode of *Wallander*.

31 May 2016

We drove down to Edinburgh and I waited at Tranent while Elaine went for a dental appointment. I hadn't been to the house for several weeks, and it was good to be back. Since my retirement, this has been like a second home for me, and as I sat and looked out to the garden, I remembered how simple life had seemed only a couple of years ago. Jim, Janette, and I spent many days together, along with Sam, chatting, listening to Jim on the piano, and simply enjoying the wonderful view over the Forth and across to Fife. Jim and Janette have been just like parents to me, and rather like my own childhood home, their house always seems safe and secure. Lately, of course, things have been harder for all of us; my MND is progressing, Janette is still in hospital recovering from her recent operation, and Jim is feeling lonely at home.

When Elaine returned, we went to Haddington to see Janette. She has lost a considerable amount of weight, and although she has very little appetite, the nurses (and her family) are trying to persuade her to eat more. Janette is being a little stubborn about this, and she doesn't enjoy being told what to do, but during our visit she did eat a small bowl of semolina with cream and jam. She has been in hospital for almost two months, so she is keen to get home. I hope this happens soon. It was certainly great to see her, and despite everything she has been through, she still has a twinkle in her eye.

1 June 2016
Yesterday, I went from one walking stick to two. Ever since my recent falls, I have known that Louise, my physiotherapist, would be concerned about my ability to continue to walk with only one stick. At my appointment, she asked me to try two sticks with wrist supports. It felt awkward at first, because I am not used to the grips around the wrist, but the support they gave me made me feel more stable. We then practised the movement of feet and sticks. Louise said that moving the right stick forward with the left foot and vice versa was the ideal way, but I found it hard to get the coordination right. She said it would be fine to move the two sticks forward and then move my legs, and I certainly found that easier. We then practised opening doors, moving around in a circle, and getting things out of my trouser pockets. Trying to release one hand to do these things without losing control of the stick is not so easy, and I will have to practise more.

I then told Louise that I was finding it difficult to do my exercises every day, and that I was feeling guilty about this. She told me not to worry about it anymore. She explained that it was now more important for me to keep my energy up, and the exercises were probably tiring me out too much. I fully understand the logic behind this, but it is a clear indication that my MND is moving on to a more advanced stage. At the end of our session, Louise walked with me to the hospital café, helped me buy a sandwich, and took me back to my car. She also told me that the next time she needed to see me, she would come up to see me at Cornhill.

When I got back to the hospice, Morag was there to meet me. She had spotted my car and didn't want me trying to walk in on my own. By the time I left in the afternoon, I had had aromatherapy with Susie, a haircut with Moira, and a relaxation class with Sheena. They all teased me about being pampered, and we all laughed together — the best tonic in the world. Elma decided that I was simply too busy to have my usual hand massage — that would have to wait until next week.

2-4 June 2016

It was wonderful to drive down the avenue of trees that led to Ballathie. We had booked our two-day stay a couple of months ago, and it hardly felt as if we had been away. The sun was shining brightly when we arrived, and as soon as we were in our disabled room, Elaine opened the French windows, pushed me out to the little table on the edge of the lawn, and we both settled down to read. The yellow of the April daffodils had been replaced by the pink, red, and lilac of the June rhododendron bushes. At about five o'clock, a very large number of rooks came gliding back to perch high up in the oak and beech trees opposite. The noise of their squawking was very loud, but it was also reassuring. In the evening, when we went for dinner, some of the hotel staff welcomed us back, and it felt good to be remembered. The food was as delicious as ever.

On our second morning Elaine wheeled me all along the front drive. We stopped to admire the rhododendrons, and watched the sheep and cattle grazing in the fields. It was incredibly peaceful, and I imagine the scene would hardly have been any different a hundred years ago. More reading in the sunshine was followed by more food and wine in the evening, and before we knew it, we were having a last walk up the drive on our final morning.

6 June 2016

Last night was Peter's sponsored bike ride around London to raise money for MND. He emailed to say that he was very tired at the end but he had finished the course. This morning I have been reading about one of my fellow sufferers, Lucy Lintott. At just 21, Lucy is the youngest person in Scotland with MND, and she is a great inspiration to others. Lucy has done a huge amount to raise money for, and awareness of, this terrible disease. She has travelled all around the world in a bid to see and experience as many things as possible, and she has written very honestly about her story. Lucy has her own blog, and this how she began one of her recent posts:

"Each time I write I have to be willing to open myself up, and with every post that I write, I cry without fail, and I'm sure this one will be no different!"

8 June 2016

Today was my last aromatherapy session of this series. It has been wonderful to get the stiff muscles in my legs, back, and shoulders massaged, and I savoured every minute of my final hour. As soon as we were finished, Susie booked me in for a series of therapeutic touch sessions, to begin at the end of July. It is very important for me to have things like this to look forward to, particularly in the absence of any medical treatment. One of the regulars at Cornhill, who is battling with cancer, asked me today how much time I spend in hospital. He said, "It must get you down, having to spend so much time having treatment". When I told him that I don't spend any time in hospital except for occasional outpatient appointments, and that there is no treatment available for me, he was very surprised; in fact, I'm not sure he believed me. I didn't really want to get into a discussion about this, and fortunately Hazel came to my rescue. She wanted to check my new feeding tube, so we went along to a treatment room. Hazel watched me very carefully as I walked along with my stick, and reminded me to take as much time as possible; she, like everyone else at the centre, knows that my walking is deteriorating. Having reached her room, however, the news was good. The tube was fine, the hole in my stomach was not inflamed, and my weight was unchanged from last month. None of these factors were signs of any medical improvement, but, unlike my walking, they were indicators of stability — and "stability" is as good as it gets. I felt quite pleased with myself as I walked back to the day room, and I celebrated by having my hands massaged by Elma. As she worked the lotion into my hands, and I felt my fingers loosen up, I felt very grateful indeed for the kindness that she and the other volunteers have shown me over the last six months.

9 June 2016

I received some more photos of my brother's night ride through London — some of him in the darkness with his friend Fotis, who accompanied Peter on the ride, and some others of Peter in the early morning towards the end of his ride. He has now raised over £3,300 and I am very proud of him. Niamh from MND Scotland also sent me the final draft of a press release that she has prepared, based on an interview with me at our recent MND support group meeting. She has written a piece about my story so far, and it should be released on 20 June.

After lunch Judith collected me and we went to Dunkeld. She took a very scenic route along some narrow roads. The tall rhododendron bushes were stunning and they towered above the car on both sides. Dunked is an attractive town, and Judith wheeled me around the ancient Cathedral and the grounds that surround it. We then had ice creams that melted quickly in the sun. Judith was determined to get me close to the river, and achieved this by wheeling me down a track off the square. We sat in the sun with Lockie and admired the beautiful view, surrounded by a large number of dark-headed gulls. When I got home, I promptly sank into my recliner and fell asleep. I had really enjoyed my afternoon out, but I was so tired. I know it is simply the disease, but I still find it so frustrating that I can feel exhausted after just sitting in my wheelchair.

10 June 2016

The ups and downs of living with MND. Yes, despite everything, there are ups. For the majority of the time since my diagnosis, I have managed to take all the positives I can. I have tried desperately hard to live in the here and now, and, tempting as it can be, I have rarely allowed myself to wallow in self-pity. However, some days are more difficult than others, and yesterday was one of them. In contrast to the recent glorious weather, it was wet and much colder. By mid-morning I was feeling chilly in my polo shirt and deck shoes; my feet were freezing to the touch, and my bare arms just wouldn't warm up. I feel draughts much more these days, mainly because I am so inactive, and in the end, I switched on the little heater that sits beside my chair. I then watched the service at St. Paul's to commemorate the Queen's 90th birthday. The pomp and ceremony of the occasion lifted my spirits a little, but as various bishops talked about the longevity of the Queen and Prince Philip, I found myself bemoaning the fact that they have already lived for 50% longer than I have, and that that percentage is likely to increase. To make matters worse, a number of other ninety-year-olds then got up to speak, and they all looked far too spritely. In the afternoon I put on Classic FM, pressed the "recline" button on my new chair, and tried to sleep. Knowing that time is so precious, I try to avoid sleeping too much during the day, but it felt good to shut my eyes, empty my mind, and drift away.

12 June 2016

After my rather miserable performance on Friday, I felt better over the weekend. For the first time in my life, I watched the Trooping of the Colour from beginning to end. I found myself marvelling at the fact that this was the 64th time that the Queen has attended this ceremony. These occasions are expensive, and some say divisive, particularly when so many families are grieving the loss of loved ones as a result of this country's involvement in the wars in Iraq and Afghanistan. But ceremonies involving the military and the royal family are still immensely popular.

14 June 2016

I woke up to hear that Russia has been given a suspended disqualification from the European Football Championships. I was relieved, although somewhat surprised, that England haven't been treated the same. The video evidence, however, clearly showed that Russian fans caused the trouble in the stadium at the end of match. In the days leading up to the match, a small number of so-called fans from both countries behaved in an appalling way. There is no excuse for this, but I suppose the French police must have known that a combination of thugs from England and Russia, cheap alcohol, and a violent city like Marseilles, was always going to be a toxic mix.

CHAPTER TWELVE

Up Late With David Dimbleby

15 June 2016

There was lots of laughter at Cornhill today. I arrived later than usual, at about 11.30, to find the dayroom quite full. Fortunately, there was still a spare chair in the main circle. One or two people were sitting quietly, lost in their own thoughts, but most of them were chatting away. Unless you had been told that this was a drop-in session at a palliative care centre, you would never have guessed that the room contained so many people with, or in remission from, life-threatening illnesses. The animated conversations were full of smiles and gestures, and there was a distinct lack of gloom or doom. It could easily have been any bunch of people meeting in their local club — and in a way of course, that is exactly what it is. Just like most other "clubs", this is where we meet up with friends who have something in common. In our case, it just happens to be something rather unusual that binds us together.

By mid-day, most of the group had left, but Margaret had just arrived. I told her that I had been worried because I hadn't seen her for two or three weeks, and she reminded me that she had told me that she was going on holiday. This was a cue for Elma to tease me about my memory before she started to massage my hands. After my massage was over, Margaret asked me how my fingers felt. I told her that they were much looser and that it was great to get some relief from the stiffness that I feel most of the time. I said I tried to do hand exercises each day, like clenching and unclenching my fists. At this point, Margaret looked at me with a perfectly straight face and said, "Do you have soft balls?" I knew exactly what she meant, but I couldn't help smiling and raising my eyebrows. Margaret covered her mouth with her hand, as if trying to take the words back, and then burst out laughing. Within seconds, I was laughing so much that tears came into my eyes. Neither of us could stop. Margaret got up and turned her back in an effort to bring herself under control, but as soon as she looked around, and we made eye contact, we collapsed in hysterics. Several of the volunteers came over to find out what was going on, but when I tried to tell them, I started laughing so much that I couldn't get the words out. In the end, I managed to repeat what had been said, and we all laughed together. I told Margaret that I would write about it in my blog.

17 June 2016
My voice was poor this morning. Claire, who cleans this part of the college each weekday, arrived just after nine, and as always, she popped into to see me. Most

mornings, Claire greets me with a comment on the weather, and today she once again mentioned the rain. After some beautiful weather in May, summer seems to have deserted Perthshire for the time being. Claire is used to my slow and slightly slurred speech, but I could tell that even she was struggling to catch some of my words. We got there in the end, and I settled down to some writing.

An hour later my mobile rang, and thinking about my communication problems earlier, I considered letting it go to voicemail. I have always found it hard to ignore a ringing phone, however, so reluctantly I answered it. I immediately recognised the slightly frail, Devonian voice on the other end — it was my aunt Rita, my late father's older sister. Rita is 93, and she has lived alone in her farmhouse since her husband, my uncle Stanley, died a few years ago, at the age of 96. Rita is very deaf, and in the past, I have had some frustrating phone calls with her. I have shouted in an attempt to make her hear, but my aunt hasn't heard me. A year ago, my sister had explained that there was no need for me to shout. I can clearly remember her words: "Shouting at her only makes it worse, you silly boy; all you have to do is speak slowly and clearly, and Rita's special phone will do the rest."

I decided to follow Steph's blunt instructions. Speaking slowly would not be a problem; it is all I can do, but the "clearly" part would be impossible. In response to my aunt's "Richard, is that you?" I said, "Hello Rita, Yes, it's me." To my amazement, Rita didn't repeat herself, she just said, "Oh, how are you?" The conversation continued for a couple of minutes, and then she said, "I'm going to finish now, my dear, I don't want you getting too tired." These words made me feel rather sad, but as we said our goodbyes, and I put down my phone, I felt incredibly pleased that, despite my failing voice, I had managed to have a successful conversation with my lovely aunt. Perhaps my words don't sound quite as bad to other people as they do to me.

18 June 2016

During my twenty years of teaching economics and politics, I remained thoroughly unconvinced by the promises made by politicians of all persuasions. My students quickly learned that many of the manifesto pledges made during elections would be extremely difficult, if not impossible, to carry out. Of course, in a referendum, there are usually no second chances, so the stakes are even higher. Once the vote on our membership of the EU is over, there will be no going back. The claims and counter-claims of the opposing sides have become ever more extravagant, and the whole campaign has been marked by an unprecedented level of bitterness and verbal abuse.

22 June 2016

The first time I was aware of an election or referendum campaign was in September 1964, when I was 10 years old. Along with my parents and my sister, I was staying with my aunt and uncle in Essex, and one afternoon, I was dragged away from my game of cricket to watch a very thin man talking from the back of a trailer, just down from their house. He didn't sound very interesting to me, but my mother told me that he was the Prime Minister, and he was called Sir Alec Douglas-Home. She said he used to be called Lord Home, but he had had to stop calling himself that. I asked her why he had to change his name, but my mother said it was too complicated to explain. On the night of that election in October, I stayed up later than I had ever done before. I saw the thin man from the trailer being interviewed, but I thought another man, who smiled more and smoked a pipe, looked more interesting. My father, however, clearly didn't share my view, and he was disappointed when it was announced that the new Prime Minister would be Harold Wilson. Little did I know back then that I would spend twenty-five years teaching Economics and Politics, and have to follow elections and referendums with a keen interest.

Today is the last day of polling in this latest referendum, and I'm relieved it's almost over. The campaign has been far too long, the quality of the debate has been the poorest I can ever remember, and, for the most part, there has been a distinct lack of integrity shown by all concerned.

23-24 June 2016

With no exit polls, the actual day of voting passed with little indication of what was happening. I kept an eye on the news but the only thing that was highlighted was the apparent high turnout, despite the terrible weather in SE England. Both sides claimed that the high turnout could work in their favour. After going for a lovely meal with Tim and Judith and their family, and enjoying a very strong glass of cask strength whisky, I drove home in my buggy and tried to decide whether I would stay up or go to bed and listen to the radio. At that point my mobile rang, and it was Elaine. I was relieved to hear that she had arrived safely in Nairobi, en route to an education fair at

Pembroke House Prep School. I switched on the television and saw the same face that I watched in the last EU referendum 41 years ago. David Dimbleby, like his father before him, has been an ever-present figure at elections and referendums.

Very little happened for the first hour, but then it was announced that Nigel Farage, on advice from friends in the city, had conceded that the Remain side had probably done just enough to win the day. David Dimbleby and his team reminded us all that it was far too early to make a definite prediction, but his table of pundits and MPs clearly felt that the Farage comment was an indicator of how things were going. But a little later the result from Sunderland came in. When the Returning Officer read out that Leave had polled 82,394 votes compared to Remain's 51,930, huge cheers could be heard. Leave were predicted to win Sunderland, but the extent of the victory was far greater than expected. As I heard those cheers, I knew that the UK was probably heading out of the EU. I went to bed.

At 5 a.m. this morning I woke up and put the radio on. It was clearly all over. Scotland, as expected, had voted strongly for Remain, along with Northern Ireland, but most of Wales and England, with the exception of London, had voted in favour of Leave. By 8.30, David Cameron had announced that he would soon step down as Prime Minister, Alec Salmond had called for another Scottish Referendum, and the pound had fallen sharply.

25 June 2016
I received confirmation that I do have travel insurance for my trip to Tenerife in July. When I first looked into

this in May, several companies had turned me down, and one said they would cover me but the premium would be £3000. As this was more than the cost of my holiday, I decided to keep looking. Finally, I found a firm that would do it, but only on condition that my prognosis was longer than six months from the date of departure. I told them that nobody has told me that I will definitely die within six months, but this was far from certain. They then said they would go ahead for a premium of £400. I asked the man on the phone what would happen if they had to fly me home for some reason, and then I died five months and two weeks later. How would they know that I had died, and if they found out, would they ask for a refund of the cost of repatriation from my estate? The man said that was an interesting question, but thought we should proceed on the basis that all would be fine. We both laughed nervously.

Talking openly about my chances of dying in the near future, particularly to total strangers, is an odd experience, but it doesn't bother me anymore. The poor people who have to ask these questions are normally far more embarrassed by the situation than I am.

26 June 2016

I stayed in bed until quite late, listening to Clare Balding's programme on radio two. She is an outstanding communicator, and very versatile. Although her background is firmly in horse racing, she has branched out into many other fields, and this summer I am sure she will play a leading role as a presenter during the Olympics and Paralympics. As I listened to the music on her show, I was feeling a little sorry for myself. I didn't think I would make it to chapel, and I was missing Elaine. However, there was an interesting guest on the show, talking about her Buddhist beliefs. She mentioned the central roles that pain and suffering have in Buddhist teachings — the idea that the pain of loss, or a serious illness, can soften us, make us less self-centred, and more compassionate. The guest then told of how the people of Nepal, from where she had just returned, were patiently getting their lives back together after the devastation of the recent earthquakes. She described how she had watched an old man as he picked up large stones and slowly moved them from one pile to another, as part of the process of re-building his house. After listening to this, I told myself that things could be far worse, and that I must pull myself together. I promptly pulled myself out of bed, over-balanced, and fell on to my knees. It took me several minutes to haul myself back up, and by the time I was in a standing position, I was feeling rather self-centred again.

28 June 2016

It is great to have Elaine back. People have been very kind to me while she has been away, but I never feel quite right when she is not here. As soon as she arrived back yesterday, she heard that Janette has had a relapse after her latest operation, so this morning, Elaine had to drive straight back to Edinburgh to see her in hospital. With all the usual end-of-term activities to attend to, hundreds of reports to write, and her Commemoration Day speech to finish for Saturday, she certainly has her work cut out. I spent part of the morning trying to work out how England managed to lose to Iceland last night, and catching up on the fall-out from Brexit.

29 June 2016

Brexit continues to throw up more questions than answers. Can the Conservatives find a leader who is capable of unifying the opposing elements of the party? Can Labour find a leader who is supported by the party rank and file and capable of winning a general election? And can the SNP find a way of keeping Scotland in the EU, without triggering another referendum on independence? One of the most interesting revelations that has emerged is the sheer number of Leave voters who are now claiming that they regret voting the way they did. "I was persuaded by the fear that was spread about mass immigration", "I didn't realise the implications of leaving", and "I voted without thinking" were some of the explanations that I heard on the radio as I drove into Perth. These comments were beginning to make me angry.

Within ten minutes of arriving at Cornhill, any anger that remained had quickly subsided. Being with people who really do have things to worry about, and seeing their kindness and humour show through, puts things firmly into perspective. I chatted and laughed with Louise, Laura, and Elma, and then Margaret offered me a cancellation slot for a session of therapeutic touch. Lying on my back, fully clothed except for my shoes, and covered from the neck down by a blanket, I was amazed by the effectiveness of Margaret's light touch. The heat that I could feel as she barely touched my face and head was incredible. As she continued to stroke my arms and legs through the blanket, and I listened to soothing music, I felt utterly relaxed. By the time the treatment was over, I was not asleep, but in a calm, trance-like state. Thoughts and worries about the referendum were long gone.

1 July 2016

Today, I find myself absorbed by death, not my own death, but the appalling death of 20,00 young men who went "over the top" in the Somme area of Northern France, exactly one hundred years ago this morning. As a boy at school, I developed a keen fascination for the writings of those who served during the First World War. I studied the contrasting poems of Rupert Brooke, Siegfried Sassoon, and Wilfred Owen, and I read, and re-read, Goodbye to all That, by Robert Graves. As a seventeen-year-old, I was absolutely certain that the death of those 20,000 young men, and that of millions of others who died during that war, was a futile and terrible waste of life. I announced that I was a pacifist and embarrassed my father by refusing to wear a poppy on Remembrance Day.

Now, 45 years later, how do I feel? I still prefer the haunting words of Owen's *Anthem for a Doomed Youth* to the blind patriotism of Brooke's *The Soldier*, but I recognise that war is more complicated and contradictory than it appeared to me as a schoolboy. Like many people, I have been swayed by arguments in favour of taking military action, only to regret things later. The case for British intervention in Afghanistan and Iraq seemed strong at the time, because they were "good causes". Initially, when British casualties were reported, it strengthened the resolve to avenge these deaths, but, as more and more coffins arrived home, watched by millions on television, public opinion changed, and the calls for our troops to be withdrawn became louder. And now, after all that anguish, we are faced with the threat from ISIS. I don't see that being resolved by peaceful negotiation; there could be many more deaths to come.

2 July 2016

Yesterday was Commemoration Day at Glenalmond. There were two chapel services in the morning, one for non-leavers and one for all the leavers and their families. I went to the second of these with Jim and Tom, and, as always, we particularly enjoyed the music. John Wright, who has taught at the college for 37 years, gave a wonderful address on behalf of all those who are leaving this term; it was an emotional farewell and he fully deserved his standing ovation. Prize giving came next. Tom wheeled me into the sports hall, which was packed with hundreds of pupils and parents. There were fine speeches by Lord Menzies, the Chairman of Council, the Captains of College, Elaine, and Lord George Robertson, who as guest of honour, also awarded the prizes.

As I watched Elaine on the platform and listened to her speak about her first year as Warden, the achievements of the pupils, and her plans for the future, I felt incredibly proud. Having heard a great number of head teachers speak in schools and conferences over the years, and observed their tendency towards pomposity, my collective term for a group of head teachers is a "swelling". Elaine is as determined as the next head, but she is not motivated by the trappings of power, or by feelings of self-importance. She is genuinely pupil-centred, and this is what drives her forward and guides her decision-making.

4 July 2016

With one week to go before we leave, I went through all the paperwork for our holiday. In recent years, we have booked our flights and accommodation independently, but this year, with the complications of my MND, we have done everything through one company called Disabled Access Holidays. The firm has been very helpful and efficient in terms of flights, accommodation, and transfers, but I'm finding it hard to accept that the "disabled passenger" to whom they refer is actually me. The wheelchair assistance at the airport, the disabled lift on and off the plane, the wheelchair-friendly transportation to and from the hotel, and the specially adapted hotel room, including a wheel-in shower, are precisely the things that will make this holiday possible for me. I am very grateful to have them, but every time I see the wheelchair symbol on the letters, vouchers, and flight details, it reminds me of how rapidly my life has changed. I understand what has happened to me perfectly well, but I suppose part of me is still in denial — these are things that have always happened to other people.

As if to reinforce my changed circumstances, a lady rang from Perth and Kinross Council to talk to me about the adaptations that they are planning for the new house. She confirmed that tenders have been accepted for a wet room, a ramp, and an electronic entry system for the front door. I hope that this work can start fairly soon. I am certainly looking forward to living on the ground floor.

5 July 2016

Today, I couldn't get my trousers on. The stiffness in my arms and legs has been getting gradually worse for months, but up until now I have managed to sit on the edge of my bed and bend forward far enough to get my feet, one at a time, into the right trouser legs. This morning, however, I just couldn't manage it, and after several attempts, I was forced to give up. As I pulled myself up to a sitting position, I felt exhausted, so I let myself fall backwards. I lay there on my back with my legs dangling over the side of the bed, unable to get up. Initially, I saw the funny side of the situation, and I managed to laugh, but then I cried with frustration. Elaine heard me from the bathroom, and quickly came to the rescue. As she put my legs into my trousers and helped me to my feet, I said, "Sorry". Elaine told me I had nothing to apologise for, and we both smiled — but we both knew this marked the beginning of a new chapter.

CHAPTER THIRTEEN

Hiding Away on Holiday

7-8 July 2016

Somehow, over the last two days, I have managed to get myself dressed without any help. Not having to bother about socks certainly helps, although the "summer" temperature in Perthshire leaves me with cold feet. It was strange not going to Cornhill this week — the first time I haven't been for several months. I missed seeing all my friends, and I shan't see them again until we get back from holiday at the end of the month. Yesterday, Judith, along with her daughter and Lottie, tried to take me to a little beach area, down by the river, which runs behind the Glenalmond Mill. We drove the buggy along a rough track, but it was too difficult to get to the river. Sitting in the buggy, knowing that the water was just around the corner, but not being able to get there, was very frustrating. We changed plans and went up to Woodhead, the house we are moving to in August. I managed to get the buggy into the garden, and after driving around the rhododendron bushes, we sat there in the sunshine and had a beer.

This morning I watched the highlights of last night's Euro semi-final between France and Germany, and switched on the news. I was faced with reports from Dallas about the shooting of five police officers by snipers, following a demonstration. There was debate about the tactics used by the police, but once again, it raises the whole issue of gun laws in America. Whatever other mistakes Barack Obama may have made, he has shown great courage, in the face of a very powerful gun lobby, by trying to get some gun controls introduced in his country. The ease with which people can buy lethal weapons in most American states is frankly staggering. If Donald Trump becomes the next president, things are likely to get far worse.

10 July 2016

I have just spent five minutes picking up euros. I tried to check the amount in the wallet that came from Thomas Cook, but I couldn't grip them properly between my fingers and I dropped notes all over the floor. In the middle of picking them up, the phone went, but by the time I had hauled myself up it had rung out. As soon as I bent down again, my mobile went, but I couldn't get to that in time, either. After checking recent calls, I realised it was Peter, so I rang him back. He was with Max at his weekly tennis coaching. We talked about my holiday, which begins tomorrow, and his recovery from his recent fall from his bike. Peter said he was going to watch the Wimbledon final on a big screen at the tennis club and then he was meeting his friend Fotis in a pub to watch the final of the European championships. We agreed that it would be good if France could win the tournament.

Elaine has finished cutting and filing my nails and trimming the hair on my neck — more jobs that I can't manage any more. She is determined that I will look neat and tidy for my holiday. I still feel guilty that I can't help with the packing, but Elaine tells me to just relax and let her get on with it. After my near fiasco with the visa waivers when we went to America at Christmas, I think she is determined to do it all herself, and I don't blame her. I press the remote for my recliner, lie back, look out of the window, and watch the rain pouring down. The two-week weather forecast for Tenerife South says the average maximum and minimum temperatures will be 95 degrees F by day and 75 degrees F by night — a little warmer than Perthshire.

Andy Murray has just won Wimbledon. He played so well, and his return of serve, from one of the biggest servers in the game, was quite incredible. He cried (again) but he spoke very well. He was generous in his praise for Milos Raonic, and even thanked David Cameron for coming to watch. Unlike her predecessor, Nicola Sturgeon did not unravel a Scottish saltire in a cheap bid to make a political point.

11-25 July 2016

I spent most of the first week of my holiday in self-imposed isolation, on the little terrace outside our room. The journey from Perthshire to Tenerife had gone as smoothly as possible. Ed met us at Edinburgh Airport and he moved our luggage to the bag drop while Elaine took charge of my wheelchair. We did some shopping, and were then taken in a lift vehicle to an emergency exit door at the back of the aircraft. A smiling hostess opened the door from within and I only had to hobble a few yards to my seat. The flight was fine, but my right leg was aching badly by the time we came into land. When everyone else had disembarked we were collected and taken by lift straight to the luggage collection point, and within a few minutes I was being pushed up a ramp into a van, ready to go to our hotel.

Our room was large and had an adapted bathroom. Our terrace was in the corner of the large pool area and only a few yards from a lovely bar and restaurant. The whole place was beautifully landscaped and spotlessly clean, there were lifts and ramps in all the right places, the food was good, and the staff were delightful. The same can be said of the newly developed area around Plaza del Duque - very attractive walkways down to a white-sand beach, lovely bars and restaurants, stylish shopping areas and beautiful apartments — and despite a few inclines, they were all accessible by wheelchair.

So, why did I not take advantage of all these facilities? Well, I did try sitting by the pool on our first day, but I felt too self-conscious in my wheelchair. I was the only disabled person there, the only one not lying on a sun bed, and the only one unable to enjoy a cooling swim in the beautiful pool. Stupidly, I thought everyone was looking at me. After a short while, I asked Elaine to wheel me back to our terrace, which was only 20 yards away. She was reluctant to leave me there on my own, but I insisted she returned to her sun bed. Over the next few days I read books, watched the Open golf on TV, and listened to the test match. Elaine pushed me out for lunches and dinners, both in our hotel and in local restaurants, and I thoroughly enjoyed myself.

On day nine, I suddenly decided that I would try to get onto a sun bed. It turned out to be easier than I had thought, and as I lay in the sun beside the pool with a glass of beer by my side, closed my eyes, and listened to the water lapping gently against the side, I almost felt normal.

The runway at Tenerife Airport is right next to the water, on the southern tip of the island, and as we prepared to take off last night, I couldn't help wondering if it would be the last time I would see a foreign land. We had a good flight home and landed at Edinburgh just after midnight. There was a delay before the lift vehicle arrived, and by the time we had collected our bags and met Ed in arrivals, it was nearly 1 a.m. When I finally got into my own bed at 2.15 a.m., I was exhausted.

26 July 2016

After only a few hours' sleep, I woke up with a terrible toothache. One of my back teeth had been feeling sensitive for a few days, and during the flight home it had begun to feel worse. I had taken a painkiller the night before, but by morning I knew that I had to get to a dentist quickly. Elaine rang my dental practice, and fortunately they could fit me in that afternoon. More painkillers made things a little more bearable, but unfortunately my colitis had also flared up. The combination of MND on the one hand, and colitis on the other, is not a good one. The former makes it impossible to move any quicker than a very slow shuffle, but the latter requires frequent and urgent journeys to the loo. My dentist quickly decided that my tooth needed to be taken out, so after three injections to freeze the area and a considerable amount of pulling, the tooth finally popped out. Initially, the relief was huge, but a few hours later, when the effects of the anaesthetic had worn off, the pain was as bad as it had been before. More painkillers helped a little, but the colitis got worse. By the end of the evening, I was feeling utterly miserable. I even joked with Elaine that it might be best to simply have me put down.

27 July 2016

I woke up with a dull ache rather than a terrible pain, and I decided that I could face the world after all. We drove to Cornhill, and seeing all my friends again proved to be just the tonic I needed. It had been a month since my last visit and I had missed everyone more than I realised. These are the people who understand my situation better than anyone, and I understand them too. We accept each other for what we are, and we don't have any unreasonable expectations in terms of behaviour. Within minutes of our arrival, we were immersed in the banter between the medical staff, the volunteers, other "service users", and their carers. Louise, my physiotherapist, arrived to see me, Margaret took Elaine away for a session of therapeutic touch, and Elma gave my hands a massage. Over the next hour, I also chatted to Moira, Morag, the other Louise, Diane, Laura, and Stuart. It was great to see everyone again.

In the afternoon, Peter, Juliet, and Max arrived. A day earlier, and I would have been hopeless company, but their timing was ideal. They had arrived in Scotland by train, spent a day and night in a very busy Edinburgh, and were now based in the Crieff Hydro, an ideal place for Max. As always, it was wonderful to see my brother and it was really good to catch up with Juliet. I hadn't seen her for many months and, like Elaine, she has a unique understanding of the trials and tribulations that terminal illness brings to family life. I wore out my voice as time went by, so I had a rest while Elaine showed them around the school. We then enjoyed a curry for supper. A few more painkillers helped me have a good night's rest.

29 July 2016

After our very enjoyable dinner at the Crieff Hydro the night before as guests of Peter and Juliet, we were later to bed than usual, and we slept in. I left Elaine sleeping, and decided to try and get myself up. Having nearly slipped in the shower the morning before, I made do with a wash at the sink. This involved standing over the basin and pushing my forehead against the mirror in order to keep my balance. Once that was accomplished, I didn't have the energy to stand and shave, so I sat on the loo and did my best to tackle my stubble without the aid of a mirror. Having rested for a few minutes, I had enough energy to stand again and clean my teeth, then I made my way slowly back to my bed, and started the slow process of dressing. Five minutes later, I woke up Elaine so that she could see how clever I had been. This was a selfish and rather childish way of celebrating my little achievement, but I wanted to prove to her that I could still just about manage on my own.

I spent a few hours reading in the morning. Elaine had read eight books during our fortnight away, and I was keen to finish my fourth. After lunch, Cameron and his girlfriend, Alana, arrived. They are staying for the weekend, and it is great to see them. This is the first time I had met Alana, and it was the first time Elaine has seen her since her time at Loretto. She is a lovely girl; she has just left school and is eighteen months older than Cam. We joked about her being a cradle snatcher, but the two of them look very good together. Peter, Juliet, and Max arrived a little later. Max loves to be active and soon he was asking Peter to go outside and play on the slopes. He is a clever boy, and has inherited his cricketing talents from his father and his musical ability from his mother.

1 August 2016

My life is about to change this month, and that brings feelings of relief and anxiety. I am relieved that we are moving into a new house and that I will be able to live on the ground floor. Currently, I only climb the stairs once at night and come down in the morning, but each journey makes me more nervous and leaves me exhausted. The knowledge that I will never see the upstairs of the new house, however, is very depressing. I know that confinement to the ground floor and dependence upon an electric wheelchair, are necessary for my safety, but they are stark examples of the way my world is shrinking. Over the last three weeks it has been wonderful having Elaine on holiday, but it has also made me realise that very soon I won't be able to cope on my own. Showering and dressing are becoming increasingly difficult, and although I strive to manage on my own, these basic tasks are beginning to frighten me. Elaine is very happy to assist me, but she has a job to do, and when she is away on business I will simply have to swallow my pride, surrender my dignity, and allow carers to help me.

2 August 2016

This morning I was struggling to be positive, and when two old friends of Elaine arrived for lunch, I considered hiding away in my room. Despite having always thought of myself as a people person, meeting and talking to strangers can now feel quite daunting. However, Elaine persuaded me to say hello, and I am delighted that I made the effort. June and Sheena turned out to be very entertaining. They had both worked at Dollar Academy with Elaine back in the 90's and the three of them were keen to catch up on each other's news. I can no longer talk very much during a meal, having to concentrate very carefully when swallowing, so I was happy to listen to their stories. After lunch, both guests were patient with my rather slurred speech, and we had a very enjoyable chat.

3 August 2016

Wednesday is hospice day, and I am always keen to see the gang at Cornhill. This week, I had therapeutic touch with Margaret, while Elaine enjoyed having a hand massage with Elma. I also had an appointment with Hazel, my dietician, and this gave her the chance to meet Elaine and check that I have been giving her accurate information about my eating habits. Before we left, Elma gave my hands a massage, and then Margaret arrived. This was the first time I have seen her since her famous comment about "soft balls". It was wonderful to say hello and give her a hug.

4 August 2016

A day of phone calls and visits connected to health issues. Unfortunately, my colitis has not cleared up, despite doubling my normal daily dose of Asacol. Having lived with this condition for nearly forty years, I know all the symptoms, but these, combined with the mobility problems of MND, have been making me anxious. I rang the gastroenterology department at Perth Royal Infirmary for advice, but my consultant was on holiday. His secretary was very sympathetic when she rang me back, but said I should contact my GP in the first instance. She assured me that the GP would be able to help. I was a little sceptical, because in the past an appointment to see a consultant has sometimes taken up to a month. I was nervous about talking on the phone due to my poor speech, so Elaine rang for me. The GP on call couldn't have been more helpful. She said she was happy to come straight out from Perth to see me at home, but also offered to fax through a prescription for a course of steroids to the local chemist. An hour later, Elaine returned with the tablets and I started my course of treatment immediately.

In between these calls, Fiona, one of the local district nurses, arrived to re-fill the balloon that holds my feeding tube in place. This little procedure that used to worry me when I first had the tube fitted is actually very straightforward, and it was all over in five minutes. We then had a talk about the need for me to get more care on a daily basis. I explained that my specialist MND nurse was coming soon to discuss this, and Fiona told me that I must try not to worry. She then reassured me that her team would always be available, for as long as I need them. Hearing these words brought a tear to my eye.

Although part of me hates asking for help, I realise that I really don't have any option. There are simply too many things that I can't do any more, and I am just so grateful that there are people there for me. Elaine cannot possibly be with me all day, and if I keep falling over I am very likely to get hurt.

6 August 2016

For the second day running I woke up at 4 a.m. and couldn't get back to sleep. So many things were rushing through my mind, and after a few failed attempts to use my relaxation and mindfulness exercises, I got out of bed, and sat in a chair. I started to write notes on Elaine's phone about things that need to be done in the next few weeks, such as packing the rest of the house up, and sorting out utilities for the new house. I'm not sure why I'm suddenly not sleeping well, but perhaps it could be a side effect of all the steroids I'm taking. Emma is staying with us for the weekend and it is always good to see her. She is very direct, very funny, and a great friend.

In the afternoon, Elaine's parents, her brother, and her uncle and aunt arrived for tea. Elaine's mum, Janette, has had a very tough time in hospital over several months, so it was wonderful to see her up here again. She also has a walker to help her move around, and we joked about the two of us having races around the house. I took Elaine's aunt, Margaret, for a drive in my buggy. We went into the college quad, and I showed her the chapel and the library. She borrowed a short raincoat from Elaine, but being so tiny, it almost came down to her ankles. In the evening we went up to look at the new house. While everyone else went upstairs, Janette and I sat in my wet room, Janette in her walker, and me on my new loo seat. We laughed about the clever loo, which functions as both a toilet and an automatic bidet — or as I prefer to call it, a wash and blow-dry. I tried out some of the buttons on the side to see if all the gadgets were working, but it wasn't connected to the mains. The relatives gave their seal of approval to the house and left for Edinburgh. Elaine, Emma, and I went back to enjoy a bottle of Prosecco.

8 August 2016

Elaine's first full day back at work, so the alarm went off at 6.55 a.m. As I have been waking up at 4 or 5 a.m. for the last week, I was actually pleased to get up rather than lie in bed trying to get back to sleep. I hit the snooze button to give Elaine a precious extra five minutes, and went to get washed. The pressure in our shower had suddenly gone, so it took me ages to wash my hair. Completing this comparatively easy operation is difficult enough when you can only use one hand (the other one has to hold on to the wall rail to prevent over-balancing), but trying to do it under a trickle of water is very frustrating and tiring. By 7.30 a.m., however, we were having breakfast. I took my eight steroid pills in a bowl of natural yoghurt with honey, and by 8 a.m. Elaine was in her office and I was writing my blog and watching a replay of the Olympics. The BBC's coverage is very extensive, and after watching Adam Peaty win gold in the 100m breaststroke final with a new world record time, I knew I would be hooked for the duration of the games. My emotional lability (a tendency to swing from one emotion to another) certainly kicked in as I watched, and for much of the day I was either laughing or crying, or doing both at the same time.

9 August 2016

My new electric wheelchair arrived, and I'm unsure how I feel about it. On the one hand it is the final confirmation that my walking days are over, but on the other, it gives me an opportunity to continue to move around independently. Four people from TORT (Tayside Orthopaedic and Rehabilitation Technology Centre) came with the chair, and for an hour and a half they worked around me with spanners and screwdrivers to ensure that everything was right. Manufactured in Germany, this wheelchair is designed for indoor and outdoor travel, and it has something called mid-wheel drive, which allows it to turn on a sixpence. It also has adjustable foot pedals, adjustable armrests and a movable headrest; it reclines and tilts, and it has four different speed levels. All of these functions can be operated by a simple joystick, which can be moved with one finger. When fully charged, the chair will run for up to 10 miles, both on and off road.

As I was given a "driving test" around the house, I gradually became more excited about my new machine. I tried out the various switches and gadgets, and went for a slow spin around the kitchen table. The steering is very sensitive, the seat is very comfortable, and the chair feels really stable. It is being stored in the new house until we move next week, and I am looking forward to my first outdoor trip.

10 August 2016

Dee, my MND specialist nurse, came out to see me. As expected, we talked about the need for me to have more care on a daily basis, and we discussed my emotional state. Both issues are important, but Dee and Elaine know that I am reluctant to face them. Dee made it very clear that daily care is something that I need, on grounds of health, safety, and convenience. I realise that it would be foolish and irresponsible to refuse the help that is available — I need assistance with daily living, and Elaine needs the reassurance that I am getting it. Having agreed that Dee would get a care package assessment organised, we talked about the swings in emotion that I am experiencing. I said I would rather not take medication for this, but I agreed to have another session with my neuropsychologist.

At Cornhill I had a wonderful session of therapeutic touch. Last week I found it difficult to let go, but this time the heat from Margaret's hands as she gently touched my head and limbs, combined with the soothing music in the background, quickly transported me to a very relaxed, and almost trance-like world — I could have stayed there all day!

12 August 2016

The first day of the grouse-shooting season has become a flashpoint for tensions between the game industry and conservationists. As a child growing up on a farm on the edge of Exmoor, rural pursuits like shooting, fishing, and hunting were simply a part of country life. I appreciate why the killing of birds, animals, and fish can upset people, particularly those who live in towns and cities, but the claim by some that rural people are cruel and unfeeling monsters is complete nonsense.

We left the shooting parties of Perthshire behind us and drove down to Edinburgh for an appointment with our solicitor. Edinburgh traffic can be frustrating at the best of times, but during the festival it often grinds to a halt. We couldn't park on George Street, so Elaine had to push my wheelchair up through Charlotte Square. We were glad to leave the city behind as we made our way out towards East Lothian. We went through the pretty village of East Saltoun, where Elaine's mum was brought up, and arrived at Leaston, the beautiful home of Duncan and Hilary Menzies. Duncan is Chairman of Glenalmond's Council (Governing body), and Hilary has also been a governor. They are both passionate about the college, and they have been very supportive of Elaine and me during our first year. Over a long and relaxed lunch, which included some lovely food and wine, Duncan and Elaine caught up on school affairs. Hilary and I chatted about all sorts of things, ranging from mindfulness to the benefits of cooking with an aga. It was after four o'clock by the time we rose from the table, and after talking so much I had very little voice left.

14 August 2016

We left for Edinburgh again — this time to see Cameron's band, Chameleon Lady, perform on an open-air stage next to St Giles Cathedral. My blue badge allows me to park in some fairly unlikely places, but even with this advantage the only space we could find was some distance away. Edinburgh cobbles are a terrible surface for wheelchairs, and only a few yards from the car, the bolt that secures one of the footplates was shaken loose, and my foot hit the ground. Elaine managed to find the bolt and secure it again, but it was a tiring push for her, and a bumpy ride for me, as we made our way through crowds of tourists along the roads that led to the Royal Mile. We arrived at the stage to find a large crowd listening to the band. Cameron looked good in his bright blue suit, and his singing went down well with those who were watching. At the end of their set they sang the ever-popular Proclaimers song, *500 Miles*. Cameron was in his element as he encouraged everyone to join in, and the band fully deserved the ovation they were given by the crowd. On the way home Elaine called in to see Alice, and then we stopped for some shopping and a take away at Kinross. I have always enjoyed a chicken burger and chips, particularly with lots of mayonnaise, but I have always tried to limit my intake of fast food. As an MND sufferer, however, it is essential for me to keep my weight up, so I now enjoy such things without any feelings of guilt — there have to be some compensations.

Tonight we watched Max Whitlock, Justin Rose, Andy Murray, and Jason Kenny win five more GB gold medals. All their performances were great to see, but Max Whitlock's achievement in winning two gold medals for gymnastics in one evening was quite incredible.

CHAPTER FOURTEEN

Confined to the Ground Floor

16 August 2016

The removal van arrived at 8.30 a.m., but instead of spending the day packing and carrying boxes, I was forced to stay in my chair while everyone else worked around me. Jim, Janette, and Ed arrived at lunchtime to help Elaine. Jim was looking quite sporty in a red pair of shorts, but his daughter didn't approve of the socks that he was wearing with them. A little later, Dr. Bateman arrived for a home visit. With everything else going on, I had forgotten my appointment, but it was really good to see him. He is a consultant in critical care and long-term ventilation, based at the Euan MacDonald Centre in Edinburgh. I first met him very shortly after my diagnosis in May 2015, and I was immediately struck by his sensitive approach. On this occasion we discussed my breathing and sleeping, and then had a long-ranging chat about all sorts of MND-related issues. He told me that he would be seeing me every three months from now on, but was at pains to reassure me that he thought my breathing was still very stable.

At 7 p.m. Elaine came to collect me. I took one final photo of the view that I have enjoyed so much over the last year, said goodbye to the Warden's House, and we went up the drive to our new abode. There were boxes all over the place, but it has a very homely feel. I watched Team GB win even more gold medals in the cycling, and enjoyed a short walk to my new bedroom. It was wonderful to be able to do that without having to climb a staircase.

17 August 2016

My first morning in my new wet room proved to be a surprise for me and for someone else. The door into the room has still to get a slider fitted, so it was wide open. As Elaine was the only person in the house, this didn't worry me, so I got straight into the shower. I felt much safer on the non-slip surface and decided that I would let myself drip-dry while I cleaned my teeth and flushed my feeding tube. As I sat on my perch stool, syringe in hand, completely naked, I heard someone knocking on the front door. I shouted that they would need to wait, but to my surprise, I heard the sound of a key in the lock. I shouted, "Hold on!" but a few seconds later a young man appeared in the open doorway. I'm not sure which of us got the biggest shock, but as soon as the poor chap saw me, he turned on his heels, and ran out of the house. Elaine heard the commotion and came downstairs to investigate. She went out to find a slightly bemused painter, who had been given keys to the house.

As the house was still full of packing boxes, I decided to go to Cornhill for as long as possible. Elaine made me a packed lunch, and I arrived at the hospice fairly early. I have been told not to attempt the walk from my car to the hospice entrance, so I tried to ring the office to let them know that I was outside. The staff, quite rightly were busy looking after patients and visitors, so I was not surprised that my call went to answer phone. I decided to ring another number, which I believed to be the reception desk, but to my surprise, I heard a voice say, "Good morning, Community Mental Health". I didn't know quite what to say, and I was worried about my slow and slurred speech. After a pause, the lady on the other end said, "Are you, all right?" I managed to say, "I'm trying to get into the hospice." The voice at the other end sounded very concerned: "You can't get into the hospice? Do you need help?" I realised that the situation was in danger of getting out of control, so I said, "Don't worry, I will be okay," and hung up. At that moment, Morag arrived to collect me. As we went into the building, I told her what had happened, and we ended up laughing so much that I started to cry. When we arrived at the day room, I was still incapable of talking, so Morag told everyone the story, and we all started to laugh again. I should make it very clear that our laughter was not in any way intended to be disrespectful towards anyone suffering from, or involved in, mental health.

After a brief return to normality and a cup of coffee, I told Hazel, Louise, Margaret, and Elma about my unfortunate experience in the wet room. This resulted in more hysterics and plenty of teasing about my "flashing" behaviour. Elma gave my hands a massage, and then I went off for my last session of therapeutic touch with Margaret. This week, I relaxed quickly and drifted off to sleep. At the end, Margaret gave me the name of the music CD she uses during her sessions. I will get this as a download, and use it at home in my recliner. I then spent an hour chatting to (but mainly listening to) another visitor to the day centre. Eileen is tiny, has a great sense of fun, is full of energy, and, most of all, she loves to talk. She helped get my lunch box open, and as I ate my sandwich, I listened to her stories. My day at Cornhill ended with a relaxation class, led by Sheena, and then Morag escorted me back to my car.

18 August 2016

Another strange thing happened to me in my wet room yesterday morning. I needed to use my new Clos-O-Mat loo, but only in a standing position. To keep myself steady, and avoid any mishaps, I held on to the top of the uplifted seat, and as soon as I had performed the task, I pushed on the large flush button with my free hand. Immediately, a short pipe appeared from the side of the bowl. As I lowered my head to look at it, a fierce jet of water shot into the air, and drenched my face, neck, and chest. The water, of course, would have been directed at the other end of my torso, if I had been sitting on the loo, but the weight of my hand on the seat had activated the automatic "wash" mechanism. I went into the kitchen, water still dripping from my head, and told Elaine and Ed what had happened. If I was expecting any sympathy, I was mistaken — they thought it was hilarious.

Yvonne, an OT from the wheelchair service, arrived later in the morning to give me further training on the use of my chair. She asked me to practise moving forward and back and using the joy stick, and gave me clear instructions about the positioning of my head, where to look with my eyes, when to start cornering, and the best speed setting. After a few collisions with furniture and skirting boards, we embarked on a series of little journeys around the house, simulating the main actions that I will need to perform when on my own. The visit to the wet room involved a three-point turn, and the turn from the bedroom into the kitchen looked impossible. However, after a few more practice goes, and a few more bumps, I managed to get in and out of these rooms without knocking into anything. By the end, I was really pleased with myself, and as Yvonne congratulated me, I could feel tears in my eyes. It was very similar to the satisfaction I felt when I took my first drive in a car some 45 years ago. Yvonne said she would be back as soon as the ramp for the front door is installed, and then we could go for a trip around the college campus. I am looking forward to trying out the chair at full speed on the main drive.

20 August 2016

While Elaine was away shopping, I practised driving around the house and finished up in front of the French windows in the sitting room. The pots outside are full of flowers and the bird table that Jim brought me has centre stage. The sun was shining and I watched blue tits, robins, and the occasional black bird come to feed from the bags of nuts that hung from the table. Earlier in the day I had downloaded the CD that Margaret plays at Cornhill. It is called *Perfume*, and was composed by Stephen Rhodes. It contains some of the most beautiful and relaxing tracks that I have ever heard. As I put my chair into full-recline position, closed my eyes, and listened through my earphones, I was quickly transported to another world. I am not a particularly religious man, and I have few expectations in terms of an afterlife, but lying there, transfixed by the soothing sound of the music, I could imagine myself drifting peacefully away to some heavenly place. When it is time to go, this is what I want to hear.

22 August 2016

Elaine worked from home this morning while I caught up on my writing. In the afternoon, Martin Hatton, a social worker from Perth and Kinross Council, arrived to do an assessment of my care needs. Martin is a tall man with lots of personality, and he has an infectious sense of humour. His opening statement of, "Well, I don't suppose you were queuing up to get MND?" was a good way to break the ice, and we spent the next two hours discussing the care plan options and pathways that are available. My reticence about having too many visits per day were noted by Martin, but he quickly convinced me that my needs were probably greater than I was willing to admit. He explained that given the way my mobility has already declined, and will continue to do so, there was little point basing my care needs on a "good day". He said he needed to know that my "bad days" were going to be catered for, too. By the time our discussions were over, I was finally reconciled to the idea that I would soon have people coming into the house three or four times a day. This is, however, far more support than I ever thought I would need. It is double the number of hours that my eighty-eight-year-old father had at the end of his life. How can things have reached this stage already?

23 August 2016

May, one of Elaine's oldest friends (in years known, not years lived) joined us for breakfast. If Elaine is very 'Edinburgh', then May is very 'Glasgow.' She shoots from the hip, has pink hair, red glasses, and wears brightly coloured clothes. Whatever the differences in terms of personality, the two of them share a passion for teaching, May knows Elaine very well and refers to her as "my big little sister". She had intended to return home after supper last night, but after giving in to the temptation of some red wine, she stayed over and the two friends sat up and talked long after I had retired to bed.

This morning when the two of them had left, I was expecting a quiet day on my own, but an hour later, Jeremy arrived from TORT with one of the technicians. Jeremy wanted to check out the feasibility of installing a remote wireless system for me to activate the front door. The two men spent some time testing equipment from different parts of the house, and Jeremy then reported back to say that soon I should be able to open the front door by pushing a button on my phone. Another man then arrived to fix an automatic closing device on the front door, and they said everything should be up and running within another week.

24 August 2016

After a week spent indoors, today was my first trip outside the new house. Tom had stayed over last night, and before he left for Glasgow, he helped me get into my car. Although I am still confident about my ability to drive, I do now accept that I need assistance getting in and out of the vehicle. At Cornhill I drove up to the front door, and as agreed last week, the lady at the reception desk called for help from upstairs. Louise appeared only a few moments later, and we walked carefully into the building and went up in the lift. It was very busy in the day room so I took a seat across from the main group of visitors. This gave me a lovely view across Perth and out to the hills beyond. I stayed there for over two hours, alternating between chatting to the staff and resting my voice. After my weekly hand massage, I went along to Moira's "salon" for a haircut. Two things struck me about this visit, compared to my last appointment some six weeks ago. Firstly, I noticed that it took me longer to get to the room at the end of the corridor, even with someone to hold on to, and secondly, as Moira chatted away while she cut my hair, I found it increasingly difficult to speak clearly in response. As I sat in the chair, I tried to convince myself that I was just having a bad day, but then I felt a twinge of panic as I realised that it was probably a clear sign that my mobility and voice are steadily deteriorating.

26 August 2016

Every day since we moved we have had visitors, including family, friends and health professionals. Yesterday it was the turn of Sheena, my OT from Cornhill. Sheena wanted to have a look at the new house and assess its suitability. After a good chat about the general lay out, I moved into my new wheelchair and took Sheena on a guided tour around the ground floor. Over the last week I have often glanced up the stairs and wondered what it looks like up there, but I have forced myself to stay focused on downstairs. We went through the routes between the bedroom, living room, and the kitchen, and then discussed the wet room. Sheena wanted to be sure that I will be able to access everything when I am confined mainly to my wheelchair. I was able to demonstrate that I can drive the wheelchair into the wet room and manoeuvre it around the space, but this led to some interesting questions. How will I get into the shower cubicle? How will I actually wash myself properly? How will I get on and off the loo? How will I shave and clean my teeth? How will I get dressed? It was clear that the wheelchair on its own will not provide the solution. Currently, I can just about manage these things on my own, but each task is getting more difficult and more tiring. The wheelchair will get me to the right area, but that is all. To be able to perform the actual tasks, I will need assistance. We were back to the need for carers. Sheena knows that this whole issue is something that I am struggling with and she sympathises with my feelings in terms of lost independence. However, she also knows that this is something I must come to terms with. We sat and discussed the care package options that Martin Hatton had outlined earlier in the week, and I promised Sheena that I would not be resistant to his proposals.

27-28 August 2016

On Saturday evening Elaine was hosting a buffet supper and drinks for all the staff to mark the beginning of the new academic year. I had pondered over whether to go for much of the day, but in the end I was glad that I made the effort. We went down to the Warden's House early so that I could eat my food at the kitchen table before anyone else arrived. Holding a plate in one hand while getting food into my mouth with the other, whilst using a normal fork, is getting beyond me. The effort of holding the plate is very tiring, and my stiff fingers and wrist make it difficult to get a conventional fork into my mouth without spilling food. I could have taken my funny cutlery with big handles but I felt better hiding away from public view. Once I had eaten, Elaine transferred me to a sofa, and I spent some very enjoyable three hours chatting to a variety of staff and their partners, and drinking plenty of red wine. The summer holiday has been a welcome break for the teachers, who often work seven days a week in term time, but most of them said they were keen to get going again.

Yesterday was our last Sunday before term officially begins at Glenalmond. Elaine didn't go down to her office, but she had to spend most of each day working at home. She sat in her study next door to the sitting room, and I tried not to distract her too much as she dealt with a stream of emails and finalised her notes for the various addresses that she will have to make over the next few days. This will include talks to the teaching staff, the support staff, new parents, new pupils, and an assembly for all staff and pupils. Unlike many head teachers that I have observed over the years, Elaine's delivery tends to be very consistent. She is direct, but friendly, she talks to rather than down to people, and she avoids jargon and pomposity.

29 August 2016

Today, I had a home visit from Moira, my neuropsychologist. I first saw Moira nine months ago, and in January of this year she gave me an open appointment. At that stage I was using mindfulness to stay in the present and I was generally feeling quite positive. Following recent changes to my life, which have included the deterioration of my mobility and voice, along with moving house, Dee, my MND nurse, suggested that it might be a good idea to see Moira again.

Moira has a very calm manner, and she is a very good listener. This morning, she wanted to assess how the changes that have been going on in my life may be affecting my mood and behaviour. In response to Moira's gentle but probing questions, I tried to explain how I feel about the losses that MND brings. I told her that one of the most difficult things to accept is that the disease is so progressive, and that although the rate of progression varies over time, it feels inexorable. I told Moira about the anxiety I feel about having carers in to look after me, and I mentioned the times when my thoughts can become dark. I can't remember her exact words, but Moira reminded me that it is "fine not to feel fine". She also said that, given my situation, she would be more concerned if I had said that everything was fine all the time. This thought has stayed with me for the rest of today, and it has been quite a relief. Moira is coming back to see me in three weeks.

30-31 August 2016

On Tuesday morning Judith picked me up in her Mini and we drove to Crieff, along with Lottie and my lightweight wheelchair. I have missed my regular trips out

with Judith — her directness and sharp sense of humour
are good for me. There is plenty of empathy and kindness,
but no sentimentality. We stopped in the high street so
that Judith could post some parcels and she came back
with two coffees. We then drove to Macrosty Park and
enjoyed our drinks at a picnic table. Lottie was impatient
to start her walk, so as soon as we had finished we joined
all the other dog-walkers on the paths that crisscross the
park. As Judith pushed me along, I enjoyed the sunshine,
and Lottie went exploring — she never strays far, and
when other dogs approach, she is tentative about meeting
them. After another brief stop in the town, we made our
way back to Glenalmond. The back road is a beautiful
run, with some lovely views towards the Sma' Glenn and
the mountains beyond.

Wednesday was Cornhill day, but by nine thirty the
house was full of people. Claire had arrived first, closely
followed by Jeremy and Bob from TORT, who wanted to
set up my new phone system and electronic door opening.
A few minutes later, Lynne arrived to see Jeremy, and
then the electrician came in to talk about light sensors. All
of these people were there for my benefit, and I am very
grateful to them; however, it was a relief to get into my car
with plenty of help from Claire, and head off to Perth. As
soon as I parked, I saw Hazel walking towards the
hospice. I called out to her from the car window, and a
few minutes later she appeared with a wheelchair to take
me up to the dayroom. One of the staff (who I have been
referring to as Carol) came over to chat. As "Carol"
approached I was surprised to hear someone call her
"Laura". When she sat down I told her that I have been
calling her Carol in my blog. Laura said she wasn't having

that and I would have to change it. We had a good laugh about it, and for the rest of the morning she called me "Paul" every time she saw me. Hazel collected me for a chat about my feeding tube and my water intake. She explained that I needed to take in more liquids to avoid getting dehydrated, either by drinking more or through my tube. She said it was important that any carers who might look after me in the future could give me water through my tube.

1 September 2016

In recent months I have been in danger of getting paranoid about the advances that are being made in treating all sorts of diseases — except mine. Hardly a week seems to have gone by without the announcement of a medical breakthrough that will hopefully lead to a cure for something. This year I have read about developments that will tackle forms of blindness, multiple sclerosis, Parkinson's, Alzheimer's, and, of course, many forms of cancer. I'm delighted that so many people who would have faced a terminal prognosis a few years ago are being given a real chance of survival. I see tangible examples of this at Cornhill. The vast majority of the patients are suffering from cancer, but many of them are in remission. I have to admit that I occasionally feel jealous of those who have cheated death. However, things are rarely as simple as they seem, and I realised this on Wednesday, when I chatted to a man I hadn't seen before. He seemed to be fit and well, so I assumed he was another cancer survivor. It transpired, however, that his wife had died of cancer earlier in the year, very soon after she had been given a terminal prognosis. There were tears in his eyes as he told me how wonderful everyone had been at Cornhill, both during his wife's care, and for him during his bereavement. I felt terrible for having made assumptions that were entirely unjustified.

2 September 2016

Today, Judith sent me a meditation app (*Headspace*), which included a ten-day free trial. I shall try it out tomorrow morning. Recently, I have been waking up very early. Rather than lie in bed with thoughts buzzing around in my head, I have started to move into the sitting room and watch the arrival of dawn from my recliner. I think that might be a good time to meditate. After a quiet morning, Jim and Janette, along with Jim's sister, Kay and her husband, Jimmy, arrived in the early afternoon. We sat and chatted, then had tea and cakes, before going on a tour of the house. I have not seen the upstairs, and unless someone carries me up there, I never will. However, by listening to the various comments given by visitors, I'm building up quite a clear picture of the layout. Jim, in particular, wanted to have a good look at each room, and his descriptions of furniture and fittings were very detailed. At five o'clock Janette caught me yawning. "Richard, you're getting tired, we should go and let you rest", she said. As the youngest person there by far, I was embarrassed by this, but as soon as they had gone, I put my feet up and had a sleep.

3-4 September 2016

Yesterday morning was a Saturday, but as term has started, it was a normal day for Elaine. She left at 8 a.m. and I decided to try my first 10-minute introductory session of meditation. A calm voice talked me through suggested ways to sit for meditation, and then went on to explain how breathing plays a central role in bringing thoughts and feelings back towards the body. One message I took from this first session is that meditation is not about forcing things — it is more about letting go. When I opened my eyes at the end of the ten minutes, I certainly felt much more relaxed than I had been at the beginning. Elaine appeared briefly at lunchtime, but she left quickly to watch the first hockey matches of the term. She came back for dinner and promptly left again to see how the evening activities were going — the joys of a boarding school.

This is Sunday morning, but I remained at home while Elaine went to chapel. I felt rather lazy for staying in my dressing gown until she returned, but the effort of having a shower and shaving had left me feeling tired. I couldn't face the prospect of trying to get dressed on my own. For the first time, I really started to think about the difference that carers would make to my daily routine. Elaine had to go back to school for much of the afternoon, and then, just when she deserved a break, she set off to do a weekly shop in Perth. My sense of frustration and feelings of guilt over not being able to help with household chores are still strong.

CHAPTER FIFTEEN

The Carers Arrive

6 September 2016

This afternoon Martin arrived with two ladies from Rigifa Care Services to have a meeting with Elaine and me. The aim was to discuss the draft care plan that Martin had prepared, following his talks with several health care professionals. Martin included details about MND in his paper, much of which he sourced from the information available on the MND Association website. Neither of the ladies from Rigifa had worked with anyone suffering with MND, so we started by having a chat about my symptoms and the way they have, and probably will, develop. Because I have been living with the disease for a couple of years, I sometimes forget how few people know much about it. When Martin said, "Richard, you're the expert!", I realised that, within the group, he was completely right. Of course, knowing all about my current symptoms doesn't necessarily mean I understand my actual care needs, either for the present, or the future. After some discussion about risks and practical necessities,

I agreed to the basic proposal of having a carer come in four times a day, but I was resistant to the idea of having someone stay overnight when Elaine is away on school business. I understand that this level of care will become necessary in the future, particularly when I lose the ability to move unaided, but at the moment, I want to keep some degree of independence. I am confident that if a carer makes sure that I am safely in bed at night, I will be fine until someone arrives to get me up in the morning. I suspect this issue will require further negotiation, but it is certainly my preferred option.

Not long after our meeting, Judith came over to take me out for a spin in my lightweight wheelchair. The weather has suddenly turned warmer, so it was good to get outside. On our walk we met several pupils in the grounds, and as always, they greeted us warmly — another reminder of how fortunate I am to live in this community.

7 September 2016

I had a very good day at Cornhill, but I nearly lost my voice. As soon as I arrived in the reception area, I was teased about my pink polo shirt, with various comments about my feminine side coming out. I hadn't even given it a thought, but I noticed that all the other men were wearing clothes in more traditional "male" colours, like dark blue, black, or white. Louise introduced me to two trainee nurses who were visiting Cornhill for the day — I assume this is part of their training in palliative care. The girls asked if I would mind answering some questions, and I said I would be happy to do so. We then had a good discussion about my journey with MND, including how my symptoms have developed over the last four years.

Louise, my physiotherapist, then arrived. I felt embarrassed because I had forgotten that she was coming up to see me, but it was great to see her again. The trainee nurses asked if they could observe, and Louise went through my mobility issues. She confirmed that there was little to be gained by doing my old exercise programme, because it would now cause too much fatigue. Of course, what Louise and I both know, is that the majority of the exercises that I was doing a year ago are now completely beyond me. It is quite frightening to think that only twelve months ago I was still able to touch my toes, balance on one leg, and slide myself up against the wall from a squatting position. I prefer not to think about what I will (and will not) be able to do in another year's time.

As soon as Louise had gone, I had my usual hand massage with Elma. She is going on holiday to Italy for the next two weeks, but she has kindly asked Margaret to do my hands while she is away. Hazel then came to find out how my meeting with Martin had gone. She told me that she would be happy to train any carers to flush my feeding tube. Just as I was about to leave, Di said that someone had cancelled their session of therapeutic touch and asked if I would like to take it instead. I happily agreed, and a few minutes later I was enjoying the warm and relaxing benefits of the treatment.

8 September 2016
Ed came up to do various jobs around the house, including putting up pictures and curtain rails and sorting out the cables that connect all the electric appliances that

surround me. These include telephones, an automatic door entry system, a laptop, an alarm system, a standard lamp, a modem, and the remote control for my recliner. As a sound engineer, Ed is used to cables, but he likes them to be tidy. Of all the jobs he completed, the one that pleased me the most was that of filling the feeders that hang from the bird table outside my window. I never thought I would get so much pleasure from watching birds. Today was a very good one for wildlife; in addition to all the blue tits, chaffinches, robins, and blackbirds, I saw three rabbits and two red squirrels.

Just before lunch, Elizabeth Peters, an OT for Perth and Kinross Council, came to look at the adaptations that have been done to the house. Sitting on my electric chair, I gave her a guided tour. She was pleased with the wet room and the layout of the bedroom, and she said she was impressed with my driving skills. Elizabeth was sorry that the ramp was not fitted yet, but said there was little she could do to cut through the red tape that was holding things up. I told Elizabeth about our meeting with Martin and the proposed four carer visits per day. She thought this would be ideal and agreed with my view that overnight carers were not required for the time being. Perhaps I will win that argument after all.

10 September 2016

Lorna and Nick arrived yesterday for a short visit. I am always exited to see my daughter, but this time it is very special because she has her husband, Nick, with her. This morning, Megan and Euan also came up to see me. This was the first time that I have seen both of my girls with their respective partners, and I found the whole experience rather emotional. I'm delighted that they are both in happy relationships, and I'm proud of their achievements — I just wish that I could look forward to seeing more of their lives unfold in the future.

Today was also Glenalmond's Open Day, and fortunately, after a few days of heavy rain, the weather suddenly improved. The buildings and grounds at the college are magnificent, and they look even more spectacular in the sunshine. Elaine and her team have worked hard on preparing talks, tours, activities and concerts, and she was very pleased with the results. Over 200 people attended the event, and the teachers and pupils did a wonderful job of making them feel welcome. Everything was rounded off with a barbeque on the front lawn, as the pipe band went through their impressive repertoire.

11 September 2016

Today we had a celebration lunch to mark Lorna and Nick's recent marriage. My brother Peter, and his son George travelled all the way up from London; Elaine's family (minus Jim, who is sadly in hospital) arrived from Edinburgh and Glasgow, and some of Lorna's old school friends joined us, too. After champagne and some lovely food, Elaine read out some words that I had written, and we rounded off the occasion with a toast and some wedding cake. I was upset that my voice wasn't strong enough to deliver my little speech, but I was proud of the way Elaine did it for me. My final words were as follows:

"Parents want many things for their children — fulfilment of academic potential, successful careers, and financial security, are just

some of them. But when all is said and done, what matters most to me is that my children are happy. Lorna, I have never seen you happier than you are now, and Nick, you are largely responsible for that. I am so pleased that we could have this celebration here today, and on behalf of everyone, I want to wish you both all the happiness in the world".

13 September 2016

Lorna and Nick were no longer here when I got up this morning. They had a very early flight to Manchester, before flying on to Saudi Arabia via Abu Dhabi. Their luggage got lost in Abu Dhabi on the way over here and it was only delivered on Sunday evening, less than 36 hours before their return. They coped with this much better than I would have done! After the excitement and anticipation of seeing my daughter, her rapid departure came as a blow. I spent part of today thinking about the things we had talked about. Did I say all the things that I wanted to say? Did I cause Lorna too much worry about my MND?

Much of the rest of the day has been taken up by electrical and mechanical problems. Firstly, I discovered that my intercom system wouldn't allow me to unlock the front door unless someone presses the entry system from outside. This is fine if someone is out there, but it won't be much use when I want to leave the house on my own. I emailed Jeremy to ask for his assistance. Next, the CO_2 alarm went off. The piercing noise was very loud, and had I been able, I would have moved outside. Instead, I phoned Elaine at her office, and then tried to cover my ears. Eventually, one of the college maintenance team arrived and managed to silence it. As soon as all this was over, I tried to make a call on my new phone and discovered that it was dead. I thought that it might simply need charging on the base set, but that didn't work. I sent another email to poor old Jeremy.

14 September 2016

This morning, for the first time, I didn't attempt to walk into Cornhill. Instead Louise, as bright and cheerful as ever, came out with a wheelchair, and that was where I stayed until I returned to my car, two hours later. The loss of independent movement has been gradual and frustrating, but I'm now relieved to get pushed around by other people. Shuffling around very slowly with my stick whilst gripping hold of someone's arm and constantly worrying about falling is not a mark of independence — it is simply frightening. Once I get into a chair, however, I feel safe and less anxious. With Elma away on holiday in Italy — and having a great time, I hear — Margaret kindly gave my hands a massage. I had been busy talking to other people before this, so she suggested that I sit back and relax while she manipulated my fingers and worked on my palms. I felt a little self-conscious at first, as I closed my eyes, and listened to all the people chatting around me, but soon I felt very calm. Morag (known by everyone as "the boss") is always busy, and I haven't seen much of her in recent weeks. Today, however, after spending time with a new visitor, she came over for a chat. I talked to her about my carers starting next week, and she gave me some good practical advice, mixed with plenty of humour.

Not long after I got home, Judith came around to see me. She persuaded me to go out for a "walk" with Lottie. It was a lovely afternoon, and I sat back in my wheelchair and enjoyed the beautiful shades of green as Judith pushed me around the grounds. The Week magazine has just published its annual guide to independent schools, and it chose Glenalmond as having the most beautiful setting of any school in the UK. I cannot say that this surprised me — the buildings, the grounds, and the views are all magnificent. As we made our way up a fairly steep incline, two young pupils came over and kindly offered to help. One of them then took over from Judith and pushed me quickly to the top. The boys looked really happy as they went off to their house — there were no signs of the homesickness that I had felt during my own first weeks at boarding school.

16 September 2016

The day started well with my first session of meditation since I signed up for a year's subscription to *Headspace*. This session introduced the idea of how meditation can affect those around you, particularly partners. Elaine and I have both worked in boarding school education (as teachers, house-parents, and as head teachers) for many years, and our lives have often become saturated with pastoral and educational issues. After a long, and sometimes stressful, day at work, Elaine needs to escape from these pressures, but I can sometimes make this difficult for her by asking too many questions and offering too many opinions. My meditation session reminded me that the calmer I remain, the better it will be for those around me.

Sadly, the calming effects of my meditation did not last long. In the afternoon, we discovered that Jim, who has been in hospital for a few days, has been diagnosed with cancer. This is a terrible blow for Jim and all the family.

18 September 2016

This afternoon Roger arrived and stayed for a meal. He was on his way back up to Aberdeen from Edinburgh. Roger's son, Alistair, is in Cam's year at Loretto, and his two daughters were also at the school when Elaine taught there. Roger lost his wife to cancer only a few years ago, so he knows all about the loss that terminal illness brings. He also appreciates the effects of my condition on Elaine. Despite this common ground — or perhaps because of it — our conversation was not gloomy. We know the challenges that lie ahead but we also recognise the importance of trying to remain positive.

19 September 2016

Standing naked, and being showered and dried by a total stranger, is all part of having a carer, and I was apprehensive when Lorrain arrived for her first visit this morning. I thought the whole business would be very awkward, but due to Lorraine's confidence and good humour, I felt very little embarrassment. Lorraine stayed right behind me as I shuffled down the hall with my three-legged walker, and as I moved carefully around the wet room, she kept close to me in case I lost my balance. I know that I will have to get used to the rest of the team over the next few weeks, but I now feel much more comfortable about the whole thing. Elaine is away on school business for the next six days, and I know she will be much happier knowing that people are coming in to support me.

As soon as Lorraine left, Bert, an architect from Perth and Kinross council, dropped by to look at my wet room sliding door. The firm who did the alterations to the house chose to fit a heavy, solid door. This is very secure, but it is hard to slide open or shut. I had tried to explain to them that due to my MND, the strength I have in my hands and arms would continue to deteriorate. The man I spoke to, however, simply said that the door would loosen up the more I used it. Fortunately, Bert understands the problem rather better, and he is going to get the firm to fit a lightweight door that will slide more easily.

Next, I had a visit from the doctor. He came to see me about a possible urinary tract infection, but said he thought I might have an enlarged prostate. He told me he would return soon with a community nurse to give me an examination, and warned me that there is a chance that it could be prostate cancer. I said that if it proved to be the case, I imagined the MND would "get me" first. He declined to answer.

No sooner had the doctor left, when Moira, my neuropsychologist, arrived for a home visit. I told her that my carers had just started and then told her about the doctor's visit. She asked how I felt about all this, and I said fine. It is easy to say, "I'm fine" when you don't actually mean it, but this time it was true. Recently, I have enjoyed doing my meditation each day and I'm managing to remain calmer about things in general. Moira and I agreed that there really is little point in worrying about things over which we have no control, or that may never happen.

22 September 2016

I have never known Cornhill to be so busy. As well as the regulars who drop in each week, a number of new people came in for a visit. For most people, stepping into a hospice for the first time can be a nervous and rather stressful occasion. Hospices are associated with terms like "end-of-life care", and "life-shortening illnesses", and in addition to that, there is the whole business of joining a new "club". Morag and her team, however, are very good indeed at welcoming people. As soon as someone new comes through the door, they are immediately greeted, given a seat with a little space, and offered a cup of tea or coffee. On Wednesday, this process seemed to repeat itself many times, and at one stage, the day room was completely full. Margaret kindly did my hands again, and I listened to various conversations that were going on around me. I am more hesitant about joining in these conversations now, because my words come out more slowly — I tend to listen, nod my head and smile, but not say much.

23 September 2016

People seemed to arrive all day. As soon as Claire had left in the morning, one of the college ground staff came to cut the grass for the final time this year, and when he had finished, someone from a flooring company arrived to check the laminate in the hall. Then, Jeremy came by to make some adjustments to my automatic door-entry system. We tested it and discovered that I can now open the door, even if no one talks into the intercom system. This will be great for taking my wheelchair outside — all I need now is the damned ramp.

24 September 2016

Today was very quiet, but I enjoyed Lorraine's company during her four visits. It is extraordinary how used to each other we have become in the space of only a few days. Lorraine has a very cheerful manner, and we have quickly established a routine for each of her visits. The mornings, in particular, have been a great help. Having (gracefully, I hope) surrendered my independence in terms of showering and dressing, I feel far less tired at the start of each day, and it is a huge relief to know that someone is there to support me. I no longer have to try to hold a bar of slippery soap in my stiff and awkward fingers, and being able to sit in my shower chair while Lorraine dries my hair and back is wonderful!

26 September 2016

A busy start to the week saw a number of visitors in the morning. As soon as Lorraine had given me my breakfast, Claire arrived to do the cleaning. It seems to be part of the daily routine now that as one goes, the other arrives. Jeremy popped in an hour later with a replacement phone, and then Heather, another carer, arrived for a familiarisation visit. I have become rather attached to Lorraine so it will be strange to have someone different, but I'm sure we will get along fine. In the middle of Heather's visit, my GP arrived with Linda, one of the community nurses. After Linda had helped me to undress and manoeuvred me into the correct position on my bed, the doctor performed his little "internal" examination. He said that he couldn't detect any enlargement of my prostate, and given that nothing had shown up on the blood tests he did last week, he could almost certainly rule out prostate cancer. He said he didn't know what was causing my problems, so a visit to a consultant urologist would be necessary. Before the doctor had left, Sylvia, Judith's new neighbour, arrived with her two daughters. Unfortunately, my sitting room was so full by this point that Sylvia retreated and said she would come back another time. Finally, just after lunch, a lady from the home vent team arrived with a machine for me to do an overnight sleep test.

I spent a quiet afternoon doing some meditating and watching a film about the Second World War. The film was very good, but I was distracted by thoughts of Elaine. She had only been away for six days, but I was missing her, and when she finally arrived back at eight thirty, I was very relieved to see her. She was very tired, but before we could sleep she had to take a glowing sensor from the machine that had been delivered earlier and attach it to my earlobe. The machine records my breathing overnight, and indicates whether or not I need any artificial ventilation. To date, this has not been necessary, but it probably will be in the future.

27 September 2016

I went out for a wonderful drive with Judith. We drove to Crieff, picked up some petrol and an ice cream, and headed for the Sma' Glen. The drive through the glen is lovely and at Amrulee we took the narrow, winding road up towards Glen Quaich. The views over the lochs and across to the mountains were stunning, and the light, due to a combination of sunshine and storm clouds, was amazing. I am not surprised that this drive has been described as one of the most beautiful in Scotland.

28 September 2016

As usual, my morning at Cornhill was busy. It was good to see Elma again, and she showed me her holiday snaps before giving my hands a massage. Morag, Louise, and Sheena were all in great form. In contrast, my afternoon at home was very quiet, and I was glad. I like to think of myself as personable, and if I know I am going to have a visitor, I can prepare for it by resting beforehand. However, if people simply turn up out of the blue, I find it more difficult. I simply don't have the energy these days, and the sound of my intercom at unexpected moments can sometimes be less welcome than it used to be.

29 September 2016

Today is Michaelmas Day, and it's my birthday. My mother always said people told her she should have called me Michael, but she preferred Richard. I have reached sixty-three. I spent a while thinking about this. Should I be sad because it might be my last birthday, or should I be happy that I have reached another landmark? After a few miserable thoughts, I decided that the answer must be the latter. Sixty-three is not "old" but it is not exactly young. It's not even middle age, so it must be a good age to reach. I decided it was definitely worth celebrating.

My whole day was punctuated by pings on my phone, telling me that people had sent me a message or posted something on my Facebook timeline. In total, I received over forty birthday wishes from family and friends. Some of these were from people who I had taught over thirty years ago, but had become Facebook friends over the last 12 months. To receive messages of goodwill from so many

people was very humbling and uplifting — we all like to
be remembered. Writing every day is becoming more
tiring; I'm not sure if I can manage it for much longer.

CHAPTER SIXTEEN

Losing Jim

2 October 2016

Today was marked by the sad death of Elaine's father. Jim was only diagnosed with cancer a couple of weeks ago, but the disease was already very advanced. He was allowed home, which was where he wanted to be, and every attempt was made to keep him comfortable. The suddenness of his deterioration was a terrible shock. Less than a month ago, he was here on a visit, but his passing prevented any more pain and suffering. Jim has been like a second father to me in the last few years, and I shall miss him very much. He loved music, and would often spend hours sitting at his piano, and he had a passion for learning that he passed on to his daughter. Jim never failed to do the Scotsman prize crossword, which he won five times, he loved watching and reporting on local football, and he enjoyed telling (and re-telling) stories about his cycling holidays as a boy. Most of all, however, Jim loved his family.

Elaine went down to Tranent to support her mother and help her brother make arrangements for the funeral. I wish I could help in some way. It is at times like these that I get angry about my condition. I wouldn't mind if I had a temporary disability or illness; it is the fact that I am stuck with this disease, and the certainty that it will get worse, that gets me down.

3 October 2016

A visit from Judith and Corinne today cheered me up no end. I know that Judith misses her friend since she moved at the end of last term, and this was the first time that I had seen her since June. Corinne is a very good cook and she brought me some homemade ready meals. This led to some teasing from Corinne about Judith's limited culinary repertoire, and her preference for cooking either mince or fajitas. Only true friends can insult each other so openly, and we all laughed together.

4 October 2016

Claire had kindly filled up the bird feeders, so I spent a long time watching a family of blue tits tuck into the seeds and peanuts. I'm not sure if robins do take food directly from hanging feeders, but the one in my garden spends most of its time picking up any spillages from the ground underneath. In the evening Elaine returned from Tranent. She was tired after three days of supporting her mother, making arrangements for her father's funeral, and dealing with visitors who wanted to pay their respects. She said the most difficult thing was being in her parents' house and expecting her father to walk into the room at any moment — even though she and her mother knew this would never happen again.

5 October 2016

I had a different carer scheduled for the morning shift. I thought Heather may be a few minutes later than Lorraine has been, but after sitting on the edge of my bed for twenty minutes I decided there must have been a mix up. I shuffled along to the wet room with my walker, thought about trying to shower myself, but decided against it. Instead, I had a quick wash, flushed my feeding tube and cleaned my teeth. By the time I got back to the bedroom I was tired, but luckily Heather arrived at that moment. She explained that her rota times had prevented her from getting here any earlier, and said she would try to get it sorted out for the next time. Recently I have become more frustrated by changes to routines, so this morning I was a little more anxious than usual. Fortunately, Margaret had a cancellation for a therapeutic touch session at Cornhill, and she offered me the slot instead. Within a minute or two any stresses or strains from earlier in the day were eased and I was soon totally relaxed in response to the warmth of Margaret's hands. I'm now back home and looking forward to a lazy afternoon watching a film that I recorded last night.

8 October 2016

My voice has been getting weaker for over a year now, but the rate of deterioration has been very gradual. In recent weeks, however, I have noticed that things are getting worse. I can talk quickly and clearly in my head, but it all goes wrong when I open my mouth. Firstly, there is the delay between thinking of something to say and translating it into a spoken word. I open my mouth, but the movement of my tongue and lips is slow, and for a second, nothing comes out. Secondly, there is the problem of poor quality. In my head, I know what I want to say, and I know how to pronounce the words, but my tongue and mouth can't get into the right position to formulate the right sound. It feels as if my mouth has become partially paralysed. The result of all this is that my speech is both slow and slurred, and to me it sounds more like a drunken stupor.

None of this is very good for my confidence. If I'm with Elaine, close family, or people I see frequently, like Judith or Lorraine, I don't really give it a thought, and I'm fine at Cornhill, where everyone knows me. However, when I meet people for the first time or try to speak on the phone I become more self-conscious, and this in turn makes me more anxious. It is very tempting to avoid the problem by staying at home and only communicating by email or text. Eighteen months ago, soon after my diagnosis, I spent all those hours recording sentences on my computer for an American firm called Model talker. The synthesised voice they sent me is now on my iPad and linked to an app called *Predictable*. I know that I should be practising on this and building up phrases for the future in preparation for the time when my voice dies completely. Part of me, however, is reluctant to do this, because it feels like giving in to the disease.

10 October 2016

A letter arrived from Perth and Kinross council informing me that the building warrant for my ramp has finally been signed. This doesn't mean that it is about to arrive, but it does mean that it can now be built. It has been five months since the application for a ramp was made to the council, and I have had my electric wheelchair for over two months. Recently we have had some lovely early autumn weather, and it's been so frustrating not being able to take the chair outside. A number of people have told me that they have tried to move the process along, but it seems the bureaucratic machine that controls such things cannot be hurried. If I had a long-term, stable disability, this delay would be more tolerable, but given the progressive nature of my condition, it is difficult to accept.

I also received an email from an ex-pupil of mine. He had left Loretto twenty-five years ago and wrote to say that he was sorry to hear about my MND. He was also kind enough to say that he had very much enjoyed being in my business studies class, and this had encouraged him to take the subject at university. Messages such as this are very humbling and they cheer me up no end. I am very lucky to have had the chance, as a teacher, to make a little difference to the lives of others.

16 October 2016

My cousin Roderick and his partner arrived for a visit. Roderick is the son of my aged and very deaf aunt, and, like me, he grew up on a farm near Witheridge, in North Devon. Roderick has only been to Scotland once before, and that was a quick, two-day visit to a sheep dog trial, many years ago. This time, he is spending a week touring around in his "new" car. I use the word "new" with some reservation. Roderick, like many farmers, changes his tractor more often than his car. His last car finally gave up the ghost a month ago with 176,000 miles on the clock. Roderick has replaced it with a "new" model that has only done 93,00 miles. Roderick brought me some apple chutney from his mother. For a lady in her mid-nineties, Rita is quite remarkable. She lives alone in a fairly remote farmhouse, she drives into the village most mornings to pick up her paper, she cooks every day, and she never misses a service in her local church. This is the church where her late husband played the organ every week for over seventy years, and won his entry in the *Guinness Book of Records*.

17 October 2016

Elaine worked for most of the first weekend of half-term, but today she finally took a day off. Just before my carer arrived in the morning, she moved upstairs and continued sleeping for a couple of hours. When she came down, we sat together, drank coffee, and planned our day — a simple but rare pleasure. Elaine went shopping in the afternoon and returned with two new pairs of trousers for me. Over the years, my waist size has grown from 32 inches to 34, and now, suddenly, it seems to have expanded to 35. Normally I would have been embarrassed by this expansion, but given the strong tendency for MND sufferers to experience rapid muscle wasting and weight loss, I suppose I should be grateful that I have gone up another size.

19 October 2016

Today was Jim's funeral. This was a very sad event, but it was an opportunity to celebrate his life. The chapel was full of Jim's family and his friends from all walks of life. We sang his favourite hymns, Edwin read a lesson from Corinthians, Cam read the Desiderata, and Tom sang *Ae Fond Kiss*. Elaine delivered a wonderful eulogy perfectly capturing Jim's personality, his talents, his achievements, and most importantly, his values.

20 October 2016

Today 1 I forgot that my hospital appointment was early in the morning. Realising that there wouldn't be time to wait for Lorraine to give a shower, I tried to wash myself at the sink. It is extraordinary how a task this simple, one that I have performed thousands of times before, has now become so difficult. Even washing under my arms poses quite a challenge. Firstly, I have to force my stiff fingers open to hold the face cloth flat in my palm, then I have to dispense liquid soap on to the cloth without squirting it into the sink. Next, I have to lift my free arm into the air and hold it there, and finally, I have to turn the hand holding the cloth far enough around to wash the right area. Cleaning my teeth without either sticking the brush down my throat or getting toothpaste over my face is also quite a performance. By the time I had finished I felt quite exhausted. Of course, Elaine would have been delighted to help me with all this, but, as usual, I was feeling stubborn.

Having managed to get to the urology department at Perth Royal Infirmary, I was immediately asked if I could give a sample. I explained that I had had to go before leaving the house, so a nurse gave me a beaker of water to drink. Elaine tried to explain that, due to my MND, drinking water was very difficult, but I don't think the nurse understood why this should be the case. In the event, I managed to drink it all, sip by sip, and after a few minutes I was wheeled to a tiny room, which contained a machine with a large upward-facing funnel. The objective was for me to pee into the funnel, so that both "flow" and "volume" could be measured. We explained that for me to stand and perform this task on my own might be difficult. There was just enough room for Elaine to stand behind me and hold me steady, whilst I tried to direct matters at the front. It took quite a while to complete this operation, and we laughed so much that I nearly fell over. When we saw the consultant, he was very sympathetic about my MND; he said he understood why I would prefer not to have any more surgical procedures, and told me to carry on taking the pills. Just before I left, he took my hands in his, smiled and said, "God willing, we will keep you going". Unsure as I am about God's role in all this, I was very touched by his words.

21 October 2016

This afternoon we drove to Crieff and Elaine pushed me around Macrosty Park. The weather was mild and the leaves on the trees looked wonderful — all different shades and colours. Several people, many of them with dogs, greeted us as we passed. We couldn't help contrasting this behaviour with what usually happens in large cities, where most people rush by with their heads down, too busy to pass the time of day.

24 October 2016

I met a new carer this morning called Liz. She arrived with Lorraine and shadowed her whilst Lorraine got me showered and dressed, and gave me my breakfast. After coming in every day for the last month, Lorraine has got to know me very well, and she knows exactly where everything goes. We have a good routine, and it will be strange not to see her while she is on holiday next week. I will miss her cheery manner and her great sense of humour.

Moira, my neuropsychologist, visited me just before lunch, and we had a good talk about mindfulness. I told her that for the last month I have been using daily exercises provided by a firm called *Headspace*, and that I have found it very helpful as a way of keeping in the present, and coping with anxiety. Moira was pleased with my progress since our last session and we agreed to see each other again just before Christmas.

In the afternoon Hilary came to see me, and we went for a drive to the Sma' Glen. The sun was shining and the colours were wonderful. We parked by the river and I admired the view while Hilary took her spaniel, Bertie, for a walk. We returned to the house and I talked very openly and honestly about the emotional aspects of living with MND. I laughed and I cried, and Hilary was very understanding.

26 October 2016

The alarm sounded at 4.50 a.m. this morning, and Elaine was collected at 5.30 a.m. by Gary, the Glenalmond taxi driver. She is off to an education fair in Dubai, and needed to catch an early flight from Edinburgh to Heathrow. She worries about me when on these trips, but at least she now knows that my carers are coming in every day. Having resisted this for so long, I am now delighted to have the support and companionship that the carers provide.

1 November 2016

Ever since my diagnosis was confirmed, I have known that my breathing will deteriorate as my respiratory muscles weaken, and that respiratory failure will almost certainly be the cause of my death. In recent months I have been preoccupied with the weakness of a different muscle — namely my tongue, and its effect on my voice. Losing my speech is bad enough, so I've tried not to increase my anxiety by worrying about my ability to breathe.

Today, however, Dee, my MND nurse, visited me. She was pleased with my emotional state, but she did ask if I had done anything about a living will. I said that I had thought about it at the time of my diagnosis, but had not taken it forward. Dee suggested that I contact my GP and discuss it further. As soon as she said this, I wanted to ask the inevitable question, "Are you telling me that my respiratory muscles are about to fail?" Perhaps I was afraid of the answer, or perhaps I didn't want to know, but I didn't ask the question. I did, however, promise to contact my GP.

2 November 2016

At Cornhill I spoke to Morag about my conversation with Dee. As always, Morag was direct and down to earth, and she reminded me that that it was fine to feel upset about these things. It's strange, but sometimes I almost feel as if I need permission to express these feelings. Within a couple of minutes I felt much better — back in the present, and able to laugh again. I was certainly given plenty of attention during my visit this morning. At one point I had my OT sitting on one side, Louise, my physio, on the other, and Elma on a stool in front of me, giving my hands a massage.

4 November 2016

Today I had another day out with Judith. She picked me up mid-morning and we drove through the Sma' Glen and across to Aberfeldy. The trees, lochs, and mountains looked spectacular in the sunshine. Judith wanted to find somewhere "interesting" where she could push me around in my wheelchair, but finding a parking space proved to be difficult. In the end we parked at the bottom of the town and we went into the park so that Lottie could have a run. I could see the golf course through the trees, and although the view was very good, it reminded me how much I miss playing.

With Lottie safely back in the car, Judith decided she would push me up the hill to the Waterfall Cafe. By the time we were half way up, she was having second thoughts, but after a breather, we made it to the top. We managed to find a space at a table, and I felt like a young child as Judith took off my coat, scarf and gloves, and then buttered my roll. Dependence on others in the privacy of your own home is one thing, but it is harder to cope with in public. A little boy was sitting at the next table, and I caught him looking at me a few times. At any moment I expected to hear the words that I remember asking my mother in a similar situation, namely, "Why is that man in that funny chair?" But this little chap was either far too polite for that, or perhaps he was thinking about something entirely different, such as the ice cream he hoped he might get next.

6 November 2016

I nearly fell in my wet room this morning. I was standing still while Liz dried my back and legs. To keep myself steady, I was holding on to a pole from the ceiling that supports the little gate at the front of the shower. As Liz passed me the towel so that I could dry my front, I forgot to hold on with one hand. I let go of the pole, tried to take the towel, and fell forwards. Fortunately, Liz grabbed me around the waist and held me long enough for me to take hold of the pole again. We laughed at the thought of us both toppling into the shower, but it also gave me quite a shock.

9 November 2016

Last night I stayed up to watch the US election results. All the polls seemed to predict a victory for Clinton, but just after 3 a.m. the Florida result came in for Trump. The TV pundits changed their position, Jeremy Vine got very excited as he leapt around his electoral map of America, and suddenly it became clear that Trump was probably going to become the 45th president of America.

There are definite parallels between what happened in the UK in June and what has just happened in America. Similar socio-economic groups voted for "change" and many moderate people did so despite having serious reservations about the views of politicians like Nigel Farage and Donald Trump. I have just heard Trump pay tribute to Hilary Clinton, and say that he wants to be a president for "all" Americans. Share prices in the UK are beginning to recover, but the Mexican peso is tumbling.

10 November 2016

Today was Elaine's birthday. In recent years we have celebrated this occasion by going on a short city break. We enjoyed wonderful trips to Rome, Florence, and Venice, and spent many hours exploring these places on foot. We took in many of the cultural sites, but we also enjoyed just wandering around with no particular route in mind, soaking up the atmosphere, and watching the world go by from a bar or café. Now these trips are impossible, and even the simple business of buying a gift and a card has become difficult. This year, I got a card during my trip to Aberfeldy with Judith, and I ordered some gifts online. Yesterday, I desperately tried to undo the cardboard packaging, but I didn't have the strength to break the sticky tape. Lorraine kindly did that part for me. Wrapping the gifts up was totally beyond me, so I put everything in a gift bag. I then spent five minutes getting the card out of its cellophane wrapper, and several more trying to write something legible. The most upsetting thing of all, however, was not being able to get up, hold Elaine in my arms, and give her a proper hug.

11 November 2016

One of the doctors from the local surgery came to see me to discuss my living will. She acknowledged that this was never an easy conversation to have, but said it was better for everyone if it was done. Unlike many GP's, she had come across a patient with MND before, so she had a good understanding of the issues facing me. I said that when my breathing becomes impaired, I am willing to have non-invasive ventilation. This is basically a mask to provide air and oxygen. I made it clear, however, that I do not wish to have invasive ventilation, whereby a tracheotomy tube is placed through my neck and into my windpipe. After some more discussion, I also decided that I do not want CPR in the event of cardiac or respiratory failure.

I felt relieved that I had made these decisions, but I learned that things weren't quite as straightforward as they seemed. Living wills are called Advanced Decisions in England and Advanced Directives in Scotland. However, whereas these decisions are legally binding in England, they are not in Scotland. Technically, this means that people in Scotland can be kept alive until a judge makes a ruling, despite having made their wishes clear to partners, carers, and doctors. My doctor reassured me, however, that such things very rarely happen.

13 November 2016

Sadly, due to the lack of a ramp to get my electric wheelchair out of the house, I was unable to go to chapel this morning for the Remembrance Day Service. It is on occasions like this that I feel I'm letting Elaine down by not being there to support her. It is illogical, of course, because such decisions are out of my control, and Elaine fully understands that, but I still feel guilty. Instead, I watched the BBC coverage of the ceremony at the Cenotaph. David Dimbleby's commentary was excellent; he was respectful and remorseful, and, unlike many I have heard speak on these occasions, he resisted the temptation to glorify the act of war.

14 November 2016

Last night Elaine took me to Glenalmond's Autumn Concert. We got there very early and I secured a spot for my wheelchair at the end of the front row. I have to say that in over forty years of attending school concerts, I have never seen anything better. The performances, in terms of quality, variety, and delivery, were simply outstanding. The music department here is a very vibrant place; it is full of enthusiasm and energy, and the relationships between the staff and pupils are excellent. No wonder the pupils enjoy performing so much.

CHAPTER SEVENTEEN

Like a Child with a New Toy

15 November 2016

MND Scotland has been trying to find a local therapist for me for over a year, and today I finally met her. Kirstie lives near Crieff, she is trained in both massage and reflexology, and she will be coming to see me for ten sessions, with the option of ten more. Before we could begin, we had to go through some questionnaires about my condition, and I had to sign up to a series of rules for "clients". One of these did make me laugh, as it required me to promise that I wouldn't attempt to form a relationship with my therapist. We then had a discussion about my ability to undress for a massage. Kirstie explained that it would be all right for her to pull my tee shirt and jumper over my head, but it was against the rules for her to undo my trousers. I said if she could help me to my feet, I could unhook my trousers and lower them to my knees, as long as she was allowed to pull them off. Kirstie said that would be fine, so we proceeded in that way.

I lay on my electric wheelchair, in a reclined position, and thoroughly enjoyed my massage. Kirstie used a combination of oils that are good for reducing stiff muscles, and by the end of the hour, I felt both loose and relaxed. Ten minutes after Kirstie left, I was sound asleep.

16 November 2016

Having missed Cornhill last week, it was good to see all my friends again this morning. The car park was full, so I parked illegally near the front door. Morag came and collected me, and when we reached the day room I was surprised to find it so packed. The soft recliner chairs were all taken, so I remained in my wheelchair and sat at one of the tables. I recognised the man next to me, but I knew I hadn't seen him at Cornhill before. It turned out to be Ian, a fellow MND sufferer from Comrie, who I last saw at a support meeting just over a year ago, when he was visiting the hospice for the first time. He has a slow-onset form of MND, and has had the condition for eight years. When two people with MND meet each other, it is almost impossible for them not to talk about their symptoms. Ian and I briefly did that, before discussing our strategies for remaining positive.

A few minutes later Margaret came and sat with us. We hadn't met up for a while, so it was good to catch up. She told me that during her recent trip to Somerset, she had been bitten by an insect on a very sensitive spot. A consequence of this was that she had great difficulty in sitting down. I tried to sympathise, but I found it impossible not to see the funny side of the situation. Not for the first time, we both ended up in hysterics. Later, when Louise took me back to my car, I was relieved to find that I hadn't been given a ticket. A blue badge, particularly outside a hospice, softens the approach of even the most hardened traffic warden.

18 November 2016

Some cold weather arrived this week. Sitting inside all day with the heating on, I can't really feel it, but I can certainly see it. From my chair I have a lovely view into the garden, and this morning everything was covered in a blanket of frost, including the roof of the bird table. Although different birds visit my table, a familiar group arrives every morning. A family of blue tits hover around the feeders, constantly pecking at the seeds and peanuts, two blackbirds take food from the actual table, and a lone robin hops around on the ground, picking up the seeds that the tits have dropped from above. In recent weeks, however, I have had a new visitor. A cheeky red squirrel has been climbing up the leg of the table, leaning across to the suspended feeder and chewing at the peanuts through the wire mesh. Watching all this activity is a simple pleasure, but a very real one.

20 November 2016

This morning the *Sunday Post* published an article about my journey with MND, written by Bill Gibb. Niamh Callan from MND Scotland contacted me a few days ago and informed me that Bill was going to run it. I wasn't convinced that my story would stand on its own, but Bill used a reference from my blog about the film *The Theory of Everything* and the impact it had on me. He also included a photo of Eddie Redmayne, who played the part of Stephen Hawking so brilliantly in that film. The *Sunday*

Post has the second biggest circulation figures in Scotland, and is also sold in the North of England. If the article makes a few more people aware of the impact that MND has on those affected by it, then I will be happy.

22 November 2016

At last, after weeks of waiting, the ramp for my electric wheelchair is finally being installed. A team of men arrived this morning, and for most of the day they've been preparing the foundations. Kirstie arrived in the middle of all this to give me a reflexology treatment. While she massaged my feet, we listened to some zen relaxation music, and did our best to ignore the background noise of drilling.

24 November 2016

Yesterday I couldn't get out of the front door due to the work on the ramp, so I didn't make it to Cornhill. Today, however, all the work was finished, and Lorraine kindly offered to escort me on my first outdoor trip in my electric wheelchair. The temperature was below freezing, so she wrapped me up in a scarf, warm coat, and gloves. I got myself into my chair, engaged the lowest speed setting, opened the front door with my remote control, and pushed the joystick forward. I felt a great sense of independence as I moved through the doorway, went down the ramp, and drove off down the drive. Like a child with a new toy, I was soon keen to see how fast I could go. I selected the highest speed setting and pushed the joystick. To my delight, the chair moved much faster, and soon I was waving goodbye as Lorraine tried to keep up. Next, I steered off the tarmac and onto the grass to test the chair's "off-road" capabilities. It went over bumps and rough ground without difficulty, and I even managed to take it around the back of the house and into the garden. The whole experience reminded me of the first time I rode my red tricycle around the bungalow where I was born, when I was about three.

26 November 2016
Jesus Christ Superstar has been playing for forty-three years. It's a sung-through musical, without dialogue, and it demands a big cast of capable singers. I've seen very few schools attempt to stage it, so I've been eagerly awaiting Glenalmond's production. Tonight's show was a huge success. The set was spectacular, the musicians (most of whom were students) were excellent, and the quality of the overall singing and acting was better than I've ever seen in a school musical. So often in musicals the acting can be wooden in comparison with the singing, or vice versa. This evening, however, the cast stayed in character throughout the show. To pick out one cast member or scene for particular mention is a little unfair, but Herod's Song, early in the second act, was simply brilliant. This was the third performance out of four, and the theatre was packed with proud parents, staff, and members of the local community.

28 November 2016
Tom, Cam, and their girlfriends came to see *Superstar* last night, and they stayed over. I had warned them that I would be moving around this morning with very little on while my carer got me showered and dressed, so they sensibly stayed upstairs until I was up. The morning

turned out to be busy. Claire was here before the youngsters had left, and as soon as she went, Kirstie arrived to give me my reflexology therapy. Just after Kirstie departed, a GP from the local surgery came in to check on my cough, which despite a course of antibiotics, has stubbornly persisted for over three weeks. I've been worried that the cough, which seems to get worse when I talk, is connected to my MND.

29 November 2016

My bird table is becoming more popular. The lone robin seems to have found a mate, and another pair is also visiting, along with two or three chaffinches. The most surprising visitor, however, arrived this morning, when a pheasant suddenly appeared. It landed at the far-end of the garden, walked straight up to the table, and proceeded to eat all the seeds that had been dropped by the other birds. The smaller birds didn't seem phased by the appearance of such a large creature — they simply carried on as normal. Later this morning, Judith took me for another run in my wheelchair. We went all the way down to the main building, and I just managed to get over the barrier that leads into the quad.

1 December 2016

Yesterday I had an interesting time at Cornhill. In addition to seeing all my usual friends, I met two trainee nurses, who are currently working in the inpatient clinic at the hospice. They were lovely girls, and we chatted for some time about my experience as a visitor to Cornhill, and my journey with MND. Hazel joined us for part of the time, and she explained to the girls how my peg works. She also took the opportunity to put me on the scales. Knowing as I do that MND leads to muscle wasting, I can get a little paranoid about maintaining my weight. I was delighted to discover that I was exactly the same weight as I was three months ago. Information like this doesn't indicate that my MND is stabilising, but it does give me hope that my condition is not rapidly deteriorating. It may only be a straw, but it's one that I need to grasp.

2 December 2016

I've been trying to find a hairdresser who would be willing to come to the house for some time. Lorraine and Heather have both been making enquiries, but to no avail. Today, however, a lady called Annemarie came out with Heather, and she gave me a short back and sides. As I sat in the middle of the kitchen and the hair piled up on the floor, I wondered if I would have any hair left, but when I finally saw myself in a mirror, I was pleased with the result. Soon afterwards, Judith collected me to go to the lunchtime concert, and as I went down the drive in my chair, I was glad for my woolly hat and scarf. As always, I enjoyed the music. These weekly concerts provide an opportunity for pupils of all standards to perform in front of a supportive audience. Today the performances ranged from beginners playing in public for the first time, to music scholars who play like seasoned professionals. A group of visiting pupils from Hong Kong came along to watch, and one of their girls played the guitar and sang beautifully, in both Cantonese and English.

4 December 2016

This morning I fell whilst using my three-wheeled walker. I know this sounds unlikely because the three wheels provide a good base, but I simply lurched to the right as I went along the passage, and tipped over sideways. I fell straight into the little landing at the bottom of the stairs, and knocked my head against a heavy mirror. As I lay on my back, my brain told me to turn over, get into a kneeling position, and pull myself up. My body, of course, thought differently. I managed to roll onto my side, but there was no strength in my arms to do anything else. At this point, Elaine arrived, having heard the noise of me crying. For five minutes she tried to get me up, firstly by lifting me from behind, and then by trying to pull me up from the front. I only weigh twelve stone, but my dead weight was far too heavy. We sat there together, not sure whether to laugh or cry, and then the doorbell went. It was Heather, my carer. Heather wedged my feet against her shoes, and the two of them managed to haul me to my feet. Fortunately, apart from a bump on my head, the only other injury was a bruise on my side. I fear, however, that apart from transferring from one chair to another, my days of walking will soon be over.

5 December 2016

Today I have been thinking about my father. He died three years ago, but this would have been his ninetieth birthday. Dad left school at fourteen, at the beginning of the Second World War, so that he could help my grandfather run the family farm in Devon. His heart was never really in farming (he would rather have been an accountant) but he ended up staying on the farm for his entire working life. Partly because of this, I enjoyed a wonderful early childhood. I watched the local blacksmith put shoes on horses at the nearby forge; I played football and cricket for hours in our fields; I made secret dens in the hayloft, and I looked after tame lambs. Dad always made it clear, however, that there was no pressure for me to follow in his footsteps. He knew from hard experience that once you start living and working on a farm, it can be very difficult to escape. When I was thirteen, he asked me to take our dung spreader down to a field on the edge of the village. I jumped on the tractor, and half way down the street I pressed the wrong button. The spreader started to turn and cow dung flew all over the post office. From that moment on, Dad encouraged me to go into teaching.

7 December 2016

Alison, my speech therapist, came to see me at Cornhill this morning. Her comments are always practical and constructive, and today we discussed the best type of replacement iPad I should get to use with my synthetic voice. When we meet, we often talk about the need to plan ahead for the time when I will have no voice, but we never put a timescale on it. As Alison always reminds me, every case of MND is different, so it would be wrong to make generalisations. My voice certainly wasn't strong during our talk today, because I had already spent time chatting away to the staff. This had included time spent with Elma, Margaret, and Louise, and then with Carrie, one of the auxiliaries from the wards downstairs. Carrie is always in lively form, and she is certainly never short of something to say. I mentioned my wish to spend my final days in the ward downstairs if I don't have them at home, and Carrie promised she would help look after me when the time comes.

9 December 2016

I am going to have to buy a replacement peanut feeder for my bird table. My friendly red squirrel has been visiting every day, and he (or she) has worked out how to knock the end of the feeder so that all the peanuts fall to the ground. He then sits up on his back legs and eats away to his heart's content. This is a lovely sight, but my blue tits are not amused.

11 December 2016

This evening I went to a wonderful Advent Concert at Fowlis Wester Parish Church, led by the Glenalmond chamber choir. Tim Ridley, the Director of Music, directed proceedings with his usual wit and enthusiasm, and a packed congregation joined the choir for some of the carols. For me, the most remarkable features of the concert were the choir pieces, most of which were sung unaccompanied. A single note on the piano from Tim was all that was needed, and off they went. I sat in an alcove next to a huge Christmas tree and thoroughly enjoyed the performance. My only regret was that I couldn't join in with any of the carols. At least I can still sing the words in my head.

The church at Fowlis Wester is very old, and it still has a leper's squint — a low window from which lepers and other "undesirables" could watch proceedings from outside, without infecting the able-bodied congregation. It did cross my mind that in medieval times, perhaps I would have been asked to use the window myself.

13 December 2016

My neuropsychologist visited me this morning. I told Moira that my biggest cause for concern at the moment is the continued deterioration in my speech and my fears about life in the future with no voice at all. I also admitted that I have not been working on producing more "ready-made" synthetic voice sentences on my iPad. We both acknowledged that my failure to address the issue is simply an avoidance tactic on my part — if I refuse to recognise the problem, it may disappear. Of course, it won't disappear, and I promised to take action in the New Year.

Half way through our discussion, my squirrel appeared outside the French window. Moira had never seen a red one before, and she was fascinated to see it climb up my bird table and stretch across to the peanut feeder. She said she could watch this performance for a long time, and said it was very therapeutic. I'm very fortunate to have such an interesting window on the world.

15 December 2016

If anything can shake me out of my occasional bouts of self-pity, it is the appalling situation in the Syrian city of Aleppo. I am not naive; I know that all modern wars result in civilian casualties, but the sight of so many innocent children being maimed and killed is difficult to take. The pictures we see on television every night of buildings being shelled and homes destroyed are shocking, but perhaps our ability to be truly shocked is reduced by the sheer scale of the destruction. Sadly, this kind of inhumanity is nothing new. As a child, I vividly remember watching footage of women and children being burned by napalm during the war in Vietnam.

17 December 2016

I have taken delivery of a key safe. After my fall a fortnight ago, I suddenly realised how vulnerable I am when alone, and how dependent I am on others for assistance. If Elaine had not been in the house that morning, I could have been in real trouble. I would hopefully have been able to press my community alarm (if I had been wearing it), but unless I had been lying right next to my walker (which I wasn't), I would not have been able to reach the remote control to open the front door to my rescuers. Once I have given the alarm company, my carers, and my friends the combination for the key safe, I will feel a little less anxious.

18 December 2016

During the last week or so my red squirrel has become frustrated by his inability to break into my new, heavy-duty peanut feeder. He has repeatedly visited the bird table, swung on the feeder, and gnawed away at the wire, but as yet he has not broken in. He has had to make do with the scraps on the ground, left behind by the blue tits. This has made him more aggressive towards the black birds and robins, which normally have this area to themselves. This morning he decided to call in reinforcements. Three squirrels took it in turns to attack the feeder, but as yet, they have not had any success.

This afternoon Elaine is busy writing cards, and just like yesterday when she decorated the tree, all I can do is sit here, and watch, and feel pretty useless. At least I can still tap away on my computer, so I would like to take this opportunity to wish you, and your loved ones, a very happy Christmas.

20 December 2016

The stiffness in my arms and legs is beginning to prevent me from sleeping. I prefer to sleep on my side, but my shoulder quickly begins to ache in this position. Turning over is a huge effort in itself, and my legs go into spasms just before they straighten. If I place a pillow under my knees (or more accurately, if Elaine does that for me), the aches are reduced for a time, but when they return, I am forced to try and turn on to my side again. To achieve this, I have to lift my knees high enough so that I can then kick the pillow down the bed. And then the whole cycle starts again. The only solution, I suppose, is for me to take more painkillers and sleeping pills.

21 December 2016

Elaine took me to Cornhill this morning, and the staff were keen to talk to her about the reality of my situation (as opposed to the somewhat rose-tinted impression that I tend to convey). Louise took me aside for a chat to compare the two versions, and within a few minutes I couldn't hold back the tears. It was such a relief to admit that things really are getting more difficult, and the more sympathetic Louise became, the more I cried. The whole thing was a huge emotional release, and I felt much better for it. We agreed that in the New Year I would start attending their day-care programme on Thursdays, instead of the drop-in sessions on Wednesdays. Day care is more clinical and it includes a transport service. By making this change, I am accepting the need for more medical assistance as my voice, limbs, and energy levels all continue to decline.

22 December 2016

My GP came for a home visit this morning, and after a chat about my sleeping problems, he prescribed something to ease the stiffness in my limbs, and a tablet to use if I really can't get to sleep. He reminded me that I should be careful with both of these medicines. If I have too much of the first one, I risk becoming too wobbly to walk, and if I take too many of the sleeping pills, I might become addicted to them. I'm not sure I will have time to become addicted to anything.

23 December 2016

A new carer called Emma looked after me today. Emma is an experienced carer but she is only in her twenties. I was told in September that my carers would be "mature" women, so I was slightly surprised when I was introduced to this young lady. There was no awkwardness or embarrassment, however. Emma, like Lorraine and Liz, has a great sense of humour, and I'm delighted that she is now part of my regular "team". I am very lucky to have three such lovely people to look after me; they are a vital part of my life, and I would never manage without them.

25 December 2016

I had my doubts about Christmas Day. I was looking forward to seeing all the family, but I was unsure how I would cope with a crowd of people. I love having company, but in recent months I have got used to seeing one or two people at a time. As it turned out, I really enjoyed myself. Elaine and I both went to chapel in the morning. Over a hundred and fifty people, including many young children, attended the service, and the atmosphere was very special. Whatever our religious beliefs, it is a good thing to remind ourselves what Christmas is really all about.

I lasted long enough at the dining table to eat my roast turkey, but I almost cried as Cameron cut up my food and pulled my cracker for me. I had some Christmas pudding and clotted cream on my lap, whilst sitting in my recliner, and I drank more wine than I have managed for some time. There was an absence this year of course, because Jim wasn't there. Christmas is a happy occasion for most people, but for those who have just lost a loved one, it can be a painful time, too.

28 December 2016

It was exactly a year ago today that I first attended a drop-in session at Cornhill, and this was my last visit. The Wednesday-based medical staff and volunteers have been incredibly kind to me over the last twelve months, and this morning I said goodbye to Hazel, Sheena, Elma, and Di. Margaret, Peter, and Stuart weren't in this week, but I shall miss them very much, too. Elma gave me a final hand massage, while Elaine had a therapeutic touch session with Di. Laura, Marie, and Morag did their best to convince me that I will enjoy day care on Thursdays. I am sure I will, but in terms of my journey with MND, I can't help thinking that if Wednesdays represented the end of the beginning, Thursdays signal the beginning of the end.

This is not the ideal mindset, and I will do my best to be positive next Thursday.

My brother, Peter, and his son, George, arrived in the early evening. They spent hours on packed trains from London and Edinburgh, before cycling here from Perth station. This must be the fifth time that Peter has made this long and tiring journey. We caught up on all the news from Peter's recent work at Sotheby's, including the sale of the original manuscript of Mahler's second symphony, and a copy of J K Rowling's *The Tales of Beedle the Bard*. George also told us how he is managing his time between working at an independent art school called *Fine Arts* and studying for his master's degree in photo journalism.

31 December 2016

Peter and George left early this morning on their bikes to catch a train that would get them to Edinburgh in time for their connection to London. I imagine they will have a slightly more peaceful journey travelling south on Hogmanay than if they had been coming north. So, how do I feel about the New Year? I have a tendency on New Year's Eve to dwell on the "losses" associated with the passing of the old year, rather than the "opportunities" that a new year might bring. Given my circumstances, it would be very easy to fall into that mindset today; however, I've decided that would be self-indulgent. I need to celebrate the fact that I've reached 2017 — and set my sights on 2018. I may not get there, of course, but if I stay positive, the chances will surely be better.

CHAPTER EIGHTEEN

Forced to Sleep Alone

1 January 2017

The first day of the year brings news of another terrorist attack — this time in Istanbul. I wonder if there will be any meaningful resolution of the conflict in and around Syria in 2017? Will Putin and Trump surprise us all by bringing peace to the region? I suspect that the Kurds, who have fought so bravely against Isis, will be sacrificed in any peace deal brokered by Turkey, Russia, and Iran. Whatever happens, the flow of displaced people across Europe is unlikely to stop, and this will probably mean more success for anti-immigration, right-wing political parties when elections take place in countries like France and Germany.

2 January 2017

My daughter and her partner came for a visit this morning. Meg has survived her first term as a primary school teacher, and in six months' time she will finish her probationary year. I needed to speak to her about a few "end of life" issues, and at one point I became hopelessly emotional. Trying to speak coherently these days is hard, but making any sense when I am talking through tears is almost impossible. Meg was very patient, and she held my hand as I fought to control myself. As parents we become accustomed to comforting our children when they are upset — nothing really prepares us for a time when the tables are turned.

4 January 2017

Today was Lorna's birthday. I ordered some flowers online to be delivered to her house in Saudi Arabia, but the firm emailed me to say that she wasn't in when they tried to deliver them. As I had left instructions where to leave them if this happened, I wasn't very pleased. The company wanted me to ring them but I couldn't face the prospect of trying to speak on the phone. In the end Elaine rang them and they said they would sort it out. I am still waiting to find out if the flowers ever arrived.

Tom and Caitlin arrived this afternoon. They are staying for a few days, and their intention is to spend some time walking. Tom was excited about the electric guitar he had bought earlier in the day. With two guitars, a set of harmonicas, and a piano at hand, I suspect the two of them will spend far more time playing music than hiking in the hills.

5 January 2017

This was my first visit to day care at Cornhill. When I arrived for my preliminary assessment with Morag, the first thing I noticed was her uniform. She was as friendly as ever, but the uniform was a clear sign of a more clinical atmosphere. We went through some forms, which covered everything from my sleeping habits to my bowel movements, and Morag explained how the day would unfold. Morag knows me very well, and she understands exactly why I am apprehensive about starting this new service. When she took me along to the day room, I was struck by the number of electric wheelchairs in the room. I knew that two of these belonged to fellow MND sufferers, one called Ian, who I had met previously on a Wednesday, and the other called David. I hadn't met David before, but he has read some of my blog. A few days ago, he sent me a very kind email telling me how friendly the session would be. I then recognised Bob, who also has MND, from his visits on Wednesdays. Although we all have the same disease, it has affected us in different ways. Some of our arms don't work, some of our legs don't work, and some of our voices don't work. Each of us has one, some, or all of these disabilities.

David was absolutely right about the friendly atmosphere. As well as Morag, I know Louise, Marie, and Laura, and I also met a number of other people. We all had lunch together, some of us enjoyed a relaxation class in the afternoon, and throughout the day there was a great deal of laughter. Somewhat against my expectations, I find myself looking forward to returning next week.

7 January 2017

On the national news this morning there was a story about Noel Conway. Noel is an MND sufferer who wishes to have some control over when he dies. Noel's speech is much better than mine, but he is wheelchair-bound, he cannot use his arms, and he needs regular ventilation to assist with his breathing. In his interview he spoke movingly about his desire to have some choice over the timing of his death. Noel has registered with Dignitas in Switzerland, but he will soon be too ill to travel. That is why he is taking his case to the UK courts. Parliament, who make laws, fairly recently voted against legalising assisted dying; it will be interesting to see what the judiciary, who interpret laws, decide.

At the end of the news report, there was an interview with Baroness Campbell, who is a long-term sufferer of spinal muscular atrophy. She is a vociferous opponent of assisted dying, and argues that if it is legalised, it would encourage society to view disabled people as being of little value, or even dispensable. I think the baroness, like so many people, totally misses the point. She says she "absolutely loves her life". Well, I am delighted for her, but what has that got to do with Noel Conway? Noel, like me, has a debilitating and progressive terminal illness, and he has decided that very soon he will have had enough of his life. Surely, this should be his choice. On Thursday I spent a day with other MND sufferers. We laughed a lot and if anyone had been watching us, they would probably have commented on how happy we seemed. At this moment in time, that is really good news, but it doesn't mean that this will always be the case. I am generally a positive person, but I also know that my next faculty to go will almost certainly be my breathing. I'm not sure how I will cope with that, but if I decide that I don't wish to have my life prolonged, I, like Noel, would like to be able to make that decision myself.

9 January 2017

Elaine has been fairly busy with schoolwork for several days, but we have greatly enjoyed our time together over the holiday period. With my voice deteriorating, conversation can be limited, but simply sitting together and sharing a bottle of red wine while watching a film (or the latest Scandinavian psychological thriller) is a great pleasure. Today, however, the pupils come back, and we return to our term-time routine. For Elaine, this means a resumption of her very busy workload, and for me it marks a return to a more solitary life. I do not mean to imply that I will be lonely. My carers will be here at regular intervals each day; Claire will be in every morning, and I will get plenty of other visitors. In fact, in ten minutes' time Kirstie will arrive, and I will enjoy another relaxing session of reflexology — what a great way to start the week.

11 January 2017

I have decided with considerable regret that my driving days are over. Later this week I will send my licence back to DVLC. Since my diagnosis, being able to keep driving has been a real pleasure. It has allowed me to maintain a sense of independence, and, perhaps more importantly, it has helped me feel almost normal. In recent months, however, I have found it increasingly difficult to turn my head, and this has compromised my visibility, both when reversing and at junctions. I don't have to use my bad left leg because the car is an automatic, but my right leg (the less wonky one) has now become less reliable. This means that my control of the brake and accelerator is not quite as accurate as it should be. I don't want to injure myself by having an accident, and more importantly, I don't want to risk somebody else's life.

12 January 2017

After discussions with Elaine, my carers, and the staff at Cornhill, I have agreed to use my electric wheelchair around the house. Ever since my fall before Christmas, I have felt less confident about using my three-wheeled walker. Using it makes me feel less disabled, and it gives my legs a little exercise, but from now on it will simply be a means of transferring myself from my recliner to my wheelchair. I now know that in a real sense, I will never walk again.

14 January 2017

This morning, Judith helped me get ready for a trip out in the snow. Once I was covered in coats, scarves, a hat, and a blanket, I went gingerly down my icy ramp, and then we set off around the college grounds, with Lottie running alongside. My wheelchair coped well in the snow, and it was lovely to get out in the fresh air. The campus looked beautiful in the snow, as did the mountains to the North. A group of young children were sledging down the slopes. The sun was shining, but after fifteen minutes my feet were feeling numb, so I had to head for home.

15 January 2017

Today is my brother's fifty-third birthday. Four and a half years ago, when Peter was diagnosed with an aggressive form of brain cancer, there seemed little chance of him reaching fifty, but amazingly, and thankfully, he has defied the odds. In the last couple of days we have exchanged emails about our feelings for each other, and how we have faced life with "death" on our shoulders.

17 January 2017

My bird table is getting very busy again. During the last three or four days of snow there were very few visitors, although the robins braved the poor weather every day. This morning, however, there are six robins hopping about underneath the table, collecting husks and seeds that fall from above, and four wood pigeons have joined them. A large number of blue tits are hovering around the feeders, and two black birds are sitting on the actual table. Several times already the birds have been sent scattering by the arrival of my red squirrel. He is doing his best to gnaw through the wire mesh that contains the peanuts, but so far, he has not succeeded. I can sense that he is getting more and more frustrated by this. He has now taken to wrapping himself around the hanging feeder and shaking the mesh with his teeth. Every now and then he stops, lifts his head, and looks through the window at me. It's as if he's saying, "Why don't you come and help me?"

19 January 2017

Today I travelled to Cornhill in my electric wheelchair. Claire kindly helped me into my coat this morning, and I was ready when my access taxi-van driver arrived. I wheeled myself down the ramp from my front door and then very carefully lined up my wheels with the metal tracks that extended from the rear of the van. My driver gave me precise directions until I made it safely inside, and then he secured my chair with heavy-duty straps. As we set off I was immediately struck by the height of my position, compared to a normal car seat. I felt self-conscious at first, but after a mile or two I smiled to myself and pretended that I was sitting in the Pope-mobile. At Cornhill I had a fine day; plenty of laughter with the staff and my fellow "service users", and much amusement when I, as the only English person present, collected a prize for winning a quiz on the life and times of Robbie Burns.

This week, however, has also marked another sad loss. My attempts to get comfortable at night, combined with more frequent journeys to the loo, have made sleeping a difficult and sporadic experience, both for myself and for Elaine. I constantly disturb her as I try to change position in bed, mainly because I tend to moan with the effort of turning over, and every time I get into my wheelchair, the machine emits a pinging noise as it is switched on. Very reluctantly we have agreed that after a goodnight hug, it would be better for Elaine if she moves into her "other" bedroom upstairs. Sleeping apart is something we always said we would never do, no matter how difficult things might become, but in the end, the practicalities of the situation have defeated us.

20 January 2017

Over the years we have seen some pretty unlikely people run for, and even win, the presidential race. I well remember the astonishment that people in this country felt when Ronald Reagan, a former B-list actor, stood for, and won the US election in 1980. If that was surprising, the sight of Donald Trump actually being sworn into office this afternoon was almost surreal. The contrast between the outgoing and incoming presidents couldn't be more marked. The former is dignified, modest, measured and eloquent; the latter appears brash, simplistic, confrontational, and arrogant. Trump ended his inaugural speech with the exact words he used thousands of times during his election campaign: "We are going to make this country great again". Obviously, millions of Americans cling to the belief that Trump can somehow deliver this promise. If I was an out-of-work coal miner from Pennsylvania, or a long-term unemployed car worker from Detroit, I might be tempted to cling to this hope myself. However, in today's world, where manufacturing jobs move to low-wage economies, and with automation about to explode, I think I might be disappointed. He may be chauvinistic, xenophobic, and intolerant, but we have to remember that millions of people in the UK voted for Trump-like policies in the EU referendum, just a few months ago.

21 January 2017

Meg and Euan came for a visit this morning. I tried to remain positive, but it was hard to hide my frustration at not being able to speak very well. Feeling the need to lighten the atmosphere, I decided to demonstrate how mobile I have become in my electric wheelchair. Actually, moving around in my chair is far quicker and less tiring than shuffling along with my walker. I showed Meg how I can now move from room to room in the house, and even negotiate tight corners without chipping paint off the doorframes. Meg told me she was trying to think of something to do with her class this coming Wednesday, to celebrate Burns Day. This reminded me of the time when she learned and recited her first Burns poem, when she was in primary one. I remember her practising that poem as if it was yesterday. How can that little girl be a teacher herself now? And where have the intervening eighteen years gone?

23 January 2017

I have become convinced that I need stronger medication at night. I am currently taking paracetamol and a mild sleeping pill, but this is not really helping me much. The pain in my legs, due to cramps and spasms, continues to keep me awake, and after a whole night of twisting and turning, I feel exhausted by the time morning comes. The sleeping pills make me yawn constantly but they don't seem to put me to sleep. I know that stronger medication will have side effects, but I am reaching the point where I simply want something to knock me out.

24 January 2017

Dee, my MND nurse, arrived to see me this morning. We talked about my problems with talking, walking, and sleeping. I gave her a quick demonstration of the synthetic voice on my iPad, and we agreed that I should now start using it more frequently. I have been resisting this for some time, mainly due to my feelings of pride and embarrassment. Having to write a reply to someone on a keyboard instead of speaking the words does not come naturally. However, the time and effort involved in having long conversations, including repeating myself because people can't understand me, is wearing me out.

Next was walking. I explained that other than using my walker to transfer myself straight from my recliner to my wheelchair, I no longer feel confident or strong enough to walk more than a couple of steps. We agreed that the time has come for me to get wheels on my shower chair. This will enable my carers to take me straight from my bedroom to the shower and back again. I will no longer have to hobble sideways around my wet room, bent double, like a half-demented crab. Finally, Dee said she would talk to my consultant about my sleeping problems, and was hopeful that a solution could be found fairly quickly.

26 January 2017

I took my old iPad to Cornhill today to try out my synthetic voice in a "safe" environment. I tried to demonstrate to Louise how it works, but unfortunately, the volume was not loud enough for my voice to be heard. We fiddled about with the settings, but in the end, I had to revert to my own voice. I will take in my new iPad next week, as it has a higher volume. Despite my disappointment, this was a very useful exercise. Graham, another MND sufferer, was using his keyboard to "speak" and he made us all laugh with his witty comments. The speed with which Graham communicates is inevitably a little slower than the spoken word, but his meaning is very clear, and his facial expressions show a wonderful range of emotions. The day passed quickly. In addition to a catch up with Morag, I met a new physio called Fiona, had a three-course lunch, enjoyed some reflexology with Ann, and joined in a relaxation class.

29 January 2017

Lorna and Nick have been with us for three days. It has been lovely seeing them again, and to hear about all their plans for the future. It has taken quite a time for them to find each other, and I am just so pleased to see them look so happy. Last night it was time, once again, to say goodbye. Lorna has spent almost her entire adult life living thousands of miles away, and although she has always reminded me that she is never more than a day away, our goodbyes have always been tinged with a sense of finality. Last night, we both felt this more keenly than before, and it made for rather a tearful farewell. After years of keeping my feelings under control, something for which I am now ashamed rather than proud, my illness has freed me from an emotional straightjacket. It is a huge relief to be able to express feelings of love and sadness with tears — after all, that is precisely what they are designed for.

CHAPTER NINETEEN

Are the Angels Coming?

1-10 February 2017

I have spent early February in Perth Royal Infirmary. Having struggled with my cough for a few weeks, ten days ago my condition suddenly deteriorated. In the space of three hours, my temperature shot up, I lost all power in my arms and legs, and I couldn't catch my breath – frightening symptoms for anyone with MND. As soon as Elaine found me slumped in my wheelchair, she rang NHS 24, and forty minutes later I was in an ambulance on my way to hospital. I have seen all the reports about the crisis in A&E departments, but I have to say that everything at Perth went like clockwork. There was no waiting in corridors for hours; I was assessed immediately, given a provisional diagnosis of mild pneumonia, and quickly transferred to an admissions ward. There, I was hooked up to bags of antibiotics via an intravenous drip.

The next few days passed in a haze. My temperature remained stubbornly high, I felt sick for much of the time, and although I craved sleep, it just wouldn't come. There were some very dark moments. I distinctly remember lying in a pool of sweat one night, unable to breath properly due to the constant coughing. I could feel all the tubes going in and out of my body but I couldn't move at all. At that point I really did think that a permanent sleep might be a welcome release. I had to smile early the next morning, however, when the first thing I heard was the Lord's Prayer being solemnly recited by the dementia patient in the bed next to mine. For a moment or two I thought the angels might be coming for me.

During my days in hospital, I became increasingly emotional. The mere sound of Elaine's voice on the phone, let alone the sight of her face or the touch of her hand, was enough to bring on the tears. I also found myself weeping when Karen, a physiotherapist I have known for years, came to see me, and when my nurse asked me about living with MND. After all those years of boarding school-induced stiff upper lip, I am getting better at crying.

Of course, it wasn't all sad. The nurses and auxiliaries were wonderful. They were patient, kind, polite, and so caring, and there were some interesting fellow patients. One poor chap simply didn't know where he was. Whenever he was reminded by a nurse or fellow patient that he was in hospital, he usually replied with, "Don't be silly, I'm at home, and what the hell are all these people doing in my house?!"

Last night I was finally "released", and when I got home I was delighted to find that Clare Jackson, Senior Tutor at Trinity Hall, and presenter of the television series *The Stuarts*, was staying the night. Clare was one the brightest pupils I ever taught, and I distinctly remember her reading most of my Economics library in her first term. This morning we reminisced about days at school and Clare took some photos of my red squirrel in the snow. It's so good to be back home.

12 February 2017

Although I survived my time in hospital, two high profile MND sufferers died whilst I was there. The first to go was Gordon Aikman. Gordon was diagnosed with the disease in 2014, aged just 29. At the time he was Director of Research for the "Better Together" campaign, ahead of the Scottish independence referendum. Gordon was a very political animal, and during a televised speech fairly soon after his diagnosis, he dramatically stated that he would be dead within a year. At the time, I found his remarks deeply depressing. "How dare this man condemn me and my fellow newly-diagnosed MND sufferers to death within the next twelve months", I thought. Although Gordon's prediction turned out to be wrong (both for him and for me), the emotive language he used raised public awareness and shocked politicians into action. His tireless campaigning gained cross-party support in Scotland for more MND specialist nurses, and raised more than £500,000 for research into the disease.

A few days after Gordon died, Joost Van der Westhuizen lost his battle — he was only 45. The former South Africa scrum half and World Cup winner was diagnosed with MND in 2011. He was given just a couple of years to live, but he defied the doctors' predictions to hold on for six years, all the while raising funds through his charity, the J9 Foundation.

13 February 2017

Today I had post-hospital visits from Elizabeth, my occupational therapist, Linda, my community nurse, and Hazel, my dietician. All three were as helpful and as kind as ever. Dee, my MND nurse, had already visited me on Friday. To get so much support within only three days of leaving hospital was wonderful. This, along with the excellent care I received whilst in hospital, makes me realise how lucky I am to live where I do. Every evening I see reports on television about missed targets in hospitals, the pressures on community care, and the lack of integration between these services. I know that health service employees in the Perth area, like their counterparts in other districts, are working in difficult conditions, but the service I have received has been outstanding.

14 February 2017

When I reached my recliner after breakfast this morning, I found a red envelope on the arm. After a struggle to open it, I found a lovely Valentine's card from Elaine. I was completely overcome by emotion as I read the beautiful words that she had written inside. Last night I sent an e-card to Elaine. It did arrive this morning, but the contrast between what I received from her and what I was able to give in return only served to increase my sense of inadequacy. In the afternoon Peter, Juliet and Max, who are spending a few days at the Crieff Hydro, came in to see us. Peter had found it frustrating being so far away when I was in hospital, and was keen to check on me. I think he was surprised, and relieved, to find me looking fairly normal.

15 February 2017

This afternoon Elaine packed her bags for a trip to Nigeria, China, and Hong Kong, where she is attending education fairs, meeting prospective parents, and attending events for former Glenalmond pupils. Whilst I was in hospital, she thought she might not be able to go on this trip, but as soon as I was recovering at home, I made it clear that I wanted her to go ahead. Before she left for the airport, her mother arrived. Janette is staying with me while Elaine is away. She has been just like a second mother to me, and after not seeing her much during her own illness, I am looking forward to spending time with her again.

16 February 2017

This was my first day at Cornhill for three weeks, and I was a little unsure how I would cope; however, when I arrived I was given a warm welcome by everyone. I had a debrief with Morag about my time in hospital. Morag understands me very well, and I knew there would be no point trying to pull the wool over her eyes. I was totally honest about the way the whole episode had dented my confidence. Morag listened carefully and didn't feed me any of those well-intentioned, but unhelpful lines, such as, "You will soon be back to normal". She knows perfectly well that my journey with MND doesn't work like that. I shed a few tears, Morag held the tissues, and we were soon laughing and joking again. In the afternoon, after a relaxation exercise, we all watched the best of *The Two Ronnies*. I haven't laughed so much for ages. Ronnie Corbett died of MND last year. Peter, Juliet, and Max arrived to say goodbye in the early evening. Peter, as usual, wanted to be "useful", so he filled up all my bird feeders. I hoped that this might attract my red squirrel so that Max could see him, but he didn't make an appearance.

19 February 2017

This morning the sun is shining, the sky is blue, and my bird table is bursting with activity and song. Through my French window I can see snow drops for the first time this year, and I think I can see some buds on the rhododendron bushes at the end of the garden. After my set back at the beginning to the month, I am now feeling stronger. With spring just around the corner, my spirits are beginning to rise.

20 February 2017

Today, my mother-in-law and I had an interesting episode with her mobile phone. It was frustrating for both of us at times, but also very amusing. Janette rarely uses her pay-as-you-go mobile, and understandably, she has problems remembering how to navigate her way around all the buttons. Our first problem was getting the phone charged. After plugging it in for an hour, Janette announced that the charger hadn't worked because the black line on the indicator hadn't moved and the bar was still white. I explained that if the bar was white, it meant the phone was now fully charged. Next, she decided to make a call. She said she thought the number was somewhere in the phone, but she had no idea where. We carefully made our way to the "contacts" icon via the green phone symbol, and Janette began to scroll down the list. Unfortunately, she pressed too hard as she did this and ended up ringing the wrong person.

When I eventually heard Janette talking to her son, I thought our problems were over, but sadly they were only just beginning. A few seconds into the call she suddenly shouted, 'It's not working!' She then started pressing buttons at random and quickly lost the contacts list. We began the whole process again. As soon as she did get through, Janette's first words to Ed were, "What did you do? It stopped working". Without waiting for a reply, she then started talking about other things. After a minute, however, she realised that there was no one on the other end — she had been talking to herself. After a few more failed calls, we discovered that she had been holding the phone in such a manner that she had kept pressing down on the "end call" button. Just as we thought we had communications under control, a message popped up on the screen to say that the mobile had run out of credit. The topping-up process took quite some time, and involved more calls to Ed, and a few failed attempts to enter a code and send a text message. After all that, we finally settled down for a rest, before tackling the mysteries of the microwave.

21 February 2017

This morning a young man arrived to fix the sliding door on my wet room. Yesterday afternoon I closed the door when I went to the loo, but when I tried to open it again, I found that it was stuck. I pulled away, but from my wheelchair it was hard to get much leverage. Realising that I was never going to force the door open, I began banging on it and calling for Janette. She couldn't work out where I was at first, but when she arrived we attempted to communicate through the door. My speech was so slurred that she found it hard to understand me, but suddenly I heard her trying to slide the door. Eventually, after a lot of scraping noises, the door slowly moved back, and I made my escape.

While the young man repaired the door, Bobby came in to see me. Bobby is a Sheriff in Glasgow, an Old Glenalmonder, and a great supporter of the school. We had sat next to each other at a dinner party nearly two years ago, and after learning about my illness, he had told me that his wife had lost her own battle with MND. Ever since that evening, Bobby has been very supportive of Elaine and me. He has a great understanding of the journey that we are going through. Today, Bobby told me the fascinating story of how he led an inquiry into a fire at a hospital at Port Stanley, in the Falkland Islands, back in the 80s.

23 February 2017

Yesterday a crown came loose, and in the middle of the night it fell out. Fortunately, I was awake when this happened, or I might easily have swallowed it. I imagine "passing" a crown, with a fairly sharp post attached to it, could be rather painful. I asked Demi, a new carer who started looking after me this week, to ring my dentist to see if they might do a home visit. They said they didn't provide that service, but they could refer me to a dental centre, which could collect me in my electric chair. They said this might take a few weeks and suggested I try to fix the crown temporarily with some dental cement from the chemist. Demi kindly offered to collect some cement and when she returned for her next visit, she patiently followed the instructions and stuck the crown back in.

The highlight of the day was the arrival of Elaine, back from her overseas trip. I fully understand that it is totally impossible for me to accompany her on these trips, but I still feel guilty for not being there to support her. I miss her terribly when she is away, and now that my voice has deteriorated so much, we can't really speak on the phone. Instead, I keep my mobile within reach throughout the day and night, and wait for the sound of a text message. This week, I was pleased that I managed to take a selfie and send it to her.

24 February 2017

This morning Bill, Charlie and Emma, the Chairman, Honorary Secretary, and Membership Co-coordinator of the Lorettonian Society came to visit me. I knew they were coming, and assumed the purpose might be connected with my recent resignation from the Executive Committee, due to my inability to attend any more meetings. I taught Bill and Charlie back in the 80s, and I can remember them sitting in my Economics class as if it were yesterday. We enjoyed reminiscing about the "old days", and we laughed about the fact that after 30 years at Loretto, I find myself married to the Warden of Glenalmond. I gratefully accepted a bottle of Loretto whisky and a hip flask, but then found that my main gift was an invitation from the Central Committee to become an Honorary Life Vice President of the Society. Very few people have been bestowed with this title. I was surprised, honoured, extremely touched, and delighted to accept.

25 February 2017
I never forget this day because it marks the birthday of both my younger daughter and my late sister. Meg is 23 today and Steph would have been 66. My feelings of happiness and celebration for my daughter are contrasted with my sense of loss for the passing of my sister. If Steph could hear me now, however, she would be the first to tell me that she lived her life to the full, and that I should get on with my life, and "Stop being morbid!"

27 February 2017
This evening there was an item on the Scottish news about the launch of something called "Realistic Medicine". Doctors will be expected to spend more time listening to patients with serious medical conditions, rather than simply prescribing more drugs and treatments. Quality, rather than quantity of life, is to be given more importance. A man with kidney failure was interviewed and said that, after having an open and frank talk with his consultant, he had chosen not to have dialysis; he wanted to spend what time he had left doing things with his family. I can perfectly understand his point of view. Doctors are trained in the art of prolonging life, but more treatment is not always the best treatment.

1 March 2017
I understand that this year the astronomical first day of spring isn't until 20 March. For me, however, today has always been the date when I have assumed that winter is over. Fortunately, the weather is now supporting my view. A week ago, I awoke to a fairly thick blanket of snow following some severe weather warnings from the met

office, but today the sun is shining, the sky is blue, and I can see tinges of yellow on the top of the daffodil stalks outside the French windows. I have never suffered from S.A.D., but I do find that my spirits are lifted by the arrival of more daylight, and particularly, more sunlight.

2 March 2017

It is exactly two years ago today that I was given my provisional diagnosis of MND. I have been re-reading my entry for that fateful day, which I remember as clearly as if it was yesterday. During my walk that morning through Duddingston golf course, and throughout the subsequent bus journey into Edinburgh, I constantly tried to tell myself that I was simply going for another test. I was pretty sure, however, that the Electromyogram, known as the needle test, was going to show that there was something seriously wrong.

Having survived for two years since then, and for five years since my first symptoms, I have been luckier than many. The statistics tell us that only 50% of MND sufferers survive for longer than two years after their diagnosis, and only 20% are alive five years after the onset of symptoms — either way, I suppose I am doing pretty well. Despite all the losses, I still feel strongly that my life is worth living.

4 March 2017

Emma, a former pupil of Elaine's, has been staying with us for two days. Emma is a "reader" at Warwick University, and on Thursday evening she gave a lecture to a group of Glenalmond pupils on "big data". Young people are certainly aware of the huge amount of data that businesses and organisations receive and generate, but they rarely stop to consider the ways in which this data can then be used, with both positive and negative consequences. Emma thought the talk went well. Today we have chatted about all sorts of things, whilst she has tapped away on her laptop, preparing for her next project.

6 March 2017

My GP is coming for a home visit this morning. I have been taking a new medication to help reduce the pain associated with the stiffness and cramps in my legs. The pain has been particularly bad at night, and even after taking a sleeping pill, I have been waking up frequently. It is a catch 22 situation, because when my legs ache I have to change position to reduce the pain, but rolling over from my back to my side, or vice versa, takes a huge amount of effort. I am just hoping that they can give me something that will enable me to get a good night's rest. When my doctor arrived, we discussed my sleeping problems, and he decided to increase the dosage of my latest medication. He also prescribed a stronger painkiller. I explained that I have also been suffering from dry and itchy skin. We agreed that that might be a side effect of one of the drugs, so he prescribed a cream to deal with that. He also warned me that the new painkiller might have side effects, too. I now have a great assortment of medications. Some help with other long-term conditions, several tackle the symptoms of my disease, and a couple reduce the side effects of other drugs. Sadly, not one of them actually treats my MND.

7 March 2017

My new painkiller is a liquid form of morphine. Whilst my carers are permitted to place my other pills in my yoghurt so that I can take them, the rules for drugs like morphine are different. These drugs are based on opium, and they can be highly addictive. Consequently, my carers are not allowed to administer them. Normally, Elaine will be able to deal with this, but she is away overnight. Before she left this morning, she drew up a dose of morphine with a syringe and left it in a bowl. This evening, just before I went to bed, Lorraine watched as I took the syringe and tried to squirt the morphine into my mouth. Unfortunately, my stiff fore finger and thumb didn't work very well, and most of the liquid ended up all over the front of my tee shirt. All we could do was laugh. Lorraine and Demi are perfectly capable of administering this drug, and I would trust them with my life, but I know the rules are there for a good reason.

9 March 2017

After another restless night, Demi told me I looked very tired when she got me up this morning. Claire said the same when she arrived, and as soon as I reached Cornhill, Morag made the same observation. Throughout the morning, my eyelids felt heavy and I found it very difficult to keep awake. When Ann offered me the chance to have a session of reflexology, I gladly accepted, and within a few minutes of her starting to massage my feet, I was totally relaxed. My sense of relief as I gave in to the fatigue and drifted off to sleep was quite overwhelming.

11 March 2017

A weekend at home for the pupils, so a rare chance for Elaine to catch up on some sleep. I tried to persuade her to take the whole day off, but while I watched the rugby, she worked away on reports and emails. It is always a dilemma for me when my adopted country plays my country of birth. I was delighted for Scotland when they beat Ireland and Wales, but when it comes to the Calcutta Cup, I find it impossible not to support England. Sadly for Scotland, they met England on a very good day. Scotland battled away as always, but they were never really in the game.

13 March 2017

For the last couple of nights I have taken a higher dose of morphine, just before being put to bed. It has certainly helped to reduce the cramps and spasms in my legs, and I have managed to sleep for three or four hours at a time. After weeks of hearing my carriage clock mark each hour during the night, it has been a huge relief to miss a few chimes. When I wake up in the night, I try to use my mindfulness to help get myself back to sleep, but I have to admit that morphine is more effective.

CHAPTER TWENTY

A Hospital Bed Comes Home

14 March 2017

Linda, one of the district nurses, came in today. She confirmed that following a referral from my OT, she is ordering a hospital bed for me. Only a few weeks ago, I had strongly resisted this idea. I didn't want my bedroom to resemble a hospital ward, and I didn't want to face the implications of such a change for the future. Recent events, however, have convinced me that a bed that can be moved up and down and adapted to my sleeping position is exactly what I need. We also discussed the possibility of having rails on the bed. I don't like the idea of being trapped in a cot and always having to depend on Elaine or my carers to let me out. In the end, we agreed on a compromise: I would have a rail on the right and a bed lever on the left.

16 March 2017

Despite a poor forecast, the sun came out at Cornhill this morning, so Louise took David and me out on the balcony for some fresh air. From there we had a fine view of the gardens that surround the building and we could also look across to the mountains in the distance. Having enjoyed being outside, Ann collected me for a relaxing session of reflexology, and then I joined everyone for lunch.

As I sat in my wheelchair on the way home, high up in the back of my access taxi, I felt very contented. As my world has gradually become smaller and smaller, I have adjusted my expectations and, perhaps more importantly, I have learnt how to appreciate the beauty that exists in simple things. My friend Hilary and I were talking about this earlier in the week. She has a deep love of the land and nature, and I was telling her how I now get as much enjoyment from watching the birds outside my window as I did from travelling to far-flung places. The reason, of course, is that I see the birds with different eyes. Instead of glancing at them in passing, I really see them: the colour of their feathers, the way they interact with other birds, and their ability (or not) to hover in the air. I also hear the songs that they sing.

19 March 2017

During my many years of teaching economics and politics, I enjoyed debating issues with my pupils, but when I retired I was very happy to leave most of it behind me. I am relieved that I don't have to teach the subject at the moment, because the quality of political debate appears to be in decline. This has been particularly true in Scotland during the recent referendums on independence and EU membership. The claims and counter-claims of the opposing sides became more and more ridiculous as the campaigns went on. And now, just as people thought referendums were behind them, they are facing something called "IndyRef2". I am quite relieved that I am very unlikely to be around to see it.

20 March 2017

This afternoon two men from Perth and Kinross social services delivered my new hospital bed. They had it up and ready within 10 minutes, and after giving me a quick demonstration on how the remote control worked, they left me to it. For several minutes I just sat and looked at this new and very clinical addition to my bedroom, trying to come to terms with the fact that this wasn't a temporary piece of equipment, but a permanent fixture. Once I had accepted that, I spent some time playing with the buttons on the control. One moved the whole bed up and down, one lifted the head of the bed, one tilted the bed, and one lifted the middle of the bed up. I was keen to discover if I could safely get on and off the bed without help. I knew it would have been sensible to wait until Lorraine arrived at teatime, but I couldn't resist the temptation to give it a try.

I moved my wheelchair so that it faced the side of the bed, took hold of the grab rail near the top of the bed, and pulled myself into a standing position. Keeping one hand on the arm of my wheelchair, I slowly turned around. At that point, however, I realised that I had set the bed a few inches higher than I was used to. I couldn't reach the remote control to lower the bed, and instead of turning around and starting again (which would have been the safest option), I tried to push myself up so that I could get my bottom on to the edge of the bed. Inch by inch, I managed to shift myself backwards into a sitting position.

At this point, I had to sit still and get my breath back. Next, I took hold of the grab rail with one hand and tried to swing my legs up. After two failed attempts, I finally managed to get one leg onto the edge of the bed; I then slowly shuffled my bottom across until I was lying on my back. I lay there for several minutes, but when I tried to move my arms and legs, they felt as if they were filled with lead. I rested for a little longer. Getting off the bed proved to be rather easier. I simply let my legs fall off the side, held on tight to the grab rail, and slid myself into a standing position; I then turned around, and slumped, exhausted, back into my wheelchair.

21 March 2017

The first night in my new bed was a question of trial and error. Initially, it went badly because I raised the head of the bed before I got in. This meant that as soon as I lay down, I slid down the mattress and my head came off the pillow. I reached up behind me, and using the iron rail of the bedstead, I managed to pull myself back onto the pillow. I then turned around and grabbed the remote control. Unfortunately, in the darkness I couldn't find the right buttons to press, so I spent quite a time going up and down, and tilting myself one way and then another. Finally, however, I managed to get myself into a comfortable position whereby my head and my legs were supported. I expected sleep to come easily, but it took a couple of hours for me to drop off. When I woke up the clock next door was only chiming three. I lay there for a very long time, listening to what sounded like a gale outside, and later, when I looked out of the window, snow was falling quite heavily. So much for the beginning of spring.

23 March 2017

The Good Schools Guide has been writing reviews on independent schools for many years. Their assessments are known for being candid and unbiased evaluations, and following a visit from one of their reviewers, schools are always nervous about how they will be judged. Glenalmond's latest review was published today, and it was one of the most glowing reports that I have ever read. The review, based on interviews with parents, staff and pupils, said the school was on the up and up, and praised the academic rigour, the standard of pastoral care, the strong discipline, the range of sporting activities available, and the magnificent campus. It reserved its highest praise, however, for Elaine. It mentioned the improvements that she has made since she took over as Warden (head teacher) and described her leadership as "inspirational". Elaine felt the review put too much emphasis on her, but I am delighted she got the credit that she deserves.

25 March 2017

Today is the end of term, so there are lots of happy pupils and teachers around the school. For Elaine, it will be another week before she gets any proper time off, but at least she will have part of this weekend at home. Last night I went out for the first time in a while. We went to Perth Concert Hall, where Glenalmond were putting on a special one-night performance of the *Jesus Christ Superstar* show they performed in the autumn. The event was an absolute triumph; over a thousand tickets were sold to the public, the quality of the acting and music was simply outstanding, and the cast and orchestra were given a standing ovation at the end. Perhaps I am biased, but I can honestly say that in forty years of watching school plays and musicals, I have never seen such a professional production.

26 March 2017

Just five days ago the snow was falling and we seemed to be back in winter again. Today, however, the sun shone brightly, and I decided to venture out into the garden for the first time this year. Unfortunately, I didn't appreciate how soft the ground was at the side of the house, and before I reached the safety of the patio, my heavy wheelchair slowly but surely began to sink into the mud. I tried moving forward very gradually, but that didn't work, so I switched to maximum speed. The wheels simply went into a spin, and I was forced to call for help. Elaine placed a wooden board under the wheels, and she eventually managed to pull me onto firm ground. After six months of sitting indoors, it was wonderful to sit outside and feel the warmth of the sun.

29 March 2017

For three weeks now I have had an unsightly gap in my upper front teeth. This is due to losing a crown after eating one wine gum too many. My old dental practice decided they wouldn't be able to treat me in my electric wheelchair, so I was referred to a special NHS dental centre. This morning an ambulance collected me in my chair and took me to the centre. The receptionist asked me to fill in a form recording my medical history and medication, but I explained that I can no longer write with a pen. In response, she offered to complete the form if I told her the information. I tried to start speaking, but I couldn't get my tongue around the names of the drugs. In the end, I got out my iPhone and typed the information into the "notes" section. I was looking forward to having my crown cemented in, but as soon as the dentist examined the area, she announced that the base of the tooth was fractured and the crown could not be put back. She made an impression of my front teeth and said that a temporary denture would be ready in a week. She explained that it might be six months before the root of the tooth could be removed and a new crown fitted. I looked at the dentist, began to laugh, and said, "I'm not sure I will still be alive then". For a second or two she looked rather concerned, but then she patted me on the arm, smiled, and said she would try to hurry things along.

31 March 2017

This morning was busy with home visits. First to arrive was my dietician, Hazel, who wanted to check up on my eating and drinking. I told her that I am managing to eat a soft diet with little difficulty, and confirmed that although I can't swallow thin liquids like water and wine, I can still manage orange juice and port. Hazel was happy with this, and pleased that my weight has actually gone up. She was less convinced that I should be eating so many wine gums. As soon as Hazel left, my hairdresser arrived, and proceeded to give me a short back and sides. My next visitor was my OT, Elizabeth, who wanted to check up on my new shower chair. I said it was more comfortable than my old one, but I was surprised that it can recline. I said it was unlikely that I would want to lie prostrate in the shower — and I'm sure my carers would agree.

1 April 2017

It's April Fools' Day, but I have two things to celebrate. Firstly, Lorna arrived from Saudi Arabia this morning. She has made four visits to see her old dad since last May, and it's great to see her. She joined Elaine and me for a walk/wheel around the grounds, and, as always, she enjoyed all the beautiful green scenery. Although there are a couple of parks in the Aramco compound where she lives, and her house is surrounded by well-watered gardens, she gets little respite from the sand and the desert. My second piece of good news was the confirmation that I have gained almost half a stone since my time in hospital. Weight loss for people with MND can be a very serious business. It usually indicates muscle wastage, and for those who don't have a feeding tube, it can be very difficult to put the pounds back on again. I am very fortunate — not only can I still eat soft food, I also have a tube in place for the future.

2 April 2017

A lovely day with the family. In addition to Lorna, Meg, her partner Euan, Elaine's son, Tom, and his girlfriend, Caitlin, were all here for the day. It is very rare for us to have so many of the "children" here together, so there was plenty of news to catch up on. Lorna is now leading a team of education managers in Saudi Arabia, Meg has just completed her second term as a primary school teacher in East Lothian, and Tom is preparing for his final exams at Glasgow University, before hopefully doing a Master's degree at Edinburgh. The education thread continues to run strongly in the family. I went out in my wheelchair to explore the college grounds with my two girls, and later in the evening Tom and Caitlin entertained us by singing and playing Elaine's guitar.

3 April 2017

Lorna and I had a productive morning finalising arrangements for the purchase of her new apartment in Edinburgh. With dual citizenship, Lorna's banking arrangements are quite complicated, so she had to transfer funds between her US, UK, and Saudi Arabian accounts via online banking. In the end, however, she still had to visit a branch of her bank in Perth to make the final payment to the property company.

In the afternoon we had a visit from Diamond, an ex-pupil of mine, who lives in Hong Kong. I have only seen Diamond once since he left school in 1985, and it was wonderful to catch up with him again. We reminisced about the days when I was his housemaster at Loretto, and he told Lorna and me about his career as a fund manager and his plans for the future. I find it almost impossible to get my head around the fact that former pupils like Diamond can be almost fifty years old. At the end of the afternoon we knew that this was probably going to be "goodbye" in the final sense, and it was quite an emotional farewell for both of us. I have learnt to recognise tears as a very natural and appropriate way of showing emotion, and I find it sad that so many men still view them as a weakness. I recently watched a fascinating programme about Andrew Marr's remarkable recovery from his stroke. Sadly, Andrew (another old Lorettonian) spoke of his pride at never crying, as if this was a badge of strength. Nothing could be further from the truth.

5 April 2017

The ambulance transport for my dental appointment arrived very early this morning. The driver explained that she still had to pick up two more "customers", so she asked me to wheel my chair right to the front. After she had attached various straps to secure me in position, we set off on a mystery tour around Perth. After picking up two more people and dropping them off at Perth Royal Infirmary, we headed out to the Broxden Dental Centre. For some reason I had it in my head that my denture would be simply fitted into the space where my old crown used to be. I was quickly informed, however, that the root of the old tooth would have to be removed first. I tilted and reclined my chair until I was virtually horizontal, and prepared myself for the anaesthetic. I had to have four injections to numb the area, and it took a great deal of pulling and twisting to get the root out. After much biting on gauze to stem the bleeding, my denture was put into place. During the next hour while I waited for my ambulance to return, the plate felt very strange on the roof of my mouth, and by the time I finally got home, the anaesthetic was wearing off. I was very relieved when Elaine gave me some liquid paracetamol to reduce the pain.

6 April 2017

My dentist asked me to leave my new denture in overnight so that it could set in, and it was rather an uncomfortable experience. This morning, as soon as I got to Cornhill, I asked Morag if she would mind taking it out. I was amazed how small the plate was in reality, compared to how large it had felt in my mouth. After reassuring me that I would get used to having this foreign body stuck to the roof of my mouth, Morag suggested that we find some goals for the future in terms of my MND. I suggested that staying alive might be a useful one, but Morag laughed and said that was a given. In the end, we agreed on keeping my weight up and maintaining my ability to transfer independently into my wheelchair from my bed and recliner.

After so many "losses" in terms of mobility last year, and my hospitalisation in February, I had become reconciled to further inexorable decline this year. Over the last six weeks, however, I have increased my weight, and I have continued to manage my transfers. I told Morag that I was just beginning to hope, perhaps stupidly, that some aspects of my condition might be a little more stable at the moment; that I might possibly be on some sort of plateau. Morag said there was no reason why this shouldn't be the case. I said that I was scared of raising any hopes, but Morag said we both knew that things would develop, but that I must take the positives when I can.

9 April 2017

Yesterday I heard the very sad news that Graham Cowie has died. I remember Graham well during his time as a pupil at Loretto. He was a great character and he had a wonderfully infectious laugh. It is a great testament to Graham that so many of his former school friends have posted messages on Facebook. Very few parents choose to send their young children away to board these days, but there is no denying the strength of the bonds that are forged between those who share, and at times endure, such an experience. It has been very touching to read the messages about, and memories of, Graham, including from those who were his contemporaries at Loretto's Junior School (the Nippers) in the 1970s.

11 April 2017

When I received the rota for my carers this morning, I was disappointed to discover that I will have seven different people looking after me this week. The overall care I have received since September has been very good indeed, but an important part of my service plan was the requirement for me to have a small number of carers. This was agreed because of the rarity and complexity of my condition. For the first four months or so everything worked very well indeed. Lorraine, Demi, and Emma are all wonderful carers, and I have established a strong relationship with them; they understand my needs, and the continuity has been good. In recent weeks, however, due to changes to the administrative side of the care company, the rotas have changed, both in terms of personnel and times. Although this is frustrating, I know that I am still very lucky compared to many people across the UK. With almost a thousand carers leaving the profession every day (mainly due to long, unsociable hours and low pay), the whole system appears to be in crisis.

12 April 2017

Three good friends from Loretto visited us today. I have known Paul and Dan since the 80s, and Elaine also worked with them for many years. Dan's wife, Yasmin, who we both know well, also came. Rather than cook something more exotic, Elaine made a shepherd's pie so that I could join in. It was very tasty, but I felt slightly embarrassed that my need for a "soft" diet restricted the menu to such an extent. Swopping stories about boarding schools is always entertaining, and the hours passed very quickly. I managed to join in as much as possible, but I had to rest my voice at regular interviews.

13 April 2017

I had a wonderful day at Cornhill. Another patient and I sat around a table with Morag, Louise, and Laura, and we made rocky road cake and truffles. I found smashing up biscuits with a rolling pin to be very therapeutic, and we managed to make quite a mess with all the melted chocolate and marshmallows. The banter among patients and staff is always entertaining. We all understand the journey we are on, so the humour can be fairly dark, and any chance to seize upon a possible double entendre is quickly taken. It might seem a strange thing to say about a visit to a hospice, but I haven't laughed so much for ages.

CHAPTER TWENTY-ONE
Disability Can Be Funny

15 April 2017

After seeing so many different carers this week, three of whom I had never met before, it was a great relief to see a familiar face this morning. Demi is by far my youngest carer, but she, like Lorraine and Emma, knows me very well. One of the most difficult things about having a new carer is trying to make them understand what I am saying. Now that my speech is so compromised, it is very hard for new people to tune in to my voice. Attempting to explain where things are and which medication I need can be very difficult for me, and it becomes very tiring when I have to repeat myself again and again. There is also a tendency for people to assume that my slurred speech is somehow an indication of senility, so they start talking to me as if I am a child. Sitting in my shower chair while someone pats me on the shoulder and says, "There, there my dear, you just sit quietly and don't upset yourself" is very frustrating. So far, I have bitten my lip, but inside my head I am screaming, "I may not be able talk properly, but I'm not an idiot — my brain still works!"

16 April 2017

Elaine has just left for the Easter Day service in Glenalmond's chapel. I had hoped to attend in my electric wheelchair, but the forecast is for heavy rain. Instead, I am watching a televised service from Hereford Cathedral. Easter, like Christmas, has become a huge commercial event, with millions of pounds being spent on chocolate eggs and a whole array of other so-called 'Easter' gifts. Today only a fraction of the adults who buy these gifts, or the children who receive them, will be attending a church service. Even fewer will know why Easter falls on this day, what their chocolate eggs symbolise, or why they might roll eggs down a hill. I am sure that many of the people I can see singing in Hereford Cathedral consider this to be a great sadness; that it reflects the continual decline of religious faith in this country. To millions of others, however, it simply doesn't matter — they know that Easter has something to do with Jesus' crucifixion and his resurrection, and for them that is enough. I honestly don't know who is right.

17 April 2017

Today, I exchanged a few emails with the administrator from the company that manages my care. I pointed out that after several months of excellent service, the system seemed to be breaking down in terms of which carers I was getting and the timings of their visits. Initially, I received a rather patronising reply, telling me that the company's policy was that all carers can visit all clients, and that I would have to accept this. It was perfectly clear that this person had not read any of the information that is contained in my care plan, a copy of which is in his office. I emailed back to explain a little more about the nature of MND and some of the issues involved, such as having a feeding tube and having no proper voice. This resulted in a more conciliatory reply, assuring me that they would try to provide me with more continuity in future.

19 April 2017

Here we go again… Another election! This will be the second one in three years, and we had the EU referendum sandwiched between them. After repeatedly saying she didn't want to have an election, Theresa May has surprised most people by calling for one. This would seem to mark the end of so-called "fixed term" parliaments, and herald a return to the days when prime ministers call elections when they think they have the best chance of winning (within the 5-year time-frame).

Whatever her motivation, Theresa May has given me an opportunity that I thought I would never have again; namely, to stay up all night with a bottle of port and watch David Dimbleby host yet another marathon election-night special, along with Jeremy Vine and his high-tech version of the old swingometer. Unlike the last election, however, I doubt if I will have to wait until breakfast time to discover the result. Theresa May's ratings are so far ahead of the hapless Jeremy Corbyn, it would take a monumental cock-up for the conservatives to lose. Here in Scotland, Nicola Sturgeon says this election will not be about independence. If that really is the case, I wonder what on earth she will talk about?

20 April 2017

This week I have had two more visits from "boys" who were in Hope House with me at Loretto School. James, who left school back in the mid-eighties, arrived yesterday. James is a cartographer and photographer, and he has established a successful business making beautifully hand-drawn maps of estates and gardens. His late father was Deputy Head of Gordonstoun for many years, and we had a good discussion about the way schools have changed (and sometimes not) over the years.

Today Alex, who left in 1989, came up from Salisbury to see me. As a boy, Alex found it hard to come to terms with boarding, but he found solace in his love of pottery. When he wasn't throwing pots, he spent many hours drinking tea in my house or baby-sitting my daughter, and over his five years at school, I got to know him very well. I never had any doubt that Alex would become a successful potter, and after many years of specialising in terracotta, he has recently produced an outstanding collection of large stoneware clay sculptures. Following exhibitions at Chatsworth and Canary Wharf, Alex's work is now in high demand. Despite his success, however, he remains as modest, sensitive, and charming as ever — just as he was as a boy. At a time when pupils were sometimes judged more by their prowess on the rugby field than anything else, life for gentle souls like James and Alex could be hard. I am delighted that both of them have found happiness and fulfilment in their chosen fields.

22 April 2017

Today I met another new carer. When I saw an unfamiliar name on my rota, I was fully expecting a stressful visit, but on this occasion it proved not to be the case. Anne is a retired nurse who continues to work long after the normal retirement age, and I thought she was wonderful. She knows all about MND, having nursed a fellow-sufferer during her time spent working in palliative care, and she fully appreciates that the disease affects people in different ways. As we spent some time talking about my own symptoms and how they have developed, it was clear to me that we were going to get on very well. Anne has that ideal combination of sensitivity and humour, and I look forward to seeing her again soon.

24 April 2017

This afternoon I managed to throw orange juice all over the place. Sitting in my recliner, I carefully lifted my glass from the shelf, making sure that I hooked my little finger underneath the glass to prevent it from sliding from my hand, but just as I was about to take a sip, I coughed. This caused my hand to shake, and when I tightened my grip my arm went into a juddering spasm. The contents sloshed into the magazine rack next to me, and spilled over the floor. The cables for my laptop, phone, and recliner all got wet too. When I tried to transfer into my wheelchair I very nearly slipped on the wet floor, but I eventually managed to fetch a roll of paper towels from the kitchen. I got myself safely back into my recliner, but I still couldn't reach the floor. I dropped some towels and tried to use my foot to mop up the liquid, but I didn't make a very good job of it. I spent a frustrating hour looking at the mess around me, feeling thoroughly useless, and then Judith arrived for a visit. I hadn't seen her for three weeks, so I accused her of having abandoned me. She gave me a little Easter egg, however, so I quickly forgave her! I moved into my wheelchair again and Judith kindly cleaned up all the mess.

25 April 2017

I watched a recording of a recent programme about Billy Connolly. It included many of his old sketches, tributes from some of his more famous fans, and some interviews with the man himself. His contribution to comedy over many decades has been quite incredible. He is a very funny man to look at, he makes fun of subjects that many comics would avoid, and even people who are initially offended by his language usually end up roaring with laughter. For me, the funniest (and the most emotional) part of the show was when he joked about living with Parkinson's Disease. Finding humour in such an otherwise tragic subject takes some doing, but by laughing at his own predicament he helps people like me see the funny side of life. As they say, if you didn't laugh, you would cry.

27 April 2017

I should have known that it was tempting fate to tell people that I felt more stable recently. This week, my trousers have felt slightly looser on the waist, so this morning at Cornhill, I asked Louise if I could use their new sit-on scales. They told me that I have lost four pounds over the last month. Louise said this wasn't a significant loss and suggested that we simply keep an eye on things. I felt somewhat reassured, but the thought did go through my mind that this could be the onset of a sudden increase in muscle wastage, and the beginning of an inexorable deterioration in my condition. After sharing a few jokes and stories with everyone else, I soon became distracted from my morbid thoughts, and later on the way home in bright sunshine, I was further cheered by the sight of gambolling lambs in the fields, thousands of daffodils along the hedgerows, and the snow-capped mountains in the distance. Perthshire in the spring is a wonderful place to be.

30 April 2017

Early Sunday morning, television is crammed with programmes on politics and religion, but I wonder how many people bother to get up to watch them? Of those who do deny themselves a long lie in bed, I suspect more watch the re-run of *Match of the Day* than tune in to Andrew Marr or Robert Peston. My carer arrived at 7.30 a.m. this morning, so I had a somewhat forced opportunity to watch them all. The political interviews followed a very predictable pattern: the interviewers asked direct questions, the interviewees refused to give a straight answer, the interviewers then repeated the question, and the interviewees answered the question they wished they had been asked in the first place. One of the very few unqualified, one-word answers came from Theresa May, who, when asked by Andrew Marr if she, as a committed Christian, thought gay sex was a sin, replied with a very definite 'No'. So I learnt something after all — it just wasn't about politics.

1 May 2017

May Day used to represent the beginning of summer, back in the times when February marked the start of spring. It is hard to believe that this could ever have been the case in Scotland, where winter can seem to go on forever. Although I have lived in Scotland for some thirty-eight years, I have always retained a strong sense of being "English". I am proud of my country of birth; I still support it on sporting occasions, and it is a great sadness for me that I will almost certainly never see the beautiful patchwork fields of my native Devon again. However, May Day signals one of the few things about England that frankly embarrasses me: Morris dancing. I would like to be considered a liberal-minded man, but I have always found the sight of men dancing around with bells on their legs and waving handkerchiefs in the air to be faintly ridiculous. I apologise to any Morris dancers out there, but I would prefer to watch a man in a kilt doing a Highland Fling, any day!

3 May 2017

Elaine is away for several days, meeting up with former Glenalmond pupils in Canada and America. Whenever I hear anything about Canada these days, I immediately think about Julie, a former pupil of mine from my time at Loretto. Julie and her twin sister, Sarah, were in my Economics class back in the 80's, and they both went on to become teachers. Julie taught in many different countries before settling in Ontario, where she still lives with her two children. Tragically, Julie lost her husband, Mark, to leukaemia nearly six years ago. That event has left her with a very real understanding of the trials and challenges that a terminal illness brings. For the past year, Julie has sent me frequent messages of support in response to my blog, and although I haven't seen her since she left school, I consider her to be a very good friend. In my mind's eye, of course, I still see her as the seventeen-year-old girl who sat in my classroom over thirty years ago.

5 May 2017

Perhaps May is the beginning of summer after all. The weather this week has been glorious and my garden has been busy with wildlife. In addition to my usual birds, I have had visits from a woodpecker. On two occasions, it has swooped down and pecked at my peanut feeder, but I suspect its beak is too big to get through the wire mesh. With the French window open, I have also been able to hear the birds as well as just see them. I have decided my favourite is now the chaffinch, because it has beautiful colours and seems to sing continuously. A young squirrel has also been visiting the bird table. At first, he kept trying to get to the seed feeder, but after jumping onto the Perspex cylinder several times and sliding to the bottom, the little fellow discovered that the wire peanut holder offered a better chance of success.

7 May 2017

I have worn out my voice this week, and it is entirely my own fault. I keep forgetting that I need to pace myself with my talking in order to protect my tongue and throat muscles, rather like a long-distance runner has to conserve energy by not sprinting in the early part of a race. The "problem" has been the number of visitors that I have had. In addition to home appointments with Kirstie, my reflexologist, Moira, my neuropsychologist, and Carol, my social worker, Corinne, Judith, Gill, Jean, and Steve have all been in to visit me. I really enjoy seeing people, and talking is the most natural thing to do when they arrive. At a certain point, however, instead of doing the sensible thing, and saying, "Sorry, I don't think I can speak any more", I tend to carry on until my speech becomes almost incoherent. At that point, people realise that the conversation has become rather one-sided, and the visit comes to an end. By not being more honest on these occasions, my behaviour actually causes more embarrassment for everyone.

9 May 2017

I am really looking forward to seeing Elaine when she gets back from New York this evening. I have to say, however, that her mother, Janette, has looked after me very well over the last week. When I hear or see the term "mother-in-law", I find it hard not to think of a hippopotamus. This, of course, is the fault of Leonard Rossiter, who, when playing the part of Reginald Perrin in the hilarious 1980s sitcom, always saw a lumbering hippo in his mind's eye whenever anyone mentioned his wife's mother. Janette is a well-built lady but I wouldn't say she resembles a hippopotamus. Perhaps a water buffalo might be a better likeness? In all seriousness though, she has been incredibly kind to me over the years, and as my MND symptoms have gradually worsened, she has always been happy to help with my care. I am very proud to call her "Mum".

11 May 2017

We had a great time this morning making smoothies at Cornhill. There were only five of us attending, so we all sat around a table in the kitchen area and did our best to prepare the ingredients for Louise, who was in charge of the blender. Kath sat next to me, and as usual, we exchanged light-hearted insults. She knows that my hands don't work properly, but that didn't stop her digging me in the ribs, telling me not to be lazy, and asking me to get on with peeling and cutting up fruit. In turn, I told her not to be such a bossy-boots. In different circumstances it would be very easy to become defensive, but we all know that such comments are meant in good humour: more than that, they are actually our way of showing affection for each other. We all know that we are terminally ill, and we can certainly empathise with each other, but the last thing we need is too much sentimentality, or even worse, pity. I made a right mess of trying to peel a mango, but the resulting drink tasted very good. As well as mango and ginger, we made (with plenty of help from the staff) smoothies from blueberries, strawberries, and bananas.

12 May 2017

A transport ambulance collected me this morning to take me to the dentist. The driver had a difficult time securing my chair to the floor with various straps, and as soon as we set off there was a loud bang behind me. The driver stopped, checked the back of the vehicle, and said she thought there might be a problem with the suspension. We agreed to carry on for the time being, and we made it safely to our destination. My "temporary" denture was checked and I was asked if I would like to have a bridge fitted at a later date. I considered this option, but I said I couldn't face a lot more dental work. The dentist gave me some adhesive to keep the denture plate more secure, and my driver was waiting for me in reception.

Shortly after arriving home, Marcus and Diana, two more of my former pupils from the 80s, arrived for a visit. Despite suffering a stroke a few years ago that left him semi-paralysed, Marcus is as positive and as amusing as he was as a boy. We exchanged funny stories about life in a wheelchair and Diana laughed as loudly as I remember her doing over thirty years ago. She was a tall, strong-minded, and vivacious girl at school, and she hasn't changed at all.

14 May 2017

I missed an opportunity today that may never come my way again. After Elaine had left for chapel this morning, I opened an email that Judith had sent me much earlier. She was offering to come and accompany me to the service, so that I could hear the Glenalmond choir sing *Zadok the Priest*. If I had known that they were singing this wonderful piece, I would have tried harder to get there, instead of catching up on lost sleep. Ever since I first heard *Zadok* being sung live as a whole-school anthem at Loretto, in 1979, I have been mesmerised by its power and its beauty. Elaine knows just how much I love it, and when she returned from chapel she said she had had to hold her emotions in check while she read the lesson immediately afterwards.

This afternoon, I opened a file on my computer called "Notes on my funeral" and wrote that I would like this anthem to be played on that occasion. Some might consider this to be rather pretentious, given that Handel composed it for King George II's coronation, but this is what I would like. Of course, if I want it sung live by the college choir, I will need to get my timing right.

17 May 2017

Yesterday was not a good day. I had stayed up late the evening before, enjoying some desert wine with Elaine, Hilary and Duncan, and Sam and Niall. Along with several other members of the Glenalmond Council, they had been to a dinner in Duncan's honour, in the college hall. I am unable to get up to the hall anymore, and even if I could, I would not be very good company. Understanding as people are, they don't really want to share dinner with someone whose speech is almost incomprehensible, uses ridiculous cutlery, and tends to drop food on the table. Of course, even if other people don't mind, I do. Anyway, yesterday I felt tired because I hadn't slept well, and I found it very hard to raise my spirits. For the majority of the time I pride myself on being (or at least, giving the impression of being) positive, and any negative thoughts are usually thrown off fairly quickly. Occasionally, however, I can dwell too long on how futile my life seems to have become. It's not that I feel particularly sorry for myself; I simply become consumed by a sense of being helpless, hopeless, and rather useless. It's at times like this that I need to remember the mental toolkit that Moira, my neuropsychologist, has given me — namely, to acknowledge the losses of the past, and the challenges that lie in the future, but to try and live in the present. This morning, as I watch the birds and the squirrels feeding from the table outside my window and look at the surrounding trees swaying and shimmering in the sunlight, I am doing much better.

19 May 2017

Having got myself into a more positive frame of mind on Wednesday, I am now back in "worry" mode. Yesterday morning Lorraine told me that she had heard me coughing. I tried to make light of it, but backed up by Elaine, she insisted on calling my GP's surgery and requesting a home visit. The doctor said he would come out later. I found myself thinking about the last time that I developed a cough back in January, when I ended up in hospital with mild pneumonia. The thought of lying in bed for days, or even weeks, having drugs pumped into me intravenously and being fed through my stomach tube, was very depressing. When my GP arrived, I was very relieved when he told me that he couldn't find any sign of a chest infection. I apologised for dragging him out for nothing, but he said, "Don't be silly; you can't afford to take any chances". I'm unsure if this made me feel better or not.

This afternoon Judith came around. Having observed the deterioration in my voice for over eighteen months, she understands how tiring (and frustrating) speaking has become for me. While I sat back in my recliner, she sat next to me in my wheelchair and did some sewing. We only talked a little, but, as always, I enjoyed her company. I also found the rhythmic movement of the needle and thread very relaxing.

21 May 2017

There was another dose of politics on television this morning. Andrew Marr looked his usual smart self, but the same couldn't be said for Robert Peston, or his main guest, Boris Johnson, both of whom looked as if they had been dragged through a hedge backwards. Perhaps I should have been concentrating more on what they were saying, but as most of us know, non-verbal factors such as appearance and body language have far more impact than mere words. This might help explain why the Conservatives strengthened their lead in the polls while they repeated one short message about a "strong Brexit", but lost ground when they started to talk more about their actual manifesto. Of course, it rarely pays to be honest in politics. By telling the truth — that we cannot cover the rising cost of social care, unless we pay for it — the Conservatives have lost out. Labour, however, by promising to spend billions on public services without really saying where the money will come from, have gained.

CHAPTER TWENTY-TWO
Survivor Guilt

23 May 2017

This morning I woke up early, pulled myself out of bed, and got into my wheelchair. Although my hospital bed is much more comfortable than a normal one, it is very frustrating having to remain in a static position all night. Until recently, I always slept on my side, but I no longer have the strength to turn myself over. After seven or eight hours on my back, I am more than ready to move. I wheeled into the living room, put on the television, and was stunned by the news of the appalling suicide attack that took place in Manchester last night. I watched for two hours as more news of this terrible event unfolded. Dan Walker, who did an outstanding job anchoring the programme for the BBC, announced that twenty-two people, including a number of children, had been killed, and sixty more were injured. An atrocity such as this certainly puts things into perspective, and reminds all of us that most of our woes are not really that bad, after all.

25 May 2017

This morning at Cornhill, as I sat in the sunshine on the balcony with Morag, I was distracted from the beautiful view of the mountains by a nagging feeling that my weight was beginning to fall. Morag took me to the sit-on scales and I was surprised, and delighted, to discover that my weight is exactly the same as it was a month ago.

Armed with this reassuring information, I thoroughly enjoyed the rest of the day. This included some meringue-making in the morning, and a visit from a musician in the afternoon. Two of the inpatients from downstairs joined us for the latter, and we sat around in a circle and sang along to golden oldies from the sixties. I felt rather self-indulgent as I enjoyed all this while Ann gave my feet a massage.

27 May 2017

This was Elaine's first proper day off for over a month, so quite rightly, she enjoyed a long lie in. Lying in bed is no longer an option for me, so I was showered, dressed, and fed by 8.30 a.m. When my carer, a delightful young lady called Neschka, left, I followed her out in my wheelchair and parked in the garden. I spent a lovely hour sitting in an oasis of green, enjoying the warm sunshine, and watching the birds and squirrels feeding from the table. When Elaine appeared she was carrying her breakfast on a tray. As I tried to move my wheelchair closer to her, I pushed the joy stick too hard, knocked into the table, and spilt coffee all over the place. At moments like this, the temptation is to swear loudly, but on this occasion, despite feeling very frustrated, I sat quietly while Elaine went for a cloth and mopped up. After spending a very rare morning together in the garden, I went inside and began a long vigil in front of the television, watching the Scottish and English cup finals. My father remained a passionate Arsenal supporter right up until he died, and although I defected to Manchester United, my brother, after a childhood spent supporting Leeds United, has also become a strong Arsenal fan. I was delighted that, against the odds, Arsenal won the match.

28 May 2017

Ann, who had two spells as a nurse at Loretto, and her husband Mike came up for lunch today. I was very conscious of how slow and clumsy I have become at the table. Ann and Mike are the last people to worry about such things, but I still found it frustrating. The whole point about sharing a meal with friends is to enjoy the food along with the conversation, but when you need all your strength and concentration to achieve just one of these actions, your level of participation becomes minimal. In the afternoon we all went for a walk around the grounds with Ann and Mike's beautiful red setter. He had a great time racing around the campus while we enjoyed the sunshine, the rhododendrons, and the stunning views.

30 May 2017

Hazel, my dietitian, arrived for a home visit this morning. We had a good chat about my "input" and "output" of food and drink, and she was pleased to know that my weight is holding up. We then set about changing my feeding tube. I reclined in my wheelchair as Hazel attached a small syringe into a port on the outside of the tube, and withdrew the water from the grape-sized balloon that sits inside and keeps everything in place. Once the balloon was deflated, Hazel carefully pulled the tube out. I couldn't resist leaning forward and taking a look at the exposed hole in my stomach. It looked somewhat bigger than I had thought, so I quickly averted my gaze. Hazel took out a fresh tube, spread gel on the deflated balloon, and pushed it through the hole. She then syringed water into the new balloon via the port, and the operation was complete. Hazel asked if I would mind helping her with a questionnaire for social services. The questions were all related to my ability to perform various tasks independently, such as move around unaided, do housework, get myself dressed and showered, and go shopping. Having answered "no" to all of these questions, I then had to indicate how long it has been since I could perform these tasks. The answer in most cases was nine or ten months. Being reminded that I could do all of these things less than a year ago was a sobering thought. For the rest of the morning I did my best to think of the things that I can still do.

1 June 2017

Elaine's uncle died last week, and today she went down to Tranent for his funeral. Willie was in his late eighties and he had been married to Elaine's aunt, Margaret, for over sixty years. It is sad but true that extended family members rarely meet up except for weddings and funerals, so Elaine, Tom, and Cameron saw some people for the first time in years. Willie, like Elaine's father, had been in the Boys' Brigade for many years, and there was a wreath on his coffin in the shape of an anchor, the BB's emblem. There was also a wreath in the shape of a Maltese cross, in memory of the many family holidays that he enjoyed on that island.

3 June 2017

June is hardly bursting out all over in Perthshire, but after weeks of semi-drought conditions, I suppose the rain is just what the ground needs. The farmers will be happy too, but as a breed they are notoriously difficult to please when it comes to weather. As a child growing up on a farm in Devon, I clearly remember my father's early morning ritual. He would get up, go down the stairs, and tap on the old barometer that hung in the hall. Not satisfied that the pressure reading was always correct, he would then switch on the radio (which in those days was still called a wireless) and listen intently to the Home Service farming forecast. An hour later, when he came in for breakfast after milking the cows, he would listen to another forecast, just to be certain that he had it right. His obsession with the weather became even more acute at this time of the year, when dry conditions were vital for the harvest. Of course, my memories of those days are full of sunshine. I loved riding on the trailer behind my father's tractor and helping the farm workers stack the bales of hay and straw. I also enjoyed eating the scones topped with clotted cream and strawberry jam that my mother brought out to the fields every evening. As we sat on the bales enjoying our tea and the beautiful views towards Exmoor, my father would remind us that our family had been doing the same thing, in the same place, for over a hundred years.

4 June 2017

The usual Sunday morning political interviews on television have been replaced by coverage of the terrible attack that killed seven people, and injured many more, in London last night. National campaigning has been suspended for the second time during this election, but early indications are that polling will still take place on Thursday. Facing defeat in its military campaigns in Iraq and Syria, ISIS appears to be concentrating more and more on "soft" civilian targets in Europe. After three such attacks in Britain in less than three months, Theresa May clearly believes that a new and tougher approach is required. When she spoke outside 10 Downing Street this morning she certainly didn't shy away from confronting the problem, and her final sentences were almost Churchillian in style. In response to the prime minister's speech, Tim Farron and Jeremy Corbyn both attempted to make political capital out of this tragedy by suggesting that recent events might have been prevented if police numbers had been higher. They both know perfectly well that even if we had tens of thousands more police officers on the streets, they wouldn't be able stop the sort of suicidal attacks we have seen in Manchester and London. Even by modern standards, when the quality of political debate has fallen to a new low, their comments were totally lacking in integrity. The polls, however, continue to show Labour gaining ground.

6 June 2017

When my carer arrived at lunchtime today, she asked me how I was. I answered by saying, "I'm ok, thanks". She laughed and said, "You should be saying you feel fantastic!" I knew that she was simply trying to jolly me along, but I couldn't stop myself from saying, "I hardly think so. Now, if I could get up and walk, that would be fantastic." My carer was clearly embarrassed by my sarcasm, so I quickly apologised.

7 June 2017

I got quite a shock this morning when a letter arrived from Perth and Kinross Council. It informed me that they now intend to charge me £26,000 each year for my care, backdated to April. Last September, when my care package was put in place, I was told that due to my terminal condition, my care would be provided free of charge. They appear to have decided that I should have died by now. I have informed my MND team and they are going to see what they can do.

8 June 2017

The wheels of local government tend to turn slowly, but today things moved very swiftly indeed. This afternoon I received an email from the council telling me that they had made a mistake with my care charges. It transpires that the form my GP signed in May 2015, stating that I was terminally ill, was not checked before the bill was sent out.

9 June 2017

I fully intended to stay up to watch the election results, but I gave up at 1.30 a.m. and retired to bed. Even by then it looked very unlikely that either side would gain an overall majority, and this morning, when I re-joined the coverage on television, a hung parliament was confirmed.

In recent weeks, Theresa May has looked less confident as opposition to her manifesto has intensified, and she has looked very uncomfortable when being heckled. By contrast, Jeremy Corbyn, who has concentrated on rallies in safe Labour territory, has been seen on television being cheered by his supporters. As I write, Theresa May is heading to Buckingham Palace to inform the Queen that she intends to form a government with the help of the Unionists from Northern Ireland. She might survive as prime minister in the short term, but she will never lead her party into another election. One area where the Conservatives did well last night was here in Scotland, where they had their most successful result for over twenty years. I think a second independence referendum is disappearing over the horizon.

10 June 2017

I am unsure if I should continue with my blog. The business last week over my care charges has made me re-evaluate things. The DS1500 form, which my GP signed back in May 2015, basically stated that I was unlikely to live for more than six months. At the time, I called this my "advanced death certificate" and I assumed that even if I survived longer than that, my life expectancy would be about fourteen months. I have now exceeded my hopes, and others' expectations, by a whole year, but I am acutely aware that most of my fellow MND sufferers have not been so lucky. I called my blog "Moments with MND" because, in addition to being honest about the way the disease progresses, I wanted to convey my determination to stay positive, and enjoy the moments I had left. I am unsure if I have succeeded in my objectives, but I am beginning to experience a form of survivor guilt — the whole thing is very confusing. Perhaps Perth and Kinross Council, who are faced with the ever-increasing cost of looking after people in the community, were right in their judgement that I have outlived my right to free care. By the same token, having almost reached the one-hundred-thousand-word mark, perhaps my blog is getting a little long in the tooth.

12 June 2017

During my reflexology treatment this morning I drifted off to asleep. Even after so many sessions with Kirstie, I am still amazed how this massage technique, which is totally confined to my feet, identifies and relaxes areas of tension all over my body. Just after I woke up, my left leg suddenly became rigid. Kirstie gripped the big toe of my left foot between her thumb and forefinger and held it until the spasm subsided. I am now getting these spasms more often, particularly in my hands and legs. My muscles are no longer receiving clear messages from my brain, and they seem to be screaming out for help.

21 June 2017

I haven't used my laptop for days, but I have greatly enjoyed having my brother here for another visit. Although my voice, or rather the lack of it, prevents me from participating properly in a conversation, it has been so good to simply share the same space with him. Peter understands my situation better than most, and he hasn't put any pressure on me to continue with the blog. Early this morning, however, after Peter had departed, I realised just how much I would miss the routine and purpose that writing has given me. And then I found many Facebook and email messages from friends, former pupils, and family, all encouraging me to keep going. Thank you everyone for your support and encouragement — it means an awful lot to me.

22 June 2017

I had a good time at Cornhill, which encapsulated all the emotions that a day at the hospice can bring. During our weekly catch up, Morag and I discussed how the care-charging episode has affected my confidence. Morag's support was very welcome, and it did me good to talk it through. Predictably, it brought me to tears, but Morag knew that this would happen, so she had the tissues ready. Later on, when we were all sitting in the day room, Kath suddenly piped up with, "Richard, your wheelchair is called a Quickie". Sally, who has lost her hearing aid, looked confused, but Doris, who was sitting next to her, said, "Quickie? That meant something very different in my day!" We all agreed that, exciting as such things might once have been, our current conditions and disabilities would make them unlikely today. We laughed so much that I nearly cried again. These adolescent-like moments of humour are very precious.

23 June 2017

Janette has arrived to keep an eye on me while Elaine is away on school business. Fortunately, she didn't see my recent post when I mentioned the hippopotamus. Janette is looking very well but my carers have told her not to do too much around the house. We are going to spend the afternoon watching Royal Ascot on television, with me watching the horses while Janette checks out the hats. Next week, we will be back on the game shows.

24 June 2017

This morning, I received a very touching email from my good friend, and fellow MND sufferer, David. The only part of his body that David can now move independently is his head, so to write an email he has to point a sensor, which is attached to his glasses, at the letters on a keyboard which is fixed in front of him, via an arm attached to his electric wheelchair. This is what he said:

Hi Richard,

Don't stop your blog!

I saw your update and wanted to encourage you to keep going. You shouldn't feel survivor guilt. Easy for me to say, but really you shouldn't. Even as someone whose deterioration has been fast, I don't feel remotely resentful that yours has been slower. Swings and roundabouts...

I think many people, like me, value your blog immensely for showing that life continues after diagnosis. I hope you will consider keeping it up. As my father would have said 'keep buggering on'.

Either way, I'll see you for more fun next week at Cornhill.

All the best,

David

If anything can persuade me to continue writing, and get on with my life, it is this.

25 June 2017

It is a beautiful summer's day, and Janette and I have been watching the wildlife in the garden. In addition to the usual array of blue tits, chaffinches, and sparrows, a number of new visitors are at the bird table. The most ravenous of these are a pair of jackdaws, who are attacking the fat ball feeder with great determination. The black birds and robins can't hold on to the wire mesh, so they sit underneath and peck at the scraps that fall from above. The most beautiful newcomer, however, is a jay. With its pinkish brown colouring, and blue streaks on its wing feathers, this really is an exotic looking bird. In the two years since my diagnosis, MND has steadily robbed me of my ability to walk, talk, dress myself, hold a pen, and swallow properly; fairly soon it will attack the muscles that enable me to breathe. At this moment, however, as I look out of the French window and watch a red squirrel sitting on the wall and a family of rabbits chasing around the rhododendron bushes, I feel entirely at peace with the world.

Postscript

Since this book was finished, Richard's health has gradually deteriorated as his MND has progressed. Richard can now only swallow textured food, his voice is almost gone, his muscle spasms are more frequent, and he has been advised to use a ventilator to help with his breathing. These developments have taken their physical and emotional toll on Richard, but he continues to share his experiences with others. In November, soon after his good friend David lost his battle with MND, Richard gave a moving and inspirational chapel talk to the pupils and staff of Glenalmond, using the synthetic voice on his iPad, and he still writes his blog. If you wish to follow his story further you can do so by logging onto momentswithmndblog.wordpress.com

Elaine Selley
February 2018

27755351R00195

Printed in Great Britain
by Amazon